"A breath of spiritual fresh air in the face of the 'me' centeredness so prevalent today. Jan holds out the kingdom as the pearl of great price. Read this and then live it. You will become the likes of which American Christianity needs badly."

—DAVE SWARTZ,
author of *Dancing with Broken Bones* and
The Magnificent Obsession

✠

"Most believers are frustrated. Their lives do not match their beliefs. That disparity finally explodes and drives them to virtually abandon the Christian life. Jan Hettinga takes that reality, identifies the key issues, and leads us on a journey of discovering Christ in such a way that our lifestyle and beliefs coalesce—and results in the unsurpassed joy of practical, gut-level Christian living. This book is dynamite and must be handled with care."

—JERRY E. WHITE, Ph.D.,
president, The Navigators

✠

"How can we, God's people, survive the numbing waters of neo-paganism that the tide of post-modernity is bringing in? Jan Hettinga reminds us that the gospel is 'the good news of the kingdom of God' and that conversion is acquiring kingdom citizenship. He then spells out, in practical, thought-provoking terms, what this means. No corner of life escapes his call to 'followership.'"

—JIM PETERSEN,
author of *Living Proof, Church Without Walls,* and
Lifestyle Discipleship

FOLLOW ME

Experience the Loving Leadership of Jesus

Jan David Hettinga

Dallas Willard, General Editor

NAVPRESS

BRINGING TRUTH TO LIFE

NavPress Publishing Group

P.O. Box 35001, Colorado Springs, Colorado 80935

The Navigators is an international Christian organization. Our mission is to reach, disciple, and equip people to know Christ and to make Him known through successive generations. We envision multitudes of diverse people in the United States and every other nation who have a passionate love for Christ, live a lifestyle of sharing Christ's love, and multiply spiritual laborers among those without Christ.

NavPress is the publishing ministry of The Navigators. NavPress publications help believers learn biblical truth and apply what they learn to their lives and ministries. Our mission is to stimulate spiritual formation among our readers.

© 1996 by Jan D. Hettinga
All rights reserved. No part of this publication may be reproduced in any form without written permission from NavPress, P.O. Box 35001, Colorado Springs, CO 80935.
Library of Congress Catalog Card Number: 96-9482
ISBN 08910-99824

Cover illustration: Bill Bruning
General editor: Dallas Willard
Editor: David Hazard

Some of the anecdotal illustrations in this book are true to life and are included with the permission of the persons involved. All other illustrations are composites of real situations, and any resemblance to people living or dead is coincidental.

Unless otherwise identified, all Scripture quotations in this publication are taken from the *HOLY BIBLE: NEW INTERNATIONAL VERSION®* (NIV®). Copyright © 1973, 1978, 1984 by International Bible Society. Used by permission of Zondervan Publishing House. All rights reserved. Another version used is: *The Message: New Testament with Psalms and Proverbs* (MSG) by Eugene H. Peterson, copyright© 1993, 1994, 1995, used by permission of NavPress Publishing Group.

Hettinga, Jan David
        Follow me : experience the loving leadership of Jesus / Jan David Hettinga.
        p. cm.
    ISBN 0-89109-982-4 (pbk.)
    1. Salvation.   2. Jesus Christ—Lordship.   3. Spiritual
life—Christianity.   4. Kingdom of God.   I. Title
BT752.H47 1996   96-9482
230'.61—dc20   CIP

Printed in the United States of America

2 3 4 5 6 7 8 9 10 11 12 13 14 15 / 99 98 97

Published in association with the literary agency of
Alive Communications, 1465 Kelly Johnson Boulevard, Suite 320,
Colorado Springs, CO 80920.

FOR A FREE CATALOG OF
NAVPRESS BOOKS & BIBLE STUDIES,
CALL 1-800-366-7788 (USA)
or 1-416-499-4615 (CANADA)

CONTENTS

General Introduction **9**

The Road to God's Kingdom **13**

PART ONE: THE SAFEST LEADER TO FOLLOW

Chapter One: Where Are You Going? **17**

Chapter Two: What If We Are Wrong About God? **22**

Chapter Three: What If God Is Right About Us? **29**

Chapter Four: The Leader You Can Trust **37**

Chapter Five: Holding Back from God **44**

Chapter Six: The Great Mandate **53**

PART TWO: AN UNSAFE WORLD

Chapter Seven: What on Earth Is Wrong with Us? **61**

Chapter Eight: Diagnostic Confusion **66**

Chapter Nine: What God Told the Prophets **75**

Chapter Ten: Wiping Away God's Fingerprints **80**

Chapter Eleven: The Logic of Hell **86**

Chapter Twelve: The Ultimate Cover for Rebellion **92**

PART THREE: THE SAFE FOLLOWER AND REPENTANCE

Chapter Thirteen: From Religion to Relationship **101**

Chapter Fourteen: Getting Back on Track **111**

Chapter Fifteen: The "Slice" I Want **123**

Chapter Sixteen: What Jesus Called Good News **134**

Chapter Seventeen: The Mystery of the Kingdom **144**

Chapter Eighteen: No Formula **155**

Chapter Nineteen: The Best Example of Faith **166**

PART FOUR: THE SAFE FOLLOWER AND SANCTIFICATION

Chapter Twenty: The Process Begins **175**

Chapter Twenty-One: Strongholds and Blind Spots **185**

Chapter Twenty-Two: The Mixed-Bag Situation **196**

Chapter Twenty-Three: Passing the Fish Along **204**

PART FIVE: THE SAFE COMMUNITY

Chapter Twenty-Four: What Governs You? **215**

Chapter Twenty-Five: The Beauty of Kingdom Community **225**

Chapter Twenty-Six: The Sensational Kingdom Fragrance **234**

Chapter Twenty-Seven: Nose Prints on the Window **244**

Chapter Twenty-Eight: Finishing Strong **254**

Chapter Twenty-Nine: Rediscovering the Kingdom **260**

This book is dedicated to my wife,
Scharme Lee,
true daughter of the kingdom
and companion of my heart

Acknowledgments

This book has been a project in which many others have participated. The following contributed most:

Steve Michiels, Kevin Cavanaugh, and Nate Hettinga have been most influential in helping me distill out the kingdom concepts. All of them serve with me on the pastoral staff at Northshore Baptist Church in Bothell, Washington.

The board of overseers at Northshore believed in the message and gave me the freedom to work the writing into my schedule.

The actual work has been done by three incredible secretaries. Joni Kersten prepared the bulk of the manuscript with enthusiasm and true team spirit. I am deeply grateful for her excellent supervision of the process. Krista Kreizenbeck Baughn has stepped in and helped out with willingness and competence whenever necessary. Debbi Anderson started the project with me and kept me going when I first began to realize the amount of work involved.

The wonderful graphics in *Follow Me* were the work of Pam Mullen, the communications assistant at Northshore.

Dr. Terry Taylor, president of the U.S. Navigators, insisted that the kingdom material needed to be made available to the evangical world. Thanks also to Jon Sween, Navigator staff member and small group director at Northshore, who facilitated the initial meeting with Dr. Taylor.

My editor, David Hazard, who had the job of turning a wannabe writer into a writer. He has been invaluable in forming and shaping this book. David is a kingdom player.

Thanks to Alive Communications and my agent, Greg Johnson. Greg and I go way back. We worked together in ministry at Northshore in the mid-eighties. He consistently encouraged me to get my message into print, and finally, with his very professional help, here it is.

My deepest heartfelt thanks to these and a host of others who supported the writing process with prayer and strong encouragement.

General Introduction
BY DALLAS WILLARD

The Spiritual Formation Line presents discipleship to Jesus Christ as the greatest opportunity individual human beings have in life and the only hope corporate mankind has of solving its insurmountable problems.

It affirms the unity of the present-day Christian with those who walked beside Jesus during His incarnation. To be His disciple then was to be with Him, to learn to be like Him. It was to be His student or apprentice in kingdom living. His disciples heard what He said and observed what He did, then, under His direction, they simply began to say and do the same things. They did so imperfectly but progressively. As He taught: "Everyone who is fully trained will be like his teacher" (Luke 6:40).

Today it is the same, except now it is the resurrected Lord who walks throughout the world. He invites us to place our confidence in Him. Those who rely on Him believe that He knows how to live and will pour His life into us as we "take *His* yoke . . . and learn from *Him*, for *He is* gentle and humble in heart" (Matthew 11:29, emphasis added). To take His yoke means joining Him in His work, making our work His work. To trust Him is to understand that total immersion in what He is doing with our life is the best thing that could ever happen to us.

To "learn from Him" in this total-life immersion is *how* we "seek first his kingdom and his righteousness" (Matthew 6:33). The out-

9

come is that we increasingly are able to do all things, speaking or acting, as if Christ were doing them (Colossians 3:17). As apprentices of Christ we are not learning how to do some special religious activity, but how to live every moment of our lives from the reality of God's kingdom. I am learning how to live my actual life as Jesus would if He were me.

If I am a plumber, clerk, bank manager, homemaker, elected official, senior citizen, or migrant worker, I am in "full-time" Christian service no less than someone who earns his or her living in a specifically religious role. Jesus stands beside me and teaches me in all I do to live in God's world. He shows me how, in every circumstance, to reside in His word and thus be a genuine apprentice of His—His disciple indeed. This enables me to find the reality of God's world everywhere I may be, and thereby to escape from enslavement to sin and evil (John 8:31-32). We become able to do what we know to be good and right, even when it is humanly impossible. Our lives and words become constant testimony of the reality of God.

A plumber facing a difficult plumbing job must know how to integrate it into the kingdom of God as much as someone attempting to win another to Christ or preparing a lesson for a congregation. Until we are clear on this, we will have missed Jesus' connection between life and God and will automatically exclude most of our everyday lives from the domain of faith and discipleship. Jesus lived most of His life on earth as a blue-collar worker, someone we might describe today as an "independent contractor." In His vocation He practiced everything He later taught about life in the kingdom.

The "words" of Jesus I primarily reside in are those recorded in the New Testament Gospels. In His presence, I learn the goodness of His instructions and how to carry them out. It is not a matter of meriting life from above, but of receiving that life concretely in my circumstances. Grace, we must learn, is opposed to *earning*, not to *effort*.

For example, I move away from using derogatory language against others, calling them twits, jerks, or idiots (Matthew 5:22), and increasingly mesh with the respect and endearment for persons that naturally flows from God's way. This in turn transforms all of my dealings with others into tenderness and makes the usual coldness and brutality of human relations, which lays a natural foundation for abuse and murder, simply unthinkable.

Of course, the "learning of Him" is meant to occur in the context of His people. They are the ones He commissioned to make disciples, surround them in the reality of the triune name, and teach to do "everything I have commanded you" (Matthew 28:20). But the disciples we make are His disciples, never ours. We are His apprentices along with them. If we are a little farther along the way, we can only echo the apostle Paul: "Follow my example, as I follow the example of Christ" (1 Corinthians 11:1).

It is a primary task of Christian ministry today, and of those who write for this line of books, to reestablish Christ as living teacher in the midst of His people. He has been removed by various historical developments: assigned the role of *mere* sacrifice for sin or social prophet and martyr. But where there is no teacher there can be no students or disciples.

If we cannot be His students, we have no way to learn to exist always and everywhere within the riches and power of His word. We can only flounder along as if we were on our own so far as the actual details of our lives are concerned. That is where multitudes of well-meaning believers find themselves today. But it is not the intent of Him who says, "Come to me . . . and you will find rest for your souls" (Matthew 11:28-29).

Each book in this line is designed to contribute to this renewed vision of Christian spiritual formation and to illuminate what apprenticeship to Jesus Christ means within all the specific dimensions of human existence. The mission of these books is to form the whole person so that the nature of Christ becomes the natural expression of our souls, bodies, and spirits throughout our daily lives.

The Road to God's Kingdom
BY DAVID HAZARD

"Follow Me," said Jesus.

So many of us hear Jesus' call today and set off after Him, eager as His first-century disciples were to possess the forgiveness and freedom from sin that He promised. It's easy to read the Gospels and imagine ourselves right in among the people of Jesus' day, and to feel their enthusiasm as they responded to His call.

Peter hung up his nets and trailed after Jesus as He fished for souls during three years of teaching, healing, and performing miracles. Mary Magdalene left her bedeviled life. Andrew, and other disciples of John the Baptist, heard their new Master repeat the word that generations of Jews had waited to hear: "The kingdom of God is at hand!"

These followers recognized the beginning of the disciples spiritual path. Eagerly they left behind the lives they knew and, literally, walked after Jesus. But where would the path of discipleship lead?

The will and work of God was about to be spread throughout towns, nations, and continents—and in order for this to occur, the will and work of God first spread its rule in their hearts. After all, where two wills are at work there is only a struggle for control.

"My kingdom is a spiritual kingdom," Jesus told them. "My kingdom is within you."

So the question was this: Would they follow by imitating God and the Son of Man, humbly placing themselves—soul and being—under

13

the governing direction of the Father? Would they turn away from their self-centered, self-directed ways to take part in higher purposes?

For quite a few disciples, that was too challenging. They slipped quietly away, turning back to their trades and families. Back home in the community they could still insist, "Yes, I believe in Jesus." And how would their closest friends know if, in the innermost places of their hearts—where life is governed by unseeable motives—they had refused to follow God's royal road to heaven?

Jesus' offer of forgiveness and eternal life is as attractive now as in the day when fisherman, soldiers, and outcasts first received it. Many of us jumped from our seats when we heard His call—"Follow Me"—through the appeals of contemporary evangelists. Others were prompted by the disgusting mess drugs, alcohol, or an uncontrolled libido had left on us. Like the first disciples, many of us have set out to be Christians.

But too quickly we run into questions and confusion. Is it enough just to believe—or do I have to obey God? What is the evidence of the promised change in my life as a believer—is it a change in my doctrine only, and lifestyle choices, or is it transformation of my spirit and character? Where do my personal aspirations and dreams fit? How do I even begin, when every Christian I meet seems to have a different understanding of what it means to be a disciple?

If you have been trying to understand the true path of the Christian disciple, *Follow Me* will be a welcome "map." We present it as a foundational book in the Spiritual Formation Line, because it will help to form your thoughts about the core issues of true discipleship. Namely: When we respond to Jesus' call it begins a process of change—true change, from within. The transformation of a disciple comes as the kingdom of God—that is, the will of God—grows in us as we learn how to give Him full rule of our lives. It is the call to imitate Jesus as He fully trusted and obeyed the Father.

Ultimately, the road to the kingdom of God runs through the heart of the disciple. Or it stops outside of it. And so, it is with issues of the inner man that Jan Hettinga deals. With questions that probe . . . and new insight that can change your life.

If . . .

PART ONE

THE SAFEST LEADER TO FOLLOW

→ ONE ←
Where Are You Going?

The ultimate issue in the universe is leadership. Who you follow and what directs your life, is the single most important thing about you. Tell me who your leader is — Boris Yeltsin, Louis Farrakhan, Jeanne Kirkpatrick, Yasser Arafat, Gloria Steinem, Billy Graham — and I can immediately tell all kinds of things about you . . . even if your leader is yourself, which is what most of us prefer.

Perhaps the most obvious observation one can make about the international scene today is that there is a shortage of leadership. Strong, capable, courageous, visionary leaders are sidestepping the opportunity to lead. There are some good reasons for this, the most troubling of which is a scarcity of followers.

We live in an age of 51-percent majorities, public opinion polls, and an increasingly distrustful populace. Through ever more powerful media channels, people can require leaders to be much more responsive to their demands. As a result, non-leader politicians stick their fingers in the air to read the winds of public sentiment on nearly every issue. The leaders are becoming the followers and the followers, more and more, the leaders.

Since there is no commitment or loyalty to leaders unless they "deliver," coalitions and strategic alliances are in a constant state of flux. Leaders don't trust their followers, and followers don't trust their leaders. With rare exceptions, leaders and followers can be trusted for only one thing in today's world — to do what they think is in their own self-interest.

Also contributing to the unraveling of leadership and followership is the breakdown of the family unit. Nearly half of the children in the Western world will experience the pain of their parents' divorcing by the time they become young adults. If the research is correct, the "blended" families that result are the breeding grounds for sexual, physical, verbal, and emotional abuse. One out of four female children is molested or raped, usually by someone she thought she could trust. The number of boys who suffer similar outrage is considerably less but increasing each year.

Is it any wonder that the coming generation's motto is "question authority"? Their baseball caps and T-shirts carry the spirit of the age: "No fear," "No rules," "No boundaries," "No limits." Their music exudes a spirit of detachment and profound distrust toward anyone in authority.

And then there's the church of the living God—the one place in all the world where we should be able to look for a healthy example of how leaders should lead and followers should follow. But instead, what greets us is even more disturbing than developments in the rest of the world—disturbing because following the greatest Leader of all is supposedly what Christianity is all about. When Christians seem to struggle with leadership and followership nearly as much as everyone else, the guiding lamp grows dim.

How do we who are following the one true Governor of the universe get back to becoming people who can provide the moral leadership our world so desperately needs? It seems to me that a good place to begin would be to admit that we have misunderstood what following Jesus looks like. Somewhere we started coming down heavily on the side of performance. True, we've taken care to avoid becoming the out-of-control, sandwich-board zealot on the street corner with a "turn or burn" message. Nonetheless, we've become busy with other spiritual works and performance standards: going to events, participating in programs, learning methodologies, getting involved in "ministry opportunities," assimilating materials, practicing the five or ten steps prescribed by ministry professionals. But we have not addressed *heart* issues. We've taught people to work hard, give, go—but we have mostly ignored the fact that Jesus addressed issues of the inner life *first*. It's time to assess the results. Performance-driven discipleship has not produced strong, healthy, self-starting followers. Rather, it has created a huge pool of disillusionment and apathy.

As many of us know, struggling to change outward habit without changing the heart is a formula for frustration. It's time to go back to the development of the inner life, to the heart attitudes at the deepest level of our beings. Discipleship must be applied to the inside of us—to the self, the ego, the libido, the fantasy life of the imagination, the ambitions, the passions, the soul. Gordon McDonald calls this "the life below the waterline." *It's the part that isn't seen that shapes what is seen.* Only when we stop complying with superficial, performance-based cosmetic changes and start following Jesus from the heart will the church once again light the path for the rest of the world.

I BELIEVE—ISN'T THAT ENOUGH?

If I were to put myself inside the skin of a Christian who believes in Jesus but doesn't follow Him—what would my life be like? What would I experience? I would:

- be cynical about church and the possibility of the Christian life actually working.
- cover the fact that I was spiritually empty, dry, and unsatisfied.
- tend to be passive and apathetic. I would have good intentions but lack follow-through.
- be focused on myself—my needs, my rights, my options.
- prefer being a spectator—watching, listening, but not really participating.
- occasionally admit that I have a busy, fast-paced, cluttered life and a short attention span.
- insist on arranging my life around my personal preferences, pleasures, and comforts.
- subdivide my life so that I could move from one sealed compartment to another, keeping each strictly separate—church world, work world, leisure world, family world, and so forth.
- go through the motions, doing what is expected, more out of habit than anything else.
- be spiritually sterile, barren, and nonproductive in witness, and not troubled about it.
- experience the frustration of trying to have the best of both worlds, attempting to serve two masters—Jesus and some-*one* or some*thing* else.

- pride myself on my ability to be independent and self-sufficient.
- keep my options open and remain uncommitted in order to avoid getting tied down.
- have little or no sense of overriding spiritual purpose or cause, and prefer to drift.
- cover up a quiet desperation inside — "There's gotta be more to the Christian life than this powerless state I'm experiencing."

It didn't take me long to compile this list because it's what men and women who gather to pray for revival are praying about. When I join in half-day, all-day, or all-night prayer sessions with other Christian leaders, I take notes. I listen carefully to the concerns that the Spirit of God is placing on the hearts of those who are interceding.

ENTER THE KINGDOM

If the preceding list is even close to correct about the current state of Christian experience, we're in serious trouble. Without a massive rediscovery of what following the One who offers to be our Shepherd King is all about, the church could easily die within one or two generations. It doesn't matter if we call the needed change revival, renewal, or revitalization . . . "Please, God, send it!" What "it" will amount to is a return to following Jesus in humble, consistent obedience.

We have failed to show what discipleship means at the heart level, or how to follow Christ from the depths of our being.

Jesus Christ chose to speak of our need to enter and live in the kingdom of God. He meant that God wants to reestablish Himself as our loving leader — knowing it is best for us to follow His rule than to be ruled by our own passions or by other fallen creatures who want to dominate us. We can assume that He referred to "the gospel of the kingdom" for a critically important reason. He was offering leadership and asking for followership. Salvation was a necessary means to that end but not the end in itself. This, I suspect, is where we have drifted off course.

Today, we are experiencing a crisis of commitment for the most ordinary of reasons. We are not asking for it! We have failed to show what discipleship means *at the heart level*, or how to follow Christ from the depths of our being. Somehow, we have mistakenly assumed that saving grace must be isolated from the call to follow—the call to enter into the kingdom of God, which is where followers of God live. We have become preoccupied with offering the gift, the pardon, and the loving acceptance of God's great salvation. We have forgotten that, according to Jesus, the arrival of the kingdom—the reign of God—is the gospel.

I want to invite you to think deeply with me about the biggest of big ideas:

Is God worth following?

If He is, why don't we follow Him?

What would happen to us and to our world if we did follow Him?

It is important to think about the kingdom message of Jesus, and His call to follow. But more than that we must examine the spiritual ground of our own lives and prepare to take some new steps in the footprints of our Master. It is important to look at the paths we are now following, in terms of our real, secret, inner inclinations, and ask: *Where am I going?*

You see, *who* I am following will determine *where* I am going!

Earl Jabay asks the right question: "Do we have an idea-God, or the power-authority God of the New Testament? It is a great tragedy when God becomes someone to understand rather than the power-to-heal-and-save in surrendered lives."[1]

The heart of the Christian gospel is Jesus' offer to be the leader we can trust—and His insistence that every believer become a follower He can trust.

Come with me as we explore the eternal, majestic realm of the King of the universe.

NOTE
1. Earl Jabay, *The God-Players* (Grand Rapids, Mich.: Zondervan, 1969), p. 37.

What If We Are Wrong About God?

In today's world, it's easy to see that believing in God doesn't necessarily mean much. The vast majority of people say they believe in God. But it's abundantly clear in the so-called Christian nations of the Western world that professing belief in God and allowing that belief to make any discernible difference in your life are two entirely different things.

As obvious as this lapse of logic is, few seem to notice it. To believe in an all-powerful supreme being to whom you owe your very existence and yet to live as if you are the one in control doesn't appear strange. In fact, it feels normal.

BELIEVING VERSUS FOLLOWING

The single men's Bible study I was leading began winding down for the evening. The discussion had been especially animated and lively as we dug deep into the subject of faith. Each of the seven participants had shared struggles with taking God at His word. We finally concluded that there were two kinds of "believing"—one in the sense of recognizing and agreeing with truth, and another in the sense of learning how to bring your life in line with the truth you say you accept.

After the meeting broke up, Dan followed me into my office. Almost before I had the door closed behind us, he exploded with pent-up frustration. He threw his Bible and notebook into a chair and paced the small room like a caged bear.

"This is what always bothers me about these neat little Bible studies," Dan said. "They get out of hand. We do a nice little fill-in-the-blank lesson and learn more about God . . . then what happens? Someone can't let well enough alone. He has to ask what the biblical ideas are actually supposed to accomplish in his life. I mean, why can't people be satisfied with just finding out what the Bible says and believing it? Why do we have to make such a big deal out of *application?*"

His outburst was partly serious and partly a self-effacing attempt at humor. I knew this was Dan's way of complaining that the content of the evening had gotten too close for comfort.

> *"I mean, why can't people be satisfied with just finding out what the Bible says and believing it? Why do we have to make such a big deal out of application?"*

"Spit it out," I encouraged. "What exactly has gotten you so worked up?"

"You probably wouldn't understand the shock of this, but tonight I realized that I was a believer, but not a follower, of Christ. Intellectually I don't have a problem with the material in Scripture, but permitting it to actually change me, well, that's a different matter!"

I assured him that I *did* understand only too well his internal struggle with relinquishing control. "Believing has always come easier than obeying for me too," I admitted. "If your experience is anything like mine, following Jesus will continue to be the pivotal issue in your Christian life."

"You? I thought you had it all together. You still struggle?" He was incredulous.

"Dan, *believing* is a spectator sport. *Following* is what makes you a player. Following is where the cost of commitment shows up, and that never gets any easier. According to Jesus, there's something of the cross in it. A cross that must be taken up daily as we follow Him. The cross always means 'not my will but thine be done.' It means submission to our Lord's leadership of our lives, and that always means dying to self-in-control."

Two weeks later Dan reported our conversation to the rest of the group. He confessed his reluctance to move from believing to following Jesus, then he told us he was seriously praying about it and searching his heart, trying to understand what was holding him back. He hesitantly said he thought God had spoken to him in the quiet of his thoughts.

"Well, what did He *say*?" one guy asked.

"He asked me why I didn't trust Him. The moment I became aware of the question I knew it was focusing on the right issue. For the first time in my life I was able to admit that I've been holding out on following Christ because I might not like where He'll lead me. I know it sounds arrogant, but something in me would rather trust myself than God." Within a few minutes of Dan's transparent confession, everyone in the room admitted to struggling with similar passive-aggressive, foot-dragging behavior.

Trusting Jesus would seem to be a "given" for those who believe in Him. But it isn't. There's a sticky suspicion lurking in the back of our minds — something deep within us that is stubbornly reluctant to lower the final defenses and trust God completely. Oswald Chambers observed: "When the Bible touches the question of sin, it always comes right down to this incurable suspicion of God which cannot be altered apart from the Atonement."[1]

As I've gradually grown in the truth about my Lord and about myself, I've come to realize that I'm not alone in my reluctance to trust Him. In fact, every Christian runs up against the same inner barriers that bar the way to full surrender to Christ. Let me explain where the source of some of that chronic guardedness lies.

THE REASON FOR WARINESS

Phil and Claudia Pearson taught their five-year-old daughter, Linnea, to love and respect her pastor. She prays for me each night at bedtime; and every Sunday morning after the second service, she always finds me and gives me a big hug. One Sunday morning, Linnea gave me my usual hug, this time accompanied by a kiss. Then, with a sparkle in her eye, she said, "I've got something for you, Pastor."

Clutched in her little hand was a special offering envelope for the construction of our new children's center. Block-printed in pencil was her name and the amount of five dollars. She stood there, as proud and happy as could be.

Then she leaned close to my ear again and, with a giggle, added, "And, Pastor, don't spend it on pizza!"

I laughed at her good-humored teasing and went on greeting people. Later, as I was driving home, God used her pizza remark to further stimulate my thinking on trusting His leadership. It dawned on me that we are all deeply affected by the failures of human leaders.

All over the nation citizens have grown weary, deeply cynical, and even hardened about their government. Bureaucrats redecorate their offices with fifteen-thousand-dollar desks, or zip off for "conferences" in the Caribbean—all at taxpayer expense. And American political behavior is not all that outrageous when compared to some third-world countries, where greed and extortion in government are the *norm*. The hard fact is that leaders we have trusted have abused their power and our money with astonishing aplomb. In such a world, is it any wonder even a child would know that money entrusted to a leader doesn't always end up where it was designated?

We learn from experience, don't we? Because of leadership failure, we have found ways to protect ourselves. We have become careful, watchful, and ever more guarded the more our trust is abused. But distrust and suspicion rarely stay focused on the perpetrators who provoked them. We inevitably develop something called *transference*. If, for instance, a father is distant and unaffectionate, his children will tend to assume that all fathers behave in a similar, cold fashion. They expect to have a negative experience with fathers in general.

To illustrate this transference—in a positive sense—let me share a story from my youth. When I was young, the neighbor kids would come knocking at suppertime and my parents would invite them in to sit on the stairs while our family finished our meal. I suspected they came early because my mother was usually generous with desserts. Along with a handful of cookies or a slice of pie, they would get in on our family devotions. My father would read a chapter from the Bible in his rich baritone voice and then ask questions. Eventually our neighborhood friends began to participate in the discussions. We always ended our family time in prayer with Dad and Mom praying. Occasionally we children joined in, and sometimes the visitors prayed as well.

I remember one conversation with a friend who had been showing up for dessert and devotions at our house for several weeks.

"Does your old man have to do that religious stuff with you guys?" he asked. "I mean, is it required by your church or something?"

"No," I explained. "He talks about God with us because he thinks it's important. Nobody from church is checking up on us. We just like being close to God as a family."

My friend was fascinated with my father. When I told him that my dad came and sat on my bed each night and prayed with me, he actually teared up. "I wish I had a dad like yours," he said. "I didn't think men did that kind of thing."

My father had broken a stereotype that my friend had built out of the human tendency to transfer from personal experience to a general rule. He had assumed that all fathers were more or less like his own.

But for me, the positive modeling of my dad set up constructive expectations.

THEY'RE ALL ALIKE
Another place this transference pattern shows up is in marriage. If a woman was molested or sexually abused in childhood, an expectation is set in motion that men are preoccupied with sex. When she begins to date in her teen years, the sexual advances of her boyfriends further confirm her apprehensions. If she marries a man who is immoral, sexually selfish, and self-indulgent, her opinion hardens into the conviction that "all men are the same." Even when treated with the utmost respect and sensitivity by a man, she will only see ulterior motivation and believe he is "coming on" to her.

Similarly, the man who has lived under the thumb of a domineering mother forms a negative "projection" toward women. After watching the emasculation of his father and suffering under his mother's obsession with control, he "sees" women in general as antagonists in a battle of wills. When he marries and his wife begins to assert her will in their relationship, he concludes "women are all alike."

Transference is universal in community life as well. When elected officials routinely break their campaign promises, we eventually begin to tar all politicians with the same brush—as masters of double-talk and endless self-promotion. Transferring what we've learned about the behavior of one person, we project that expected behavior onto all others who fit the profile. It may not be fair to the next leader, but it's understandable.

THE TARGET AT THE TOP
There is yet another level to this pain-avoidance pattern of distrust. What starts out as the damage of victimization easily comes out of us as an excuse to victimize others. The prime target is the highest authority.

The written Word of God is clear about this antagonism. (I have italicized the critical words.)

- The sinful mind is *hostile to God. It does not submit* to God's law, nor can it do so (Romans 8:7).
- For if, when *we were God's enemies,* we were reconciled . . . (Romans 5:10).
- Don't you know that friendship with the world is *hatred toward God?* Anyone who chooses to be a friend of the world becomes *an enemy of God* (James 4:4).
- Once you were *alienated from God and were enemies* in your minds because of your evil behavior (Colossians 1:21).

We read this assessment of our attitude toward supreme authority and shake our heads. We are aware of our suspicion and distrust—but enemies? Hatred? Hostility? No way! Why would we believe in God if we were dead set against Him?

Humankind has long projected the behavior of human leaders on God. Experience and common sense tell us that those in a position to take selfish advantage here on earth will do so. Why would heaven operate any differently? God owns the executive, legislative, and judicial branches of cosmic government—without a system of checks and balances or an appeal process. God is accountable to no one but Himself. Judging from our past experience, such a superbly positioned ego could not help but be supremely selfish.

If God were like human leaders, our defensiveness would be appropriate. Such a self-centered supreme being would inevitably make heaven a plush, gold-lined prison. If we were to follow such thinking to its logical conclusion, hell would be the one place where some respite could be had. Eternal separation from this kind of dreadful, self-obsessed deity would be a relief.

MISTAKEN ASSUMPTIONS

I started this chapter promising to explain the source of our reluctance to trust God. We looked at the common experience of professing Christians who seem able to believe in Jesus but then find it strangely difficult to follow Him. Trusting the salvation offered in Jesus and trusting the sovereign control and agenda of Jesus in everyday life somehow get separated. I believe one of the major reasons for this is the wear and tear of living in a self-saturated environment. We automatically judge God by ourselves. In magnifying the behavior of human authorities to the divine level, we create a God we could never trust. The natural learning process that incorporates transference and projection actually gets in our way at this point. The school of "hard knocks and common sense" fails us.

In magnifying the behavior of human authorities to the divine level, we create a God we could never trust.

But what if God is the most misunderstood person in your life? What if you've been suspecting and assuming things about Him that grossly distort who He really is? You may have considered yourself a sincere Christian for years but are still experiencing the frustration that comes from consciously or unconsciously keeping your distance from Christ.

Maybe it's time to deliberately close that distance, and take another look at your Leader in a new light.

NOTE

1. Oswald Chambers, *The Philosophy of Sin* (East Sussex, England: Christian Literature Crusade, 1960), p. 13.

⇥ T H R E E ⇤
What If God Is Right About Us?

From our perspective it seems fair to ask, "Can we trust the Supreme Lord of the universe?" But what we see as healthy, normal self-defense appears much different from God's point of view. From the divine perspective the central question is exactly the opposite. His concern is the unfaithfulness, disobedience, and stubborn rebellion found in every human heart. Will He ever find people who gladly accept His authority and faithfully follow His leadership?

Put yourself in God's shoes. You created a perfect world. The ecosystem functions flawlessly. You are pleased and satisfied. Finally, you put the centerpiece of your design into place—creatures with personality, self-awareness, and freedom of choice. You call them "man" and, again, you are delighted with the result of your creative work.

This crowning creation is capable of a love relationship with you. They are not programmed to love you but choose to do so. You become companions. Enjoyable conversation flows whenever you and the humans you have made in your own image are together. It's working out the way you envisioned it could. Your heart is now involved. You love Adam and Eve . . . and they live in voluntary response to your leadership and love you in return.

And then the joys of Eden come to a heartrending halt. The man and the woman have been tempted with the forbidden fruit of independence. They forget your goodness and love. Incredibly, they forget that they owe their very existence to you. They choose to believe the big lie and bite into the serpent-sponsored notion that you are holding out on them and not being fair. You watch with dismay and deep disappointment as these utterly dependent creatures join the tempter's rebellion and attempt to take control of their lives and their planet (Genesis 2–3). And since that time, every one of their descendants has attempted to set up his or her own kingdom-of-the-will.

According to the Bible, the struggle between good and evil, light and darkness, continues to this very day as a conflict between kingdoms — mine, yours, and God's. From God's perspective, what's wrong with us started with our decision to go our own way and leave His leadership behind.

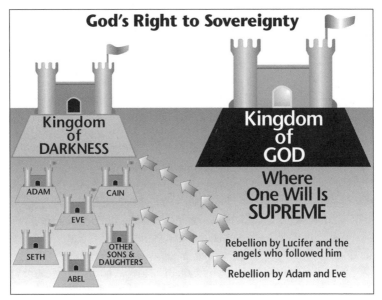

Diagram 3.1

This picture shows how humankind now stands in relation to God, with "kingdoms" facing off, each one seeking independence and wanting to be governed by its own laws. The large castle depicts the eternal kingdom of God. It is His desire for all of His creatures to be healthy, happy, and fulfilled under His reign. It was not His will for Lucifer and his fellow rebel angels — and Adam and Eve and their descendants — to revolt and set up alternative kingdoms. The surprising thing is that after the humans took over the laboratory, their Creator refused to scrub the project.

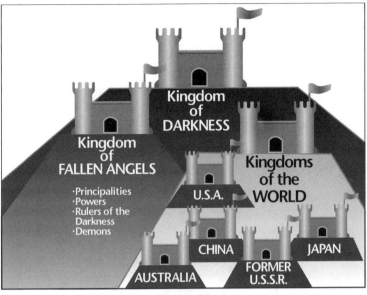

Diagram 3.2

A closer look at the kingdom of darkness brings the realization that Satan has his hands full. In the kingdom of God one will is supreme, and you become a citizen by voluntary loyalty and submission. In the kingdom of darkness the proliferation of independent selves makes things extremely complicated. You don't have to try very hard to imagine the frustration of trying to get a world of independent, strong-willed rebels to cooperate. The nation-kingdoms of this world, represented above by a token handful, operate in a constant state of competition and confrontation. This is the dangerous nature of life as we know it on planet earth.

Not only does the Devil have a difficult time getting his agenda accomplished, the leaders of the nations are in trouble as well.

At least one nation, the United States of America, actually contains many smaller kingdoms in the form of "interest groups." Each group has its own agenda and is in competition with all the others for available resources and influence. This is the breeding ground of politics. A politician is a leader who has learned the art of forming coalitions by appealing to the self-interests of various subgroups. If these leaders can attract a majority of their constituents to their array of promises, they can get elected and usually stay in power.

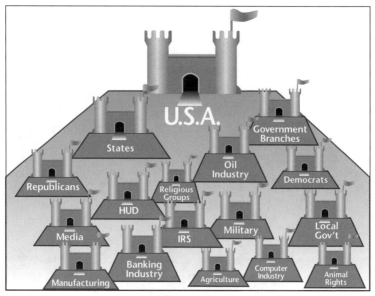

Diagram 3.3

Satan is the supreme politician. He is the master at playing to the selfish interests of the nations. In the final chapter of earth's history, when he finally puts together a global empire, he will pull it off with pure "smoke and mirrors" politics. He will promise to deliver what people think they want.

So, that's the grand scheme—but how does that matter to my life right now?

The tension between all these lesser kingdoms and wills brings incredible pressure on my life and yours. The family, for instance, is comprised of individuals who, in the likeness of fallen Adam, each have an inborn, self-centered sin nature. This manifests itself through an independent, strong will that creates competitive friction as each person attempts to get what he or she wants out of the family. The available resources, finances, time, energy, and even love become sources of frustration and conflict as each individual seeks to acquire his share and more. The home is a microcosm of the rest of the world. The same struggle for control that is a daily reality in marriage and the family riddles our schools, offices, and governments. If you think about it, you'll see the clarity that the kingdom explanation brings.

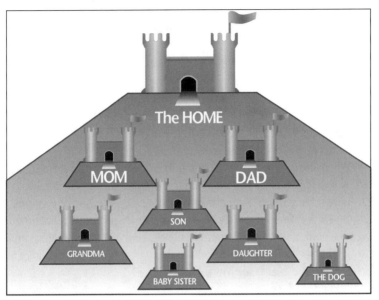

Diagram 3.4

WHO'S IN CHARGE HERE?

We have to examine ourselves and our world in light of this kingdom concept for the simple reason that it was the way Jesus thought and taught. His awareness of "realms of jurisdiction" and "authority" permeates the four Gospels. His sensitivity to the antagonism between conflicting kingdoms shows up in conversations like this one with Pilate.

> Pilate then went back inside the palace, summoned Jesus and asked him, "Are you the king of the Jews?"
>
> "Is that your own idea," Jesus asked, "or did others talk to you about me?"
>
> "Am I a Jew?" Pilate replied. "It was your people and your chief priests who handed you over to me. What is it you have done?"
>
> Jesus said, "My kingdom is not of this world. If it were, my servants would fight to prevent my arrest by the Jews. But now my kingdom is from another place."
>
> "You are a king, then!" said Pilate.
>
> Jesus answered, "You are right in saying I am a king. In

fact, for this reason I was born, and for this I came into the
world, to testify to the truth. Everyone on the side of truth listens to me."

"What is truth?" Pilate asked. (John 18:33-38)

Jesus clearly saw Himself as a King with a spiritual and eternal
kingdom. He came to earth to testify to the truth of His identity—and
to the true nature of the resistance on earth to His leadership.

It was opposition all the way.

When Jesus began to speak publicly at the age of thirty, He immediately received hostile reactions. This opposition increased steadily for
the entire three years of His earthly ministry. Not only was the content of
His message offensive—His obvious *authority* inflamed resentment.
Even the common people recognized the element of leadership that came
through in His teaching. "He speaks as one who has authority and not as
the scribes," they said (see Mark 1:22).

And it was the combination of His kingdom message and an aura of
unmistakable authenticity that set Jesus on a collision course with the
power brokers of the ruling class.

Jesus entered the temple courts, and, while he was teaching, the
chief priests and the elders of the people came to him. "By what
authority are you doing these things?" they asked. "And who
gave you this authority?" (Matthew 21:23)

They knew a threat when they saw one. Jesus set off all their sensitive alarm systems. They instinctively bristled whenever they were
around Him. Their gut reaction was hostile. This seemingly harmless
preacher and worker of miracles was *Somebody*. But who? Where did
He come from? What was His agenda? And more importantly, how
could He be safely neutralized? He must, under no circumstances, be
allowed to upset the status quo that they had so painstakingly pieced
together for their own advantage.

It was in the context of this confrontation with the power brokers
that Jesus told the poignant story of the hostile takeover of a rented vineyard (Matthew 21:33-40). The landowner had made the initial investment and had done the site work and construction. The vineyard was
fully operational when it was rented to some tenant farmers. When har-

vest time came the owner sent his agents to collect his share. The tenants chose to violently reject the owner's legitimate claim by physically beating one representative, and then killing the second. The third was stoned to death. Still, the owner tried to settle the standoff by sending more of his intermediaries. They were all treated with the same kind of disrespect and rejection.

"Last of all," Jesus said, "he sent his son to them. 'They will respect my son,' he said. But when the tenants saw the son, they said to each other, 'This is the heir. Come, let's kill him and take his inheritance.' So they took him and threw him out of the vineyard and killed him" (verses 37-39).

This was the divine perspective on the impending showdown. God was the violated owner. His servants, the prophets, had been badly treated. Now His Son had arrived. God took the risk of victimization. His own person was exposed to vulnerability. Now the case was clarified for all to see. In essence, the legal owner of the world was exposing the true nature of the tenants of His earth.

GOD'S PERSPECTIVE

The Bible records a classic illustration of how God feels about the insurrection of His creatures in several places.

> You turn things upside down,
>> as if the potter were thought to be like the clay!
> Shall what is formed say to him who formed it,
>> "He did not make me"?
> Can the pot say of the potter,
>> "He knows nothing"? (Isaiah 29:16)

> "Woe to him who quarrels with his Maker,
>> to him who is but a potsherd among the potsherds on
>>> the ground.
> Does the clay say to the potter,
>> 'What are you making?'
> Does your work say,
>> 'He has no hands'?" (Isaiah 45:9)

But who are you, O man, to talk back to God? "Shall what is formed say to him who formed it, 'Why did you make me like this?'" Does not the potter have the right to make out of the same lump of clay some pottery for noble purposes and some for common use? (Romans 9:20-21)

The absurdity is obvious. The Designer is being challenged by the rebellion of His clay product line.

In our world this kind of unjust reaction toward a legitimate leader would have provoked retaliation. History is full of wars that were started over similar situations. When the Communists revolted against the Czar of Russia in what we now call the Bolshevik Revolution, there was a terrible bloodbath. In the 1700s when the colonies revolted against King George III of Great Britain, once again, the established order did not give way peacefully to the new. When kings or emperors are challenged and their right to rule is contested, the inevitable result is war. The upstart rebels are confronted with all the power and resources at the challenged leaders' command.

> *The Creator of the earth found Himself challenged for control of that same earth — and He deliberately backed off.*

In contrast, the Creator of the earth found Himself challenged for control of that same earth—*and He deliberately backed off.* Instead of using the overwhelming forces at His disposal, He began working an amazing plan He had prepared for just such an eventuality.

→ F O U R ←
The Leader You Can Trust

I was waiting in the check-out line at the drugstore near my home. Suddenly, a blood-curdling scream and a loud commotion came from the back of the store. The clerk for my line actually reached for the phone to call 911, but at that moment a disheveled mother came marching through with a little boy under her arm, still kicking and throwing a fit. His face was knotted up with rage and was the color of a ripe tomato. I could still hear him howling after the car door slammed in the parking lot.

One of the women in line stated the obvious: "That's what I call a classic power struggle!"

Moments later, while loading my purchases in my car, I heard another squall of temper—this time from a grown man. "Jesus Christ" and "God" were mentioned in a violent and ugly way, as he cursed his wife because he'd been kept waiting a few minutes longer than he thought was reasonable. His voice contained the same rage and self-centeredness I had heard in the screams of the rebellious little boy. Both wanted their way and were willing to do whatever they thought necessary to get it.

I wish I could say that I don't exhibit the same pattern of behavior in my own life, but I can't. I am disgusted and repelled when others act it out, but when I do it, I try to cover it up or put the best face on it.

It isn't a matter of whether or not you and I have rebellious, demanding streaks in us—it's only a matter of realizing *where* they show up. Maybe you've never gone off on tantrums, but what sets you off? How far are you willing to go in order to get your way? More to the point, where do you find yourself at odds with God?

GOD'S RESPONSE TO OUR RESISTANCE

Jane will admit that she is angry with God. After being single through her twenties, she finally thought she'd found the man she wanted to marry. When he broke off their engagement she was devastated. Out of her disappointment, a deep resentment toward God began to grow. She stopped going to church because prayer chokes off in angry sobs and the Bible is an irritant. Seeing the happiness of married couples sitting around her during services is salt in the wound of her disappointment.

William bought a fast-food franchise expecting to make his million dollars quickly and retire early. Not only did he not get rich but he ended up in serious debt. The day he filed for bankruptcy, he also handed in his resignation from the Christian life. "If God won't give me what I want, why should I give Him what He wants?" he says.

We may not identify with Jane or William in the exact details of their struggle with supreme authority, but we know similar feelings. Our *excuses* for not trusting God with control of our lives may be unique, but our *resistance* is identical to everyone else's.

What's God to do with us? Here He is, the ultimate authority, the rightful leader of the universe, being constantly affronted with our anger and resentment—then our passive or active resistance. The big surprise is that He doesn't act like we do in similar circumstances. What do human authorities do when they are defied?

Let's take the United States government, for example. You look at all the taxes you pay and you get upset. The government is tapping you for more every time you turn around, so you decide you're going to join the tax revolt.

You write a nasty, hostile letter to the Internal Revenue Service and declare your independence from the tax system. Although this is the land of the free and the home of the brave, when the IRS gets hold of a letter like that, it sets in motion its enforcement policy. A process begins in which the noose of IRS authority gradually tightens. By the time you get through with your rebellion, your head will be spinning. They'll be talking about garnisheeing your wages and putting liens against your house and your bank accounts.

What happens when human authorities are faced with rebellion? They get tough.

In another more common scenario, a teenager has about had it with his parents. He says, "Dad and Mom, I am sick and tired of your rules. You're always trying to tell me what to do. Now, let me tell you what's going to happen around here. I'm going to come and go whenever I feel like it. I'm going to go to bed as late as I want. I'm going to keep my room however I please. I'll have whatever friends I want over to the house. I'll dress as it suits me. I'll listen to my kind of music and I'll play it as loud as I like it. I'm not going to put up with any more of your attempts to run my life. I am my own boss."

When parents face that kind of attitude in their children, do they respond by saying, "My, my, Son, you are finally growing up. We're so proud of you for demonstrating your independent, self-sufficient spirit"? No! They say, "Who do you think you're talking to? You're grounded! There will be no use of the phone, no use of the car, and no leaving the house except for school. On top of that, you will be expected to complete this list of extra tasks." What do even loving, highly motivated human authorities do when faced with rebellion? *They tighten the screws!*

If God reacted the way we do, we would expect Him to use threats, force, and violence to smash our pitiful rebellion. We would long ago have had our resistance to His authority ruthlessly crushed. Instead He has displayed a strange reluctance to enforce His rights as our Creator.

Certainly our defiant behavior has been a severe challenge to Him. The Old Testament clearly indicates that God has, at times, exercised His option of bringing justice and judgment upon human rebellion. The flood that destroyed all but Noah and his family tells us that God has come up to the very brink of extinguishing His creation. Apparently even His infinite patience and long-suffering love have their limits.

God's exasperation shows up in His past treatment of His chosen people, Israel. In this case a series of limited judgments was brought to bear on the stubborn rebellion of the Hebrews. They went through multiple cycles of breaking their promises and abandoning God. Then when the consequences came, they were turned back to God by adversity and suffering.

Yes, there is clear evidence that God has the power to insist on submission to His authority. But the amazing message of the Bible is that He has decided, at least for now, not to use raw power. He has decided to use another means, something none of us would have thought to use in a million years.

FACING THE ONE WE FEAR

God chose the radical tactic of *self-sacrifice* to reveal that He is the leader we can trust. In the face of our continuing insurrection, He deliberately made Himself vulnerable and allowed us to abuse and humiliate Him. Herein lies the awesome self-exposure of the Incarnation.

He was no threat. He came as a baby named Jesus. He lived among us for thirty-three years, most of them in an obscure town in a poor section of the country, and worked as an ordinary carpenter. He owned few material possessions, and His friends were working-class people.

> *God chose the radical tactic of self-sacrifice to reveal that He is the leader we can trust.*

When He went out to teach, He revealed the humble heart of a servant! That helps explain His disciples' confusion. They believed that He was the Messiah, the Christ of God. When He offered His kingdom to the crowds, they thought He intended to set up a political kingdom, to overthrow the Roman Empire. They envisioned Him establishing Jerusalem as His capital city and putting them in positions of authority at His left and right hands. His closest followers regularly bickered over which of them would be the greatest in His kingdom.

But in the Upper Room — only days after multitudes had hailed Him in the streets — Jesus quietly took a towel and basin and humbly washed His disciples' feet. He said, "I am among you as one who serves. As I have treated you, I want you to treat each other. All your concern about who is important, who is first, who is greatest is misplaced. The question is not who is serving you, but rather, who are you serving?" (see John 13:1-17). What was God in the flesh doing?

Hours later, He permitted His enemies to mock Him, whip Him, beat Him, curse Him, spit on Him, and do their enraged worst to Him. Why? Because the crucifixion of Jesus was staged, in part, to reveal a wealth of unexpected and profound truths about God. Above all, the message and significance of the cross is a *leadership demonstration*. It is the place we need to turn to face the One we so greatly fear.

Look at the cross. It is as if God the Son, with arms pinned by nails to a wooden crosspiece, is saying, "Look at Me. I am the great Ego you fear. This is the Self that occupies the throne of the universe. I understand your paranoia. You are full of fear and resentment. I know that you don't trust authority. Every authority on earth is imperfect. In their self-centeredness your parents abuse their authority. Teachers take advantage of their position. Your government leaders manipulate you and demand blind loyalty. Even religious leaders use and abuse your trust. I understand why your defenses are up. You are suspicious and cynical about anyone in authority and especially about ultimate authority. I know you think God must be the supreme egotist. It makes sense to you to judge Him by yourselves. You have naturally assumed that He is the most selfish being in the universe. After all, no one can stop Him from doing whatever He wants to do.

"Well, here I am. Nailed to your cross. Can you see who I am now? This is what I'm really like. I'm showing you that I'm humble, meek, and lowly of heart. I'm self-giving and self-sacrificing in nature. I have your best interest at heart. I will not take advantage of you because I'm stronger or smarter than you are. In fact, I'm letting you take advantage of my deliberate vulnerability."

For two millennia, hundreds of millions of people have heard their Creator's cry from the cross. They have found the cross unbelievably precious and embraced it as the ultrasound video of His innermost being. There, in terrifying yet approachable splendor, His character was exposed for all to see. At the cross, God submitted to our rebellious paranoia. He let us kill Him in our blind defiance. In the process of venting our rage and resentment against Him, He turned His victimization into our salvation.

And there He still asks us to meet Him. "Come, meet Me at the place where I humbled Myself before you; where I submitted Myself to you in all your hostility and unjust vindictiveness. Meet Me at the cross. If you cannot accept the fact that I am the leader you can trust—if you will not humble yourself to My humility and submit to My submission—then there is no hope for us ever to be reunited."

God cannot stop being God. He has the right and the responsibility to choose how rebellious human beings can be reconciled and received into His kingdom. Out of all the options that an infinite, all-knowing mind could devise, this was the best. God was determined both to maintain His integrity and salvage all who would choose to return to His kingdom. He could not compromise His authority and character, and He would not let go of His affection—for you and for me. He chose the cross as the door to His eternal love. It was brilliant. It was genius. His omniscient wisdom determined that there was no better way to reveal who He is and what His leadership is really like.

FINDING THE "WANT TO"

At a men's retreat I closed one of my Bible teaching sessions with a description of the nature of God's leadership similar to what you've just read. A few minutes later a middle-aged man fell into step with me on the walk to the dining hall.

"I've been a Christian for a long time," he began, "but I've never before seen the cross as you just presented it."

"What was it that caught your attention?" I asked.

"Remember when you were describing how the cross revealed the way Christ's ego works? Well, right then, for the first time in my life I *wanted* to follow Him. I mean, up 'til now, I knew I was supposed to follow Him, but something in me has always been reluctant."

I raised my eyebrows in a quizzical look.

He continued, "I don't know where the distrust in my heart actually came from, but it's obviously been there. There's been this fear of totally releasing the control of my life to Christ. Maybe I've been subconsciously expecting Him to exploit my trust the way my father did when I was growing up."

There was a long silence as we walked along. Then he added, "I just wanted you to know that I got in touch with following Jesus in a big way today. I think it may clear up some things in my life."

That proved to be a major understatement. Two years have passed and he's still in the life-changing process of enthusiastically following Jesus.

MORE THAN A SALVAGE OPERATION

Up until this moment you may have only seen the cross of Jesus Christ as God's means of providing salvation from the guilt and consequences of your sin. You were partially right. At Calvary the legal requirements of divine justice *were* fully met by the blood sacrifice of Christ.

But as we have seen, God was after more than salvaging our souls. He was providing the potential solution for our unwillingness to follow Him. Once and for all He revealed Himself to be the *safe leader*. That is, the One who will never trick us into trusting Him, then use and abuse us — then dump us and move on. He is the one safe leader because He has no *ego* entwined in His love for us. He does not *need* us to massage His ego, to support His public image or opinions. He offers Himself to us — both to save us from our sin in the first place, then to empower us to work out our saved-ness by relying on His love and strength. No, He is not "safe" in the sense that He indulges our headstrong or blind desires to rule our lives our own way. On that count He is fierce — because saving us from ourselves is the point.

Is following still an unresolved issue between you and Jesus? Try this exercise to find out. Imagine yourself standing before God's throne of grace. Now place all those favorite and treasured things and people that you hold dear into the hands of Jesus. As control passes from you to Him, what happens inside you?

Panic or relief? Alarm or peace?

If you aren't ready to follow yet, that's okay. Perhaps you need to learn more about this Leader's character, about the true Jesus, before you can trust Him with the most treasured things in your life.

→ F I V E ←
Holding Back from God

We reject the human tendency to abuse power. But rejecting heaven's right to lead us is a colossal blunder.

As we saw in the previous chapter, God challenged our assumptions about His character and agenda by revealing Himself in the attitude and life of Jesus. Certainly Jesus had undeniable authority. Yet He puzzled everyone, even His closest followers, by His refusal to act "presidential." Trappings of power meant nothing to Him. No bodyguards, no press secretary, no limo, no power suits, no photo ops, no carefully prescribed distance from the great unwashed pool of humanity. He didn't act the way a human being would act if he were the King of kings!

The breathtaking truth is that God in human flesh did not pull rank. He had no apparent need to be served. He focused His attention on ordinary people. He didn't seek the advantage of associating with wealthy, powerful people. In fact, His manner irritated and alienated the ruling elite from the very beginning. Not only did He *not* seek their favor, He quickly pointed out their hypocrisy.

LIGHT IN THE DARKNESS
In revealing what God is like, Jesus shocked us with God's wholeness and health. The sick and destructive self-centeredness of humanity was missing in Jesus. Yes, He was a threat—but for all the right reasons. Like a scientist presenting his life-saving research on lung cancer to a community that makes its living growing tobacco, He inevitably provoked hostility. We reacted to Jesus violently then, as now.

Why? Not because He attempts to coerce and dominate us. It is because He exposes the lies we have long embraced—our blind imagining that God wants to victimize us for His own ends, our foolish belief that the sin He wants us to quit is good for us.

Too often, we merely comply with God because we are scared of Him. We fear God because we believe He is hypersensitive to any challenge of His authority. With such a God concept we can imagine ourselves the victims of divine coercion, manipulation, and injustice. We pretend to appease the monster in the sky with subservient compliance because we think it's an advantage to get on His good side. Making the best of a system where God holds all the cards has long been considered proper religious piety. When the whole religious establishment of a culture is built around such a model of self-centered, divine egoism, it is an earthquake-sized shock to meet the true Jesus.

It is possible that, like the people of Jesus' day, we too are hiding our egoism behind our theology and "right doctrine." Secretly, we believe in a God who arbitrarily sets rules and performance standards for those under Him. The consequences are great. If we think God is selfish, then we have permission to be selfish ourselves. Jesus, like a motion-detecting floodlight, suddenly illuminated the world of His day. The darkness they thought was light was exposed (John 3:19-21). They were wrong about God and wrong about themselves.

THE GLORY OF GOD

Let me show you how easy it is to have the best of intentions and yet be off the mark. There is a mixup in some of our worship that reflects badly on the character of God. We often portray the Almighty as jealously guarding His glory, honor, and praise.

Well-worn clichés like "Be careful to give Him all the glory" still circulate widely. Pastors, missionaries, and other leaders seem to think that God is displeased when people praise and honor them for their work. They inevitably say things like, "All the praise and all the glory belong to God. I'm just His servant." Some of this may come from healthy humility. But too often we couple this kind of "evangelical political correctness" with preaching and teaching that "God is a jealous God and His glory is not to be shared with another"—and a view of God emerges. When we don't think about the implications of what we're saying, God can come out looking selfishly petty and preoccupied with His glory.

If a man demands to be recognized and honored for his accomplishments, his friends will soon be turned off by his insufferable ego needs. We find this behavior reprehensible in each other—why do we assume this is the way God acts? How did we get to where we accept the idea that massaging the divine Ego is real worship? Does God have a compelling need to be told how great He is? Does He get some sort of pleasure from the fawning, ingratiating flattery of those who are weaker?

What an unworthy concept of God!

Human despots have historically commanded adulation. Nebuchadnezzar, the king of Babylon, built a golden image of himself and decreed that all were to bow down and worship the statue at a prearranged signal. Those who refused, like Shadrach, Meshach, and Abednego, were thrown into a furnace built to incinerate the nonworshipers. Human rulers have consistently declared themselves divine and set up cults of emperor worship. Woe to the one who dared to resist the royal edict.

Just the opposite is true of our Creator. From the beginning of history, He has given amazing latitude to the independence of humanity. His creation of free will has been honored in spite of outrageous misuse of that freedom. He has never manipulated worship nor has He used His power to intimidate and coerce a fear-based response.

God desires that worship, praise, and honor be focused on Him because He wants us to know that He is the one unfailing source of all that we need for spiritual and physical life. It delights Him when the worshiper spontaneously brings honest praise from a genuinely inspired heart. Worth ascribed to worthy character, motives, and deeds is the only kind of worship that a God of integrity would find legitimate or satisfying.

To be called the greatest basketball player in history because we can dribble and shoot a basketball and because our T-shirt brags that "we are the greatest" is silly. But to be Michael Jordan, the man who led the Chicago Bulls to four NBA championships, is to actually deserve the high rank of MVP. The honor that Jordon has received is not hype. It is recognition of accomplishment.

God is to be glorified because He acts like who He is—*the greatest, the most honorable, the most trustworthy being in the universe.* He receives the glory of angels and humans because they are filled with admiration, deep respect, and appreciation for His sheer goodness and safe leadership. He deserves to be God. He has earned the right to lead. He is worthy of an eternity of heart-response worship.

We've examined the significance of what Jesus showed us about heaven's leadership. We've seen the reaction that it stirs up because it is so opposite to our own. Now, it's time to look at how this surprising revelation affects us. Let's look at four examples of what Jesus is like, and what He asks His followers to be like. Are we ready for this?

The Golden Yoke

In Matthew 11:27-30, God the Son revealed to us who the Father in heaven is:

> "All things have been committed to me by my Father. No one knows the Son except the Father, and no one knows the Father except the Son and those to whom the Son chooses to reveal him.
>
> "Come to me, all you who are weary and burdened, and I will give you rest. Take my yoke upon you and learn from me, for I am gentle and humble in heart, and you will find rest for your souls. For my yoke is easy and my burden is light."

The wonder of this revelation is shocking. God is gentle and humble of heart! This is something that you and I experience only through voluntarily submitting to His yoke. A yoke is a harnessing device by which domesticated oxen are fastened to each other and to a vehicle—a plow, wagon, or cart—they are expected to pull.

Our companion in the harness of voluntary service is Christ Himself. He is our pulling partner. He is beside us helping us carry the burden He has assigned to us. As a result, our part of the load is incredibly light.

When you work side by side with someone, you learn the most essential things about that person's character. You find out if he has endurance, reliability, and faithfulness; if he puts himself and his needs ahead of yours; whether he is self-giving or self-centered, proud or humble, gentle in using his strength or demanding and hard.

Here's the point—God is a leader who offers to be your burden sharer, your relief in weariness, your rest! This is unbelievable. Here's a leader who works alongside you, Servant yoked with servant. This is almost a ludicrous picture. Imagine a Shetland pony harnessed along-side a giant Clydesdale workhorse. Who's doing 99 percent of the work? Yet who participates in accomplishments that would be unthinkable if they had to be done in his own strength? This is exactly what Christ offers to you and me!

What I learn by being in the yoke with my Lord is how to serve. How to serve humbly, gently, faithfully. This has fascinated me to the depths of my being. Instead of using me like a beast of burden, which would have been His right as my Creator and owner, He shoulders the load beside me. Talk about appreciation and admiration! I can't get over the massive, gentle suffi-ciency that has come alongside me and invited me into the fellowship of His yoke. In submission *to* Him I have found the mystery of submission *with* Him.

> *God is a leader who offers to be your burden sharer, your relief in weariness, your rest!*

How can I do less than give Him my best and live for Him completely after all He's done for me? Appreciating the significance of His yoke creates the "want to" in following Him.

Childlike Humility

> And he said: "I tell you the truth, unless you change and become like little children, you will never enter the kingdom of heaven. Therefore, whoever humbles himself like this child is the greatest in the kingdom of heaven." (Matthew 18:3-4)

Greatness or positions of honor and respect in the kingdom of God go to those who emulate the Leader of the realm. Humility is the foundation, the very ground of being in God's kingdom. It is the essence of His own character. You can't get in the kingdom without humility — "God opposes the proud but gives grace to the humble" (James 4:6). Nor can you thrive and maximize your potential in the kingdom without it. God has a perfectly safe ego. He is safe to all those He leads. But He can only work best in the lives of followers who are willing to be ego-proofed themselves. The humble King rules in the hearts and lives of humble subjects. Childlike humility — which also produces maximum trustworthiness — is what God rewards. Our great King is the greatest because He is the most humble.

Losing to Win

> Then Jesus said to his disciples, "If anyone would come after me, he must deny himself and take up his cross and follow me. For whoever wants to save his life will lose it, but whoever loses his life for me will find it." (Matthew 16:24-25)

Following the example of Jesus will always lead to self-denial. The cross-bearing God asks all of His followers to break the awful suction of the self-centered ego by tapping into the supply of His grace through submission.

The wonder and intrigue is not so much that He asks us to develop a lifestyle of self-denial, but in the astounding fact that He behaves this way Himself. From our point of view He is in the enviable position to have it all His way. Why should He deny Himself anything? Human leaders who have money spend it. Those who have access to privileges and abundance don't hesitate to indulge themselves.

We might ask what God gets out of self-denial and the process of cross-bearing? That in itself is a question that comes out of self-centered human nature — a nature that wants to know "what's in it for me?" God enjoys His self-denying nature. As John Piper puts it: "God enjoys being God." And He seems to enjoy it when His children imitate Him. The followers of the servant-hearted King of the universe don't worship and emulate Him because they're obligated to. They follow Him because they're so impressed and enthralled with the wholeness and goodness of their sovereign Lord. Admiration and respect flow unrestrained from the hearts of the devoted followers of Jesus, the nail-scarred King. Spontaneous standing ovations spring from the souls of the servants of Servanthood. He deserves our highest praise. He is worthy of worship.

Seeing Him as He is — gentle with power, forgiving to the worst enemy — inspired this poem for me, which I have called "Scars of Love."

"Then I saw a Lamb, looking
As if it had been slain

Standing in the center
Of the throne . . ." (Revelation 5:6)
It staggers me
Stunned with incredulity
Amazed
I try to face
The pain of grace
It startles me
Shocked by suffering majesty
Awe-struck
I feel the wonder of
cross-branded love
It saddens me
Sick with Heaven's misery
Anguished
I trace humility
Scarred for eternity
"Worthy is the Lamb
That was slain
To receive honor, glory,
And power for ever!" (Revelation 5:12)

Kingdom Ambition

Salome, the ambitious mother of James and John, came to Jesus with her sons. She knelt down and asked of Him a favor.

> "What is it you want?" he [Jesus] asked.
>
> She said, "Grant that one of these two sons of mine may sit at your right and the other at your left in your kingdom."
>
> "You don't know what you are asking," Jesus said to them. "Can you drink the cup I am going to drink?"
>
> "We can," they answered.
>
> Jesus said to them, "You will indeed drink from my cup, but to sit at my right or left is not for me to grant. These places belong to those for whom they have been prepared by my Father."
>
> When the ten heard about this, they were indignant with the two brothers. Jesus called them together and said, "You know

that the rulers of the Gentiles lord it over them, and their high officials exercise authority over them. Not so with you. Instead, whoever wants to become great among you must be your servant, and whoever wants to be first must be your slave—just as the Son of Man did not come to be served, but to serve, and to give his life as a ransom for many." (Matthew 20:21-28)

Contrary to superficial first impressions, Jesus was not upset by the ambitions of Salome and her two sons. Kingdom ambitions are regarded by God as a sign of high intelligence. They reveal a superior value system. Coveting the pearl of great price or exchanging all inferior possessions in order to possess the great treasure of the kingdom is encouraged by Jesus (Matthew 13:44-46). He fully intends to set all kingdom overcomers beside Him on His throne. Revelation 22:3 reveals that "his servants will serve him" around the throne of majesty in the New Jerusalem. Then verse 5 holds out the ultimate privilege and trust a human can know: "And they will reign for ever and ever."

Now that's a high view of humankind. Our Creator believes in us and thinks we are capable of becoming part of His new administration. He intends to trust us with unimaginable power and authority. But before He grants those ultimate honors He explains what qualifies a follower of His for such immense trust.

"James, John"—you can just see Jesus looking intently into the eyes of these two gung-ho wannabes—"remember how I lead? Do you want to be trusted lieutenants? It will mean that you will have to be a servant. No, I'll make that stronger. You'll actually be a slave of those you lead for all eternity. You'll have to operate exactly like I do. I, as your leader, have come to serve and give up My rights to My life. I willingly pay the price of true leadership. I put the needs and best interests of those I love and lead ahead of My own. Now . . . are you still interested in leading with Me in My kingdom?" Bill Hybels correctly calls this the invitation to "descend into greatness."

THE HEART OF THE GOOD NEWS

The heart of the good news that Jesus came to proclaim was this: "The kingdom of heaven is near you, because I am here as its royal representative. Take a good look, watch Me, listen to Me. If you give Me a chance you will see in Me the leader your heart has always longed for.

"If so, repent . . . change sides. Surrender to My safe leadership and become a safe follower yourself. My leadership welcomes and pours grace out to those who humble themselves, who deny themselves, who ego-proof themselves. Cross-slain, cross-disarmed, cross-bearing followers are the servants I can trust."

Is it not appropriate for such a remarkably attractive, worthy supreme being to call you and me to follow Him? Why would anyone still resist once we've been exposed to what He's really like? The answer, of course, is terribly embarrassing. Even when we know the truth about Him, we still tend to deny and cover up the truth about *ourselves*. In our obsession with control every one of us is capable of incredibly creative and ingenious self-deception. Jeremiah said it well:

> The heart is deceitful above all things and beyond cure.
>   Who can understand it? (17:9)

The twist when God reveals Himself in the glory of His sheer goodness is breathtakingly beautiful. The reverse twist when humans spurn and scorn Him is horror and atrocity beyond description. It is the most unspeakable kind of injustice.

May it be the desire of our hearts to be drawn in wonder and awe to the magnificence of God's lovable humility, to overcome our unreasonable resistance to the invitation to follow Him.

⇒ S I X ⇐
The Great Mandate

*J*esus gave us a great key to understanding God's plans and priorities when He distilled the Old Testament law and prophets down to this: "'Love the Lord your God with all your heart and with all your soul and with all your mind.' This is the first and greatest commandment. And the second is like it: 'Love your neighbor as yourself'" (Matthew 22:37-39). In this succinct paragraph the Master gives us the basis for understanding that God desires a love relationship with us. It tells us that the bottom line for God is relational. Love is the goal of life. Loving God and each other is the central purpose of our existence.

In John 13:34-35 we find this reinforced. Just prior to His crucifixion, Jesus finalized His training of the disciples in the Upper Room. At this climactic moment He announces, "A new command I give you: Love one another. As I have loved you, so you must love one another. By this all men will know that you are my disciples, if you love one another." Notice how similar it is to the aforementioned commandments. What Francis Schaeffer called "the mark of the Christian"—love—is commanded by Jesus in the life of every believer. Clearly, God's intention is to offer the truth of the gospel on the silver platter of relational excellence. The loving way Christians behave toward each other is designed to catch the world's attention and create an entry point for the message of good news.

Another key to understanding God's plans and priorities, traditionally called the Great Commission, is found in Matthew 28:18-20.

Then Jesus came to them and said, "All authority in heaven and on earth has been given to me. Therefore go and make disciples of all nations, baptizing them in the name of the Father and of the Son and of the Holy Spirit, and teaching them to obey everything I have commanded you. And surely I am with you always, to the very end of the age."

At the end of His earthly ministry, just before He ascended into heaven, Jesus gave these clear instructions to His followers. The church was to be an active outreach team for the duration of its existence. Going out to make disciples of all nations has been at the heart of Christian obedience for two thousand years.

THE HEART OF GOD'S PLAN

As important as the Greatest Commandment, the Great Commandment, and the Great Commission are in shaping Christian understanding of what God is doing in the world, there is an even more significant portion of New Testament revelation. First Corinthians 15:24-28 clues us in on the overall purpose of God in Christ Jesus.

Then the end will come, when he [Jesus] hands over the kingdom to God the Father after he has destroyed all dominion, authority and power. For he must reign until he has put all his enemies under his feet. The last enemy to be destroyed is death. For he "has put everything under his feet." Now when it says that "everything" has been put under him, it is clear that this does not include God [the Father] himself, who put everything under Christ. When he has done this, then the Son himself will be made subject to him who put everything under him, so that God may be all in all.

This is a blazing burst of classified information. From the headquarters of the universe we are treated to a glimpse of the big picture. Jesus has apparently been commissioned by God the Father to resolve the leadership crisis that currently exists in the universe. This glimpse into the behind-the-scenes job description of our great Savior and Lord reveals why He used "kingdom language" and insisted on repentance as the appropriate response to His message. He came to earth with the intent of ending the insurrection of mankind against the leadership of God! He came to conquer all opposition.

That overriding purpose of God throws a floodlight of understanding upon the cross. Calvary was designed by the Father and executed by the Son as the essential means of restoring God's reign over His entire universe. It had a cosmic dimension according to Colossians 2:15, "And having disarmed the powers and authorities, he made a public spectacle of them, triumphing over them by the cross."

> *He came to earth with the intent of ending the insurrection of mankind against the leadership of God!*

And it has a personal dimension for every believer. Colossians 1:21-22 puts it this way: "Once you were alienated from God and were enemies in your minds because of your evil behavior. But now he has reconciled you by Christ's physical body through death to present you holy in his sight."

When you and I face the implications of Christ's mission on earth, we also have to face lifelong resistance to God's direction. Throughout His whole ministry, the real human problem was revealed. Even the best and most religious of us have a hostility and aggressive defiance toward God that makes us want to eliminate our Creator. When He put Himself in our hands, without defenses, we immediately took advantage of His vulnerability.

NO PLACE TO HIDE

God designed this graphic object lesson to settle the issue of who has the power problem. Human beings, in collaboration with the principalities and powers of the rebel kingdom of darkness, exposed themselves at the cross. In killing Jesus, the CEO of heaven, we demonstrated for all time the actual root cause of the break with God's kingdom. In assassinating the heir to the throne, we exposed our agenda of self-enthronement.

The Great Mandate explains the authoritative style of Jesus. He doesn't sell or market His gospel. He doesn't negotiate a compromise agreement. He simply announces His terms: "The kingdom of God is near [in me]. Repent [give up, surrender, change sides] and believe the good news!" (Mark 1:15).

The good news is that the option of surrender is open. Our insane egomania can be forgiven. Our revolution can be abandoned.

The Great Mandate also explains why His commands fairly sizzle with compelling sovereignty. When Jesus Christ has been restored to His rightful place as our Leader, authority and power emanate from His marching orders. I am so glad they do. We have a take-charge boss, a no-nonsense, make-it-happen, absolute Ruler in command. My surrendered soul is His to command, and nothing has ever fit so well or felt so right. I was made to follow Him. All the lights have gone on, all the buttons have been pushed, and all the connections made. He is my Leader! My surrender opened up the experience of life in His kingdom.

The first part of this book has introduced the Leader we can trust and follow. The next part is an in-depth look at what has happened to us because we have rejected His leadership. If there is a place in these pages where you might be tempted to skip ahead, it would probably be here. But thinking deeply about why we don't follow Him will help you diagnose your own areas of resistance—important to know if you want to find the best remedy and the life of spiritual fulfillment you've been looking for.

TAKING ANOTHER STEP—
QUESTIONS FOR MEDITATION

1. What do you expect from God? Does He seem intimidating?

2. Is it possible that you have been keeping your distance from Christ even though you believe in Him? If so, why?

3. What keeps you from trusting Him and following Him?

4. Spend some additional time rereading pages 33-36. In light of what the cross tells us, what do you think of Christ's leadership now?

5. From your perspective is God a "giver" or a "taker"? Explain.

6. What do you fear God might do to punish you if you do not follow His plan for your life?

7. Do you enjoy God? Have you found Him to be approachable, likable, lovable? Do you appreciate the safety of His humility? Explain.

8. If you were to fully accept the authority and leadership of Jesus as a way of life, what would change?

ᐳ PART TWO ᐸ

AN UNSAFE
WORLD

What on Earth Is Wrong with Us?

A friend of mine was telling me a tragic story of infidelity. His brother, a husband and father, was trashing his family for an erotic adventure with a newfound lover. He willingly placed all that he had at risk. The wife was in severe depression, the children in rebellion, the finances in chaos, and the extended family polarized. As the heartsick brother enumerated the costs and consequences that had already taken place, he was all but overwhelmed by the disaster of such self-centeredness. "How could anyone be so callously cruel and irresponsible? All he cares about is his own immediate desires. Everything and everyone that used to matter has been thrown overboard. And guess how he explains his actions? He says he finally decided to do what makes him happy, what feels good to him."

> *"Selfishness is so attractive though, isn't it?"*

We sat quietly sipping our coffee while contemplating the enormity of this private disaster. Tears began to slide slowly down my friend's cheeks. He wiped them and looked up. "I shouldn't be so shocked with my brother's behavior," he said candidly. "It isn't like I haven't thought of doing the same kind of thing myself. I guess I'm just realizing that this sin thing is worse—far worse—than I thought." There was another long pause and then he whispered, "Selfishness is so attractive though, isn't it?"

I think we would all agree that what happened to my friend's extended family was not good for the people involved. Unbridled selfishness never is. And when enough of us give ourselves permission to put ourselves, our pleasures, and our needs first, *everything* begins to fall apart.

Do you ever get sick of the savagery of the world? Of the wars, the crime, and the killing? Of politics, treachery, and the twisted weaving of popular deceits? Do you ever get nauseated by the horror and hopelessness hanging in the smog over the cities, the drug culture, the gangs, the rancid pornography? Lately I've begun to avoid the evening news. Upon reflection, I admitted to myself that I was afraid, ashamed, and saddened to be a human. Nothing seems so obvious as the need to halt this madness we call progress. No one seems to know where we're going, but we're redoubling our efforts to get there as soon as possible. Few seem willing to remember that forecasting the future must be based on an understanding and appreciation of the past.

THE OLDEST "DESIGNER" RELIGION

Discovering self, exploring self, indulging self, and defending self is, as always, the central preoccupation of man. The ancient cross-cultural "religion of me" still thrives.

Why do industrialists deliberately pollute rivers, lakes, and oceans?

Why do strip miners ravage the surface of the earth?

Why do pornographers exploit children?

Why do televangelists fleece their gullible sheep?

Why do mothers abort their unborn babies?

Why do husbands and wives abandon their marriages and families for new lovers?

Why do tobacco companies deliberately hook young people on lifetime addictions to nicotine?

Why do entertainment conglomerates continually produce movies and television shows that focus on illicit sex, filthy talk, violence, and crime?

You know the answers and so do I. Selfishness! Putting your own interests first. Getting what you want no matter how it may affect someone else. Selfishness, with its greed, envy, and jealousy. Selfishness, the breeding ground of rage, hatred, bitterness, resentment, and revenge. Selfishness—like gangrene rotting away the character and moral fiber of our communal soul.

A glance at some of the "normal activities" on this planet is not enjoyable. But before we can find and apply an adequate solution, we must first study and understand the problem. How bad is the human condition?

> Where do you think all these appalling wars and quarrels come from? Do you think they just happen? Think again. They come about *because you want your own way,* and fight for it deep inside yourselves. You lust for what you don't have and are willing to kill to get it. You want what isn't yours and will risk violence to get your hands on it. (James 4:1-2, MSG, emphasis added)

I write this book with a heart that trembles at impending global disintegration. Ethnic subcultures are deeply embroiled in conflict, a current example of which is former Yugoslavia, also called the Balkans, where centuries-old rivalries bring violence and bloodshed. Large U.S. cities like Los Angeles are stuck in the gridlock of racial strife and the violence of gang warfare. The political landscape in the United States has fractured into cultural hate groups.

Today, we are more connected by communication and media, and more educated than ever before. Yet as humans we are as divided as ever.

EXPENSIVE SELF-INDULGENCE

The global cost of self-indulgence begins with the behavior of individuals. Paul is a guy who has been out of prison now for about four years. In the early winter of 1982 he stopped one evening on his way home from work for a "couple of beers." It had been nine months since he had taken a drink. His wife had threatened to leave him if he continued to blow their money on binges. He had agreed to sober up.

The night before his return to the bars, he deliberately picked a fight. The one subject he knew he could get his wife riled up about was church. He was a wayward Protestant, she a devout Catholic. He began by telling a crude story about the pope to which she immediately took offense.

She turned on him—just as he'd planned. "At least I practice my religion," she said. "You sleep in and watch ball games on Sundays, so we both know what kind of a lousy Christian you are."

"Fine. I quit drinking, leave the friends I grew up with, change my lifestyle big-time, and what encouragement do I get? 'You're a lousy Christian,' you say. Well, miss goody-goody two shoes, I'm sick and tired of your superior attitude."

The next evening, his drinking buddies welcomed him back like a long-lost brother. The evening slipped away drink by drink, and finally the bartenders wouldn't serve him any more.

"Let me call a cab for you tonight. You're pretty drunk, Paul," offered one bartender. He refused. Twenty minutes later a patch of fog confused him. His four-by-four pickup crossed the center line and crashed head-on into a van carrying a young family. The van was demolished and four people were killed. Only the mother survived.

Paul was convicted of vehicular homicide and spent eight years in the penitentiary. His self-indulgence cruelly destroyed not only his own life and marriage but also devastated a young woman. In his sane and lucid moments in prison he counted fifty-eight people whose lives suffered pain and loss because of that one evening of self-indulgence. At times the guilt and regrets seem heavier than he can bear.

Now, take Paul's story and multiply it. In the United States alone there are an estimated 14 million alcoholics. Each year 40,000 people die or are injured in drug- and alcohol-related automobile accidents. And in other parts of the world the devastation is far worse. In many parts of Russia as many as 80 percent of the teenagers and adults are alcoholics. Enslaved to our selfish "freedoms," we have created a dangerous world.

According to the Bible, all of us are born with our *ego-immune* system damaged. The inner mechanism that was designed by God to keep us balanced as a self in proper relationship to other selves and to the Great Self of our Creator has malfunctioned. It has accelerated its strength and intensity and taken over. Now all humans have an ego that welcomes a potentially destructive self-absorption process.

"YA GOTTA SERVE SOMEBODY"

Jeff and Linda came to our Discovery class for six months and then disappeared. An attractive, intelligent couple, they appeared to have it all together. The message of Jesus had been explained in clear and interesting ways — but when the issue of *repentance* came up Jeff and Linda turned away. Submission of their lives to God was too much to ask. They were attracted to the benefits of the kingdom, but yielding control of their lives to their Creator struck them as extreme.

Now, three years later, they have resurfaced in the recovery ministry, which deals with obsessive-compulsive and addictive behaviors. Jeff is a cocaine addict and Linda is a devotee of a new-age cult. Their marriage is hanging by a thread. What happened? They rejected the leadership of God and then willingly submitted their lives to the control of lesser, false gods!

This young couple is not alone in their amazing behavior. All over this world the same people who reject the supervision of the King of the universe accept lesser, oppressive masters without so much as a second thought.

The authority we were designed to follow seems unreasonable. Yet slavery to drugs, money, ambition, workaholism, habits, dark obsessions, and authoritarian false religion seems to make sense to us.

We see a similar pattern in the lives of adolescents. As they begin to chafe under what they see as the restrictive authority of their parents, their tendency is to move toward "freedom." What does life out from under authority look like? Predictably it includes cigarettes, alcohol, drugs, sex, pornography, and the latest outlaw rock music. Added to these expressions of autonomy and independence is the "liberating influence" of teen peer-pressure. Legitimate authority is rejected and replaced with cruel and dangerous slave masters.

We insist on going our own way and doing our own thing. Then we hurt ourselves and hurt each other in the process. Bizarre as it may be, we guard each self-destructive behavior as a "sacred right" or "freedom." We resist any infringement on the "right to choose," even when the choice we want to make is deadly.

How did the predicament we are in develop on this earth? Its origin can be found in one word: *sin*. It is critical to develop our kingdom perspective in the way Jesus saw it, and to understand sin in the way Jesus understood it.

→ E I G H T ←
Diagnostic Confusion

"Come now, let us reason together," says the LORD.
"Though your sins are like scarlet, they shall be as white as snow."
ISAIAH 1:18

"I'm only human!" my friend insisted. We were sitting in a restaurant discussing a violent outburst of cursing and profanity he had unleashed on his wife the night before. This kind of "losing his cool" was a pattern in Fred's life. As I invested the time and attention it took to get inside his system of rationalization, I began to understand where he got his concept of overwhelming human weakness.

Calling sin *weakness* is an easy way to dodge the real issue. It's only one justification we have come up with to explain away this very serious problem otherwise known as sin.

When it comes to the subject of what is wrong with us, God invites us to engage the truth with our intellect. In Isaiah 1:18 He issued an appeal to every human mind: "Come now, let us reason together." The subject? Sin. Now why would God want to think deeply with us about this particular subject? Could it be that it's the one thing we all think creatively about anyway?

The interesting thing to me is that reason, logic, and research can theoretically agree with God on the subject of sin. In reality it's usually quite different. When people attempt to diagnose what is wrong with themselves, they tend to cloud the issue. It sounds so prudish, so puritanical, so judgmental to call it sin. So, we construct other definitions, as Fred did. These alternative diagnoses have deeply affected the way modern Christians view sin. After examining the current crop of definitions, we'll see what Jesus would say about our problem from a "kingdom perspective."

The following six definitions all claim the Bible as their source.

SIN AS HUMANNESS

Fred had been raised in a church where the gospel of Christ was preached. Forgiveness of sins and salvation by grace through faith was the constant theme. Along with the redemption available in Christ came a second message: "We sin every day in thought, word, and deed. Nobody is perfect. We are all sinners saved by grace. Please be patient, God isn't finished with me yet!" The bottom line was, "We are human, so we must sin."

Now there is truth in this. We are a work of God in process. Maturity in Christ is a lifetime journey. No one has arrived at sinless perfection. But when we emphasize human weakness we create "running room" for our sinful habits and patterns. If "I'm not perfect, just forgiven" is taken to its logical conclusion, we have another powerful hiding place for the selfishness from which God wants to save us. Dallas Willard, in *The Spirit of the Disciplines*, explains our low expectations this way:

> Most conservatives by the early 1970s generally accepted that being a Christian had nothing to do with actually following or being like Jesus. It was readily admitted that most Christians did not really follow Him and were not really like Him. In some circles, the only absolute requirement for being a Christian was that one believe the proper things about Jesus.[1]

This is a situation begging to be used and abused by human beings who are prone to seek the lowest levels of *commitment* to anything while still claiming *membership*.

There's something in every one of us that resists having the standards of conduct raised. We instinctively work to keep the expectations of those closest to us as low as possible. This allows us to keep many of the characteristics of the self life without feeling pressure to change. *Humanness*, *weakness*, and *imperfection* are words that tend to be useful in covering a multitude of sins.

On the other hand, there is good reason to be cautious about *perfectionism*—that is, thinking we can set out on our own to achieve sinless perfection. There is no health in moving from one extreme to another. But the *weakness-is-my-identity* kind of Christian life is a dreadful mistake. It is complacency. Understanding and compassion can become enabling, and even facilitating. According to Galatians 6:1-2, what the weaker brother needs is humble, gentle truth-telling for the purpose of victory over sin. This is to be the loving objective of the spiritually strong in assisting the weak.

SIN AS DISEASE OR DYSFUNCTION

Cassie's therapist is dismayed that the medications have only helped her depression temporarily. For other clients, whose depression is triggered by poor health or stress, medication has generally helped. Each time Cassie's problems resurface, though, they are clearly linked to issues lodged in her spirit.

"If I forgive my mother, how do I know she'll ever be made to pay for the terrible things she did to me? And the same for my stupid ex-husband. I want them to pay—but God lets them have a good life while I suffer because of their ugly behavior," she insists angrily.

If people are depressed for physiological reasons, they need medicinal treatment, because some physical problems affect the way the mind and emotions function. On the other hand, if people are depressed because they are harboring anger and the unwillingness to forgive, they need to be shown how to let go of these soul-crippling sins and led through the process of repentance. If you are a therapist or in therapy, stick with me. In no way am I bashing the science, art, and ministry of counseling. I am attempting to get a handle on inadequate ideas about sin.

Is sin *sickness*, or is it selfishness? Is it mental illness or is it rebellion against God? My conclusion is that sin produces physical, emotional, and relational dysfunction. Preoccupation with self causes various kinds of diseases.

- The sins of greed and covetousness produce a driven, workaholic, stress-filled life. The bank account may be full but the marriage is empty.
- The sin of lust produces a dangerous "every male/female is a target" mentality. Compulsive sexual obsessions take over.

Sexually transmitted diseases may lurk in the aftermath of every sexual encounter.

■ The sin of self-indulgence produces laziness, gluttony, and a sedentary lifestyle. Danger to the heart and the arteries is predictable.

■ The sins of hatred and bitterness produce internal stress and hardness of heart that make healthy relationships impossible to sustain. Eventually, inner conflict adversely affects emotional and physical health.

Am I quibbling? Is this all just a matter of where you put the emphasis? I don't think so. Each Christian-based model of sin has some truth to it. A case can be made from Scripture for a strong connection between sin and sickness. Jesus referred to Himself as a physician and to sinners as those sick and in need of His care. But it was in His treatment of the malady that He departs from the modern mind-set. He said, "I have . . . come to call . . . sinners to repentance" (Luke 5:32). For Jesus there was no substantial healing of the soul, the mind, or the body without repentance (*metanoia*, the Greek word for submission to His leadership and rejection of sin).

Here is where the sin-as-sickness idea can depart into speculation and experimentation if we are not careful. By all means, treat the symptoms with *drugs* and *therapy* as necessary. But do not avoid the underlying spiritual issues. To do so is a departure from the example of Jesus. Helping an individual deal with emotional damage is important. But all therapy that calls itself Christian must lead to the kingdom of God, not the kingdom of self. Jesus said, "What does it profit a man if he gain the whole world"—including mental and relational health—" but lose his own soul?" (See Mark 8:36.)

SIN AS IGNORANCE

Jerry fathered three children out of wedlock, then abandoned them with their mother. "But it's not really his fault," claims the social worker who is trying to find him. "It's part of the uneducated, blue-collar community he grew up in. He doesn't know any better."

The therapeutic community and the educational community are mutually dependent on one another. The study of behavioral sciences is the domain of the institutions of higher learning. It is from the fundamental misconception that sin is the result of ignorance that the educators influence the therapists. Information and its uses have long been regarded as the basis of progress. Enlightenment or the eradication of ignorance is seen as the hope and salvation of mankind. Science is the source of the only legitimate solutions.

Once again there is some truth here. Ignorance is a serious problem, and the dissemination of information is important, but it does not stop or even slow down sinful behavior.

A case in point is sex education and AIDS curricula. Never have so many known so much about sex, its options, and its consequences. Public education touts the methodologies of "safe sex." The theory behind the billion-dollar campaigns is that people are getting diseases and getting pregnant because they don't know how to avoid the results of promiscuity. Now that the theory has been tested, it has been found to be a very expensive error.

Education doesn't change sinful choices. In fact, history demonstrates that the more educated people become, the more deadly their choices become. A Stone Age native kills with a club or a spear. A nuclear physicist kills with nuclear weapons on a scale that the spear thrower can't even comprehend. Education doesn't solve the problem of violent self-assertion and aggression, it only makes people more efficient and effective. Biological and chemical weapons have replaced rifles and bayonets, which replaced bows and arrows. But aren't we far worse off?

SIN AS VICTIMIZATION

The culture of the victim has swept our world. The idea that "I can't be held responsible for my behavior because of the way I was treated by others" is enormously popular. It is becoming commonplace for admitted perpetrators to be let off the hook of justice because they were abused either as children or as adults.

I have been a pastor for more than twenty-seven years. During that time I have watched the victim mentality steadily grow. It used to be that women most often left their husbands for unfaithfulness, deadbeat laziness, or incompatibility. Now, the most common justification for the breakup of a marriage is abuse. Abuse is everything from actual physical violence to unwanted sexual pressure. For some, all conflict is regarded as verbal or emotional abuse. Even the power struggle between ego agendas is regarded as abuse.

There is absolutely no question that cruel, painful, and abusive behavior exists in marriage. Men do abuse women and women abuse men. What is alarming is the tendency to justify our own wrong behavior on the basis of what others have done to us, as opposed to taking responsibility for our own actions. Having been abused does not justify abusing. If my sin is someone else's fault, then I have no compelling need to change. I can't help my behavior. I've been damaged and programmed by the family system in which I was raised. In this view of sin the current treatment of choice is to go back into the past and affix blame. The assumption behind it? If I can understand how I was damaged, I can then make new choices to break the hold of the past.

Although there is some truth in the victim model and some help in deciphering the past, this view of sin is not setting people free. The self, however damaged, loves to hide in the victim identity. Blame provides a terrific cover for egocentricity. More and more people are discovering this model to be a convenient way to avoid taking responsibility for their choices.

SIN AS INABILITY

Some Christians start with a definition of sin called "total depravity." This does not mean that humankind is incurably self-centered and rebellious against God, it means that people are spiritually dead and completely incapable of responding to God. Only the Spirit of God can, by His own initiative, awaken and activate the spirit of men and women. This way of defining sin contains the idea that human hearts cannot choose God, unless God first chooses them. Some may conclude, "I am unable to do anything about my sin, so why bother?"

It is obvious from Scripture that God appeals to the human mind and heart as if He expects a positive response. The Bible is jammed full of commands, instructions, and divine expectations that are clearly waiting for follow-up on our part. He clearly reveals that we will be held accountable when we do not follow His instructions.

Now, this creates a serious problem for those who conclude that unregenerate humans are incapable of following God's Word. Why would God treat people as if they were spiritually capable of responding if indeed they are spiritually dead and unable to do so? Why would God waste His time appealing to men and women He had not personally "activated"?

Something more must be going on. I believe that God calls us to follow Him because following is possible. The Holy Spirit is active in the Word of God itself! Hearing the Word makes it possible to act upon it.

The word of God is living and active. Sharper than any double-edged sword, it penetrates even to dividing soul and spirit, joints and marrow; it judges the thoughts and attitudes of the heart. Nothing in all creation is hidden from God's sight. Everything is uncovered and laid bare before the eyes of him to whom we must give account. (Hebrews 4:12-13)

Yes, it is necessary for God to touch each life by His Spirit. He doesn't do this in some mysterious, arbitrary way, but through the spreading of His Word into the world. "Faith comes from hearing the message, and the message is heard through the word of Christ" (Romans 10:17). "He became the source of eternal salvation for all who obey him" (Hebrews 5:9). The entrance of His Word gives the light that activates the human spirit in much the same way as sunlight activates the germination of dormant seeds (see 1 Corinthians 1:18). As the Spirit penetrates each heart that is turned in upon itself with truth about sin, righteousness, and the judicial authority of God, an ability to respond is born (John 16:8-11).

This is the door to new life in Christ: the option to turn from *self-centeredness* to *God-centeredness* is now open. Each individual is responsible to submit to God's Spirit-inspired truth. We will be held accountable for what we choose to do.

Calling sin "inability to follow" sets up a huge hiding place for rebels. The idea of an arbitrary God, who is working out a deep scheme beneath what He is admitting publicly, reinforces suspicion and distrust toward God. A cosmic leader who has gone on record as "not wanting anyone to perish, but everyone to come to repentance" (2 Peter 3:9) and "[wanting] all men to be saved and to come to a knowledge of the truth" (1 Timothy 2:4), cannot be credible or possess integrity if He is not consistent about allowing all indeed to respond.

Others use the sin-as-inability view in quite a different way. They maintain that *they can't help their behavior*—after all, they were born this way. They are just following their genetic code. Here are some examples:

- "I am an alcoholic because it is an inherited weakness."
- "I have a violent temper because I come from a family that has passed on that pattern from generation to generation."
- "I am a homosexual because that's the way I was wired from birth. God must have intended for me to have this sexual preference because He gave it to me. I didn't ask for it. I have just known I was different from others in my gender as far back as I can remember."

The logical conclusion of such reasoning is that a lack of essential ability or capacity makes it impossible to respond to God's instructions and requirements. Therefore, my behavior cannot really be wrong or sinful. This is a clever and increasingly common way to avoid accountability for living contrary to the life of freedom God says I can live.

SIN AS MISUNDERSTANDING

There are still sizable numbers of professing Christians who are convinced that people are basically good. They tend to be involved in churches on the liberal side of the spectrum.

A lady and her friend visited the church that I pastor in Seattle. She came for several Sundays before asking if she could meet with me. When we sat down in my office, I asked her what she wanted to talk about. "Young man," she said, "you need to rethink your understanding of sin."

"And why is that?" I asked.

"You have a fine church and you are an interesting speaker to listen to, but your ideas about sin are off the mark."

"Convince me," I suggested.

She took me to Philippians 4:8 and related it this way: "If you were to look for the noble, the lovely, the admirable, the excellent, and the praiseworthy in your fellow man, you would find it. You are hung up on that depressing doctrine of sin because your focus is in the wrong place! Think positive and you'll soon see how basically good people really are."

I knew it was going to be a difficult conversation.

She waved away my explanation of a couple of clear passages on the all-encompassing sinful condition of the human heart. Romans 3:10-19, 23 didn't faze her, and I realized that this dear woman believed what she preferred to believe. Anything from Scripture that challenged her viewpoint she wrote off as opinion and "your interpretation." She represents a venerable mainline Protestant tradition. Relativism has left in its wake a generation that has corrected, modernized, and "civilized" the Bible with its politically correct view of humankind.

The sin-as-misunderstanding view is now gaining new support as the new age movement finds compatibility within churches that have cut their biblical moorings and are adrift on the sea of speculation. New-age Christianity is a do-it-yourself, mix-and-match smorgasbord of ideas. Each parishioner creates his or her own truth. As always, when we are in control, the idea of sin is modified to remove personal responsibility or guilt. The emphasis is placed on human potential and a positive-thinking refusal to see any facts that do not contribute to the glory of the new age of humankind.

IT COMES NATURALLY

Anyone who has attempted to parent a child knows from experience the extraordinary capacity for inventive self-justification that resides within each of us. Children are born masters at manipulating the data to explain why their behavior is okay. They instinctively know how to plead sickness, ignorance, victimization, weakness, inability, misunderstanding, or some combination of these classic dodges. That adults would systematize these into definitions of behavior that take the pressure off their consciences is not surprising. Without outside help we massage the truth about our behavior

> *Without outside help we massage the truth about our behavior until we get an explanation with which we can comfortably live.*

until we get an explanation with which we can comfortably live. An objective standard or benchmark must be introduced into the mix.

This is exactly what God has done. In the next chapter we will examine God's evaluation of our behavior.

NOTE
1. Dallas Willard, *The Spirit of the Disciplines* (San Francisco: HarperCollins, 1988), pp. 22-23.

→ N I N E ←
What God Told the Prophets

I made the mistake of asking Henry how he managed to place five arrows in a silver-dollar-sized bull's-eye at a distance of thirty yards. Henry is an avid archer who takes his passion for bows and arrows very seriously. For the next two hours I found myself fascinated by intricacies and complexities that I never knew existed.

Henry made a big deal of the law of trajectory. "If your aim is off even a fraction of an inch at the *projectile launch point*, the margin of error rapidly increases with the distance to the target. The point of impact on the target end can only be adjusted with a precise release at the aim point." As this champion archer continued to explain his craft, my mind was racing to the larger truth he was unknowingly illustrating.

How I wish our understanding of the life of salvation was as clear. If only we were aiming and releasing our message with the precision of the revealed Word of God. It may surprise you to discover that the crucial aim and release point for the gospel is the nature of sin. If we are off target on the question of what sin is, we will be way off target as to what salvation is. I am convinced that, as a movement, evangelicals have been drifting wide of the outreach target because of an inadequate doctrine of sin.

My family doctor is a careful, methodical man. Even when my own mind is pretty well made up about what my problem is, he invariably puts me through all the procedures: an examination, blood tests, x-rays or ultrasound, urine and stool samples, and so forth.

During one visit I asked him why he did so many tests. He said, "The most difficult and complicated part of what I do is diagnosing the problem. If I am impulsive or hasty in assessing what's wrong with my patient, the prognosis or treatment I decide to give might be useless and could well be dangerous!"

I've thought about that conversation many times. The church and the medical clinic have some similarities. Accurate diagnosis is the foundation of healing the soul as well as the body. And that's why I have such implicit trust in the Bible.

RIGHT ABOUT WRONG

For me, one of the strongest, deepest, most compelling reasons for believing the Bible is because *it has the most accurate explanation for what is wrong with us*. I have read the writings of the other religions of the world, and one of the major differences between them and the Bible is the superficial way they explain sin. The other religions have a very human explanation of evil behavior.

I have never run into anything remotely like the Bible when it comes to an accurate fix on what is wrong with the human heart. The God of the Bible evaluates, assesses, and confronts the essence of our dysfunctional behavior. If the Bible isn't true, if the answers that make the most sense aren't reliable, if this isn't God's Word, then we are truly lost. All the other explanations are not even in the same ballpark. There is literally nowhere else to go if your heart hungers for reality. But in the Bible I have found a satisfying answer to the human dilemma. When I am haunted occasionally by my own limitations and the gaps in my understanding, I come back to this assurance.

THE KINGDOM DIAGNOSIS

Next to the Law, the writings of the prophets may be the least popular portion of the Bible. There's a reason. Warnings and judgments roll on chapter after chapter. God's indictment against human sin is overpowering. The New Testament church got its definition of sin from the Old Testament, the only written Word of their day. It defines the problem for which the New Testament presents the solution. The Law and the Prophets relentlessly expose the nature of human sin from God's perspective.

For several years now I have studied the last half of the Old Testament carefully, and from that reading I compiled a huge list of God's creative descriptions of sin. I've boiled down the essence of that list into ten descriptive phrases in the language of today:

- Going our own way
- Doing our own thing
- Defiantly resisting authority
- Stubborn disobedience
- Willfull rebellion
- Defensive and antagonistic attitudes
- Self-centered focus
- Obsession with empowerment
- Compulsively competitive nature
- Addiction to control

This analysis of sin as compiled by God over hundreds of years is as powerful in provoking the human conscience today as it was two thousand years ago. We see this kind of behavior as wrong, offensive, and disgusting in others. The closer we are to selfish behavior or the more it presses in on us, the more infuriating it is. If it is done in a way that causes us loss, harm, and pain, we are outraged that anyone would so blatantly violate our rights.

Yet, when we behave selfishly, we rarely admit it. We disguise our self-centeredness and rationalize it as essential to personal freedom. We hear it every day: "I need to do this for *me*." "It's my chance to do what makes *me* happy." "I deserve the opportunity to live a little, indulge myself, have some fun."

We also justify selfishness by regarding it as part of a "healthy" process — that is, breaking free from unreasonable restraints or limits. A good example of this is the reaction of human beings in general to God's regulation of sexuality. "I'm oversexed. One man or woman just isn't enough for me." "If it doesn't hurt anybody, what does it matter what two consenting adults do?" "I'm just looking." "I'm only fantasizing — it won't hurt anybody."

It's difficult to talk to people about their sinful condition, because they don't want to listen. In the past they persecuted and even killed the prophets that God sent with His warnings, in order to shut them up. Nothing has changed. The same message receives a forceful rejection today.

It is at this point that we need to understand the seemingly heavy-handed approach God chose to take. God invented language. He designed the human brain and knows every intricate detail of our ways. So, as creative and intelligent as He is, why would He market His message with such a strong dose of the prophetic style? Why deliberately risk antagonizing and offending your hearers? What is the compelling purpose for the prophets' abrasive, in-your-face message? In my judgment it is clear that God forces the issue of sin in a confrontative way in order to make it unmistakably clear that leadership and control are the bottom line.

> *Without the prophets' perspective on sin as intentional rebellion and disobedience, the kingdom message of Jesus doesn't make sense. And without the kingdom message, repentance doesn't make sense.*

As we have seen, there are numerous definitions of sin that have, at best, a partial basis in Scripture. A church that has an incomplete understanding of sin won't understand *sin to be a leadership or kingdom issue*. Without the prophets' perspective on sin as intentional rebellion and disobedience, the kingdom message of Jesus doesn't make sense. And without the kingdom message, repentance doesn't make sense.

This is where the leadership issue is so clearly visible. If there is something in my life that I feel I must maintain control over, I won't give the helm of my heart to God. Take, for example, the person who refuses to forgive. Jesus knew that this kind of leadership impasse holds many outside His kingdom. He specifically said, "If you forgive men when they sin against you, your heavenly Father will also forgive you. But if you do not forgive men their sins, your Father will not forgive your sins" (Matthew 6:14-15). Refusing to trust God with justice and judgment means that I think I can do a better job of it than He can.

Besides, God might be too "soft" on those who have injured or offended me. I must see to it that they get what they deserve—even if I have to "play god" to do it. Letting go of my right to avenge wrong feels like too much of a risk. Why, if God treated my enemy the way He has treated me, it would be a miscarriage of justice. That rascal doesn't deserve mercy or forgiveness. He should never be let off the hook. Insisting on "payback" always places my sovereignty above God's sovereignty.

When Jesus came, He did not define the problem He was on a mission to solve—the prophets had focused on that subject. Jesus simply announced the arrival of the kingdom of heaven and of God. The ultimate Leader was making His approach. In His kingly presence our options are clear. We can continue to try to run our own kingdom. Or we can turn in submission to His.

The authority problem that the prophets had so thoroughly defined was now faced with the Authority of the universe in human flesh. He was unlike any earthly king. He was humble and vulnerable. But He was unmistakably asking for the whole world to follow Him.

As a reader you may be thinking through your own Christian pilgrimage. It's quite possible that this book is provoking the question of whether or not you really are a Christian. If that's happening, maybe you have attempted to become a Christian without a full understanding of the issue that separates you from God. By now that should be getting clearer.

Let's take a closer look at the deeply entrenched rebellion Jesus came to resolve.

⇒ T E N ⇐
Wiping Away God's Fingerprints

Without a doubt, the clearest burst of light-giving analysis of God's view of the human condition is given in Romans 1. The passage can be accurately interpreted as an explanation of what has occurred historically. All people groups have followed the same general path of self-destruction. The same assessment that applies to nations and civilizations is also a personal case study of each individual life. Romans 1 can be used as a spotlight focused on our private world or a floodlight on the whole world.

If you're a Christian, you may not think this report card applies to you. We'll see.

> The wrath of God is being revealed from heaven against all the godlessness and wickedness of men who suppress the truth by their wickedness, since what may be known about God is plain to them, because God has made it plain to them. For since the creation of the world God's invisible qualities — his eternal power and divine nature — have been clearly seen, being understood from what has been made, so that men are without excuse. (Romans 1:18-20)

God comes right out with it. From His observation of our behavior comes the conclusion that we suppress the truth about Him. It's not that we don't know about Him. The evidence of His existence is everywhere in this wonderful biosphere we call home. The billboards of creation splash the advertisements of intelligent design all around us. No thinking person can miss the obvious. As tough as it is to face and as embarrassingly true as it is, we are without excuse.

SUPPRESSING THE TRUTH

In our world today, intelligent, highly educated men and women look at the intricate design of the universe and everything in it and call it a product of time and chance. They look at things like the human eye, or brain, and say, "It's an accident!" In the face of all the evidence to the contrary, they conclude that somehow the ecosystem with its incredible life forms just evolved from some chaotic primeval soup.

That kind of behavior is exactly what Romans 1 is referring to when it says that people suppress the truth by their wickedness. God is saying, "They know. I know they know, and they know they know. They see the evidence of intelligent design. They know it couldn't have all just happened. What really is going on here is a revisionist scientific history. Politics is behind this. Smart people are denying My existence and role in creation so that they can set themselves up to take My place. They want to control their personal kingdoms without regard for Mine. In squelching the truth about Me they have conspired to get rid of Me."

And God is right about us. It would be just like us to say to each other, "Okay, this planet fairly screams intelligent design. But do you realize the options we would have if we were to wipe away the fingerprints of God? If we say there never was a Creator, do you see the enormous opportunity that would give us? We would be in charge! We can run this world to please ourselves. We can live without having to contend with any authority. No higher power, no accountability, no limits!"

EXCHANGING THE TRUTH

Several weeks ago I was reading the newspaper and having a cup of coffee in one of my favorite restaurants. An animated conversation was taking place at the next table over. I couldn't help but overhear. Two couples were discussing their work involving lobbying and influencing the state legislature on behalf of environmentalist causes. Since I am what I like to think of as pro-environment myself, I found myself fascinated as these people talked about nature with obvious reverence. It suddenly dawned on me that they were talking about "mother nature" as if she were God.

Romans 1:21-23 explains this exact behavior.

For although they knew God, they neither glorified him as God nor gave thanks to him, but their thinking became futile and their foolish hearts were darkened. Although they claimed to be wise, they became fools and exchanged the glory of the immortal God for images made to look like mortal man and birds and animals and reptiles.

Why would a lawyer, an oceanologist, a fish biologist, and a physicist be referring to nature as if it were divine? Why would they exchange the creation for the Creator? Because the creation is something we can handle—most of the time. We can measure it, utilize it, manage it—in short, we can control it. We can respect it, enjoy it, live in admiration and awe of it, and even love it. But we don't have to be personally accountable to it. We can make a god out of nature and still maintain the upper hand.

People deliberately exchange the glory of their Creator for images of themselves and created things. They exchange the truth for a lie because it is convenient. God uses the word *exchange* deliberately. It is not a mistake or an accident. It is not something we drift into ignorantly. It is a result of intentional choices.

The intelligentsia of today's world do not hesitate to claim to be wise in their dismissal of God. "You believe what? The Bible? You've got to be kidding! Where did you park your brain? Why, any thinking person has flushed that religious nonsense a long time ago."

Or they'll take the winning-through-intimidation approach: "I've got two master's degrees and two Ph.D.'s. I'm published in the most prestigious journals and I belong to the top think tanks in the country. If you listen to me you'll drop this primitive religious mumbo jumbo and develop a science-based spiritualism that puts you in the driver's seat."

Human beings refuse to believe in God, but they believe in mother nature and human potential. What happens when humans demote their Creator in order to promote themselves? They experience the wrath of God. Remember, that is how this whole section of Scripture starts: "The wrath of God is being revealed from heaven against all the godlessness and wickedness of men who suppress the truth by their wickedness" (Romans 1:18). This is where the scoffer laughs, "Sure—scare me. This is where you break out the lightning bolts and the hellfire and damnation, right?"

What a surprise it is to find out that the wrath of God amounts to God giving up on you and letting you go your own way!

> Therefore God gave them over in the sinful desires of their hearts to sexual impurity for the degrading of their bodies with one another. They exchanged the truth of God for a lie, and worshiped and served created things rather than the Creator— who is forever praised. Amen. (Romans 1:24-25)

The inevitable result is that sex becomes a primary means of rebellion. When you've liberated yourself from God's supervision, you take over the management of your own body. Rebels can't resist flaunting their sexual freedom. They defiantly establish their right to be in control of their own bodies, making their own sexual rules. In today's world a sure-fire way to provoke an explosive reaction is to question an individual's sexual autonomy. "Get your archaic, puritanical morality off my body! It's none of your business what I choose to do or with whom I choose to do it. You Bible thumpers are all repressed bigots trying to shove your 'Thou shalt nots' down everybody else's throat."

> *What a surprise it is to find out that the wrath of God amounts to God giving up on you and letting you go your own way!*

What happens next is that you lose control of being in control. Your sexual expression of spiritual rebellion takes on a life of its own. You can make the liberated choices but you can't control the consequences. Sexual addictions are just as real and even more enslaving than alcohol and drug addictions. Venereal disease lurks in the shadows of every illicit sexual encounter. Pregnancy and the expedience of murdering the baby are all part of the slippery slope of sexually acting out your defiance against God. There is an ongoing process here. A swift, powerful current captures you, obsesses you, and sweeps you along. The next rung on the descending ladder is sexual deviancy.

> Because of this, God gave them over to shameful lusts. Even their women exchanged natural relations for unnatural ones. In the same way the men also abandoned natural relations with

women and were inflamed with lust for one another. Men committed indecent acts with other men, and received in themselves the due penalty for their perversion. (Romans 1:26-27)

There is something about rejection of God and defiance toward His created design that provokes not only sexual immorality and promiscuity but also the loss of sexual identity. If there is anything that emanates from the gay rights movement, it is a radical, defiant rage. "I'm going to do what I'm going to do with whomever I choose to do it, and don't you even suggest that I might be wrong. I don't care about the risk of venereal disease or AIDS, I will express my emancipation from God by refusing His design."

INVENTING YOUR OWN TRUTH
Not all who are given over by God to the sinful desires of their hearts involve themselves with promiscuity, bisexuality, or homosexuality. But when God withdraws His influence and lets the pursuit of one's own agenda become *its own punishment*, the consequences begin to pile up. Freedom ceases to be the ability to do good, be pure, and pursue what is right. Instead it becomes only the license to indulge every whim and lust. What happens when alternative lifestyles are normalized?

> Furthermore, since they did not think it worthwhile to retain the knowledge of God, he gave them over to a depraved mind, to do what ought not to be done. They have become filled with every kind of wickedness, evil, greed and depravity. They are full of envy, murder, strife, deceit and malice. They are gossips, slanderers, God-haters, insolent, arrogant and boastful; they invent ways of doing evil; they disobey their parents; they are senseless, faithless, heartless, ruthless. Although they know God's righteous decree that those who do such things deserve death, they not only continue to do these very things but also approve of those who practice them. (Romans 1:28-32)

The bottom of the barrel is not sexual perversion. It is a depraved mind. What does that mean? A depraved mind is a way of perceiving and thinking where everything is turned upside-down. Independence is good, living in a relationship of trust and obedience to God is repulsive. The depraved mind will tolerate anything and everything except absolute truth. The strongest conviction of the heart enslaved by this condition is that everyone designs his or her own belief system. You follow your own preferences and go with what feels right to you. Anything that strikes you as authoritarian or absolutist is regarded as Stone Age ignorance or at least medieval superstition.

The bottom of the slide away from God has been reached. First they *suppressed the truth*, then they *exchanged the truth for a lie*, and now they're *into their own truth*. And yet all the while they are still religious. But with a depraved mind they construct gods in their own images and likenesses—gods with whom they are comfortable, who think like they do, who agree with them and serve them.

THE DEPRAVITY YOU LIVE WITH

This chapter may explain some things to you about what has been happening in your private world. It may be that people you love have done some deeply disappointing and heartbreaking things to themselves that have painfully affected you. In the pursuit of his or her own freedom or pleasures, your spouse may have ridden roughshod over you. In going their own way, your children may well have crushed your expectations and your hopes for them. Friends you care deeply about may be walking away from the truth of the Bible because it interferes with their lifestyles, and you may be watching them self-destruct. Or it could be that you're the one whose choices could be damaging your partner in marriage, your children, your friends, or your church family.

The Spirit of God may be tapping you on the shoulder saying, "It's time to turn around. Give it up. Come home and live under the loving guidance of your heavenly Father."

You may have gone down that ladder described by God in Romans choice by choice, decision by decision—all the while thinking of yourself as a Christian. For some reason your selfishness has soured. As you are pondering what you've been reading here, you are hearing a voice deep inside. God is whispering truth in love. A warm breeze is thawing out a corner of your heart.

What would happen if you decided to turn around? You can, you know. Why not take some time with God before we take a look at the alternative?

→ ELEVEN ←
The Logic of Hell

For a season, sin has its undeniable pleasures. Then the rebel begins to lose control of being in control. The kingdom of self, so carefully constructed, unravels to the dismay and frustration of the self-appointed king or queen, and the pain begins.

It is exactly as Dallas Willard asserts in *The Spirit of the Disciplines*: "To depart from righteousness is to choose a life of crushing burdens, failures, and disappointments, a life caught in the toils of endless problems that are never resolved. Here is the source of that unending soap opera, that sometimes horror show known as normal human life."[1]

I know of a woman who has been a professing Christian for many years. Her religious veneer has proven to be a cover for her full-blown egoism. She is a wife, mother, and church woman who has intimidated, manipulated, coerced, and dominated all the people in her life circle. For years she made her agenda work. Her husband has been passive and intentionally absent most of the time.

The children were not able to create the same distance, though. True, they did well in school, sports, music, and church—but each one slipped out of her control by developing serious obsessive behaviors. The oldest son became confused about his sexual identity. The second-born daughter was a straight-A student but developed a serious eating disorder. The third-born, also a daughter, became sexually active with a neighborhood boy, then the boy's older brother, and eventually became pregnant. Her promiscuity became a source of acute embarrassment to the family. The two younger children are still firmly under their mother's control.

This lady can't understand what has gone wrong. In her mind, she's done everything right. She has given her children all the advantages of a suburban middle-class lifestyle. They have been protected and kept in wholesome pursuits and activities. What could she possibly have missed?

When adults demand their own way, they need to consider the old Greek axiom "You build what you are." This woman's need to control and dominate was passed on to her kids from infancy. As soon as the children reached adolescence they began to act out their own version of self-centered behavior. Though all are responsible for their own choices, their mother has also promoted a spirit of preoccupation with self.

In the middle of her pain and disappointment, she blamed her husband. After all, he was never around and it was obviously his fault that the family was in such a mess. This only made the marriage worse. The church and the youth group were other obvious scapegoats. The pastor and youth pastor received a stinging assessment of their shortcomings and failure to serve her family adequately.

What is happening to her version of the "ideal Christian family"? God has permitted this woman to live a self-centered life, even though He intended that Christ be her center. God has given her what she insisted on having—control. The result is pain for herself and those closest to her.

THE PAIN ALARM

A taste of the consequences of sin is designed as a kind of strong medicine. God often gets the attention of strong-willed, self-centered people by letting their choices go sour. Pain is not necessarily a negative thing. It can be a deterrent to dangerous behavior. Yet, it is possible to sear the soul's "pain sensors" and dull the warning signals.

Does a parent's sinful selfishness have to leave an imprint upon his or her offspring? No—because many see the ugliness and feel the pain of their parents' egoism, yet choose to reject similar choices. But others become preoccupied with getting their own way too. They see advantages that can be gained by using sinful methods to get what they want. Not only do they imitate the worst examples, they add new wrinkles of their own and the pain continues.

If we stop to think about it, the existence of hell isn't hard to accept. Those who witnessed or survived the Holocaust during World War II called it hell on earth. People who grew up in homes characterized by alcoholism, drug addiction, and abuse say it was hell. If human choices produce horrible pain and consequences in this life—why wouldn't the same choices produce horrible results in the next life?

We need to think deeply about the logic of hell. Stay with me.

A LOVING GOD AND HELL

Hell is a provision of love. To force people in rebellion against God to submit to His kingdom against their will would be cruel to those people and to those who are willingly in submission to God. The Creator has no interest in disharmony and conflict in His heavenly kingdom.

So for those who refuse the offer of God's loving rule, there is a place where they can be free from it forever. The place where personal sovereignty is normal is called hell. It is a place of eternal conflict. Billions of willful, stubborn, prideful, selfish humans and fallen angels will compete for control. The result? From the sample we've already seen on earth, we can conclude that it will be incredibly painful. The "fire" that has been mocked and scorned by skeptics aptly describes the unending torment of the inward-focused ego.

If heaven is the kingdom of God where one Will reigns supreme resulting in peace and harmony, then hell is the logical opposite, resulting in pain and conflict. To a soul in rebellion, God's kingdom feels like an unbearable repression. Many respond like the adolescents in rebellion who are willing to live on the streets rather than under their parents' control and care. According to the Bible, you can choose to go your own way, but you can't control your eventual destination.

> *To force people in rebellion against God to submit to His kingdom against their will would be cruel to those people and to those who are willingly in submission to God.*

SLAPPING THE FACE OF GRACE

Such a thought infuriates those who usurp God's place. The insanity of self-enthronement steadily intensifies the closer it gets to its goal. The self-enthroned ego protects its turf. It is ready to oppose God Himself.

There's a vindictiveness in terminal rebellion. This can perhaps be most clearly seen in the attitude of Satan himself. He wants no part in heaven, where a perfectly loving and humble Ruler reigns. Perversely, he wants to *hurt* the Supreme Sovereign he rejected. So he exports his antagonism, spreads his rage against heaven, and fans the flames of humanity's egoism in order to make the loving heart of God suffer. Each soul entrapped in the pursuit of deadly "freedom" is another slap in the face of grace. Populating hell with the willingly deceived is the one way he can still make God pay for exposing and defeating him.

I know a young man who has AIDS. A practicing homosexual for eight years, he says he willingly took the risks of unprotected sex with multiple partners. And more shocking still, even after he knew he was HIV positive he continued to have unprotected sex. As he softly and disarmingly speaks of his alternative lifestyle, there is a defiance and a rage that simmers just beneath the surface.

He grew up in a Bible-reading, Christ-honoring home. He attended a strong evangelical church. He professed Christ as his Savior and was "born again" as an adolescent of fourteen. He smiles sarcastically and laughs disparagingly about his early training now. Knowing it rubs salt into my grief, he mocks the Bible and the God of the Bible.

"Why?" I ask. "Why are you so full of rage and hate? Why are you deliberately infecting others with this incurable disease?"

His eyes burn with an unnatural intensity as he replies, "I made my choices and I took my chances. Those I have infected made their choices and took their chances."

There is a long pause, and I see he is crying. Soon he is sobbing. I mistakenly assume it is grief for himself and the others who are soon to die also. But no. He raises his head and his eyes meet mine. What I see shakes me to the core of my being.

His face holds virulent hatred. He is shaking with spite. "I'm rubbing God's face in it," he says. "And I'm making sure I don't go to hell alone."

I am still deeply disturbed whenever I think of that conversation. That young man helped me understand something of the volcanic rage behind chronic rebellion. He was intentionally hurting God by destroying himself and as many others as possible. That is enmity against God in the style of Lucifer.

I'm not suggesting that all AIDS patients or all homosexuals are like this man. Most practicing homosexuals would find such destructive behavior irresponsible and even criminal, but they might also understand the deep anger behind it.

To me, this encounter demonstrates the sense and logic of hell. There are people who want nothing to do with God. They hate Him and actively oppose everything He stands for. All around us people are already entering into the rule and experience of hell. Soon they will, by their own choice, enter into its eternal reality.

TRAGIC BRAVADO

For thousands of years, *hell* has been one of the most common curse words in most of the world's languages. Yet most modern men and women ridicule the idea that hell exists. What a dreadful surprise it will be to discover that you have been granted what you have always claimed you wanted—the freedom to pursue your own independent agenda. Dreadful because the place you get to practice your own sovereignty is filled with millions of angels and other humans who have chosen the same chaos of self-assertion. Fire is an apt image of the hostilities and searing conflict of countless colliding egos.

The terror of hell is seen in small part in this life. The free will of angels and people is magnificent in its potential for good—horrible beyond description in its potential for evil. To insist on resisting the authority structure of the universe in order to carve out your own kingdom is to choose pain. To exert control apart from God is the surest way to maximize your capacity to inflict hellish pain on others.

The kingdom of God *will* come and His will *will be done* on earth as it is in heaven. The era of rebellion and insurrection on this planet will someday be over. If you don't want to be under God's leadership, there is another option. You won't be forced to submit to God. You'll be able to go your own way and do your own thing with others who are doing exactly the same. God intends to seal rebellion up in a closed system—a place called hell—that will not be allowed to contaminate His kingdom. The pain of that place will be self-inflicted *and* other-inflicted. Rebellion, revolution, and endless revenge will be all that ever happens or can happen there. God will permit those who refuse His agenda to attempt endlessly to impose their own leadership upon each other.

PLAYING WITH FIRE

I started this chapter by saying that the worst thing that can happen to human beings is for God to let them have their own way. Proverbs 14:12

sums up my point nicely: "There is a way that seems right to a man, but in the end it leads to death."

This is not what God had in mind for us! Scripture affirms that God is "not wanting anyone to perish, but everyone to come to repentance" (2 Peter 3:9). Ezekiel recounted the Lord's remonstrations for Israel to repent as follows: "Say to them, 'As surely as I live, declares the Sovereign LORD, I take no pleasure in the death of the wicked, but rather that they turn from their ways and live. Turn! Turn from your evil ways! Why will you die, O house of Israel?'" (Ezekiel 33:11).

God never intended that human beings inhabit hell. The "lake of fire" will be prepared for the Devil and his fallen angels. In fact, our Creator has done everything short of revoking free will to turn humanity back from self-destruction.

As you read this I hope you will be shaken not by a gothic vision of God's fiery judgment—but by the obvious logic of hell. Eternal damnation is scary, but even more frightening is the fact that it has already begun. Heaven can already be seen and experienced; hell can already be seen and experienced. The choice of where each of us will spend eternity is unarguably an informed choice. Which kingdom have you chosen? My purpose for including this chapter is to demonstrate the kind of fire we play with when we try to enter Christ's kingdom while still retaining our own.

If you've successfully run your own agenda while saying you belong to Christ, you should take a hard look at your life. Are you sure you don't smell smoke—in the relationships you've harmed, in the deadness you often feel toward God?

No doubt, some of the examples in this chapter have been shocking—like the angry young man with AIDS. Maybe you're wondering why I would include a chapter on separation from God in a book for Christians. No, I am not trying to manipulate you through fear. I am hoping to wake you up to eternal realities.

Why?

Because many of us have found the "perfect cover" for running our own operation, while making it look as if we are serving God. It's the cover of religion. Let's see how it works.

NOTE
1. Dallas Willard, *The Spirit of the Disciplines* (San Francisco: HarperCollins, 1988), p. 2.

→ TWELVE ←
The Ultimate Cover for Rebellion

We know we have a problem. We sense it when we are separated from God. So what do we do about it? We have, from time immemorial, gotten religious. Religion is our way of trying to bridge the gap back to God's kingdom. And have we built some incredible bridges! The problem is, they never connect to the far shore where the Ruler reigns. On our own we can only create gods after our own liking.

What *kind* of a god do we prefer? Do we want the top God—the Lord Almighty; the King of kings; the Creator, Owner, and Operator of the universe? Do we want the God who commands *all* of our allegiance? If there are less demanding options, maybe not.

RELIGION IN OUR OWN IMAGE
For most of us, our "god" is one with whom we are comfortable, a god who lets us do what we want and who gives us what we want. That's what the world of religion is tragically all about—counterfeiting divinity.

Even Christianity can quickly be emasculated into mere religion. When ego-driven theologians get through with their scholarly knives of preference and pride, the corpse of God's Word bears little resemblance to the original. There are many varieties of Christianity that are useless and benign.

On a personal level, isn't our ability to limit God to one hour on one morning per week remarkable? It's so easy to go through the motions. Church ends, we close the door on the religion category, and go home to work in the yard or watch football. Then we close the door on the recreation category and go to work or school. All the while, we insist that Christianity is important and all that, but we don't want to get carried away with it. Spirituality has its place, but you can't let it take over your life.

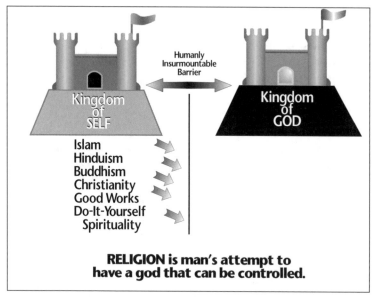

Diagram 12.1

Substitute religion has successfully helped millions avoid seriously dealing with the real Creator God and His legitimate leadership, ownership, and authority. Something in us pulls us toward the perfunctory: paying your dues, checking in once in a while, and going through the motions. As a result, religion is a terrific hiding place for rebels, some of the worst of which are in the pulpits. We must never forget that Satan loves religion, even "Christian" religion. He encourages it, promotes it, and adds his brand of spiritual flavor and fizz to it (1 Corinthians 10:18-22). If you doubt this, remember the horrible deeds that have been and are still being perpetrated in the name of various gods, including Jehovah and Jesus. This is unmistakable evidence of spiritual impersonation. Crusaders and inquisitors alike have been led astray in demonic fanaticism and then into crimes of self-righteous pride and violent coercion.

No self-made religion can bridge the gap from humanity to God. Besides, a god you can manipulate and control may be attractive, like having your own genie in a magic lamp. But he isn't real. The bridges back to God, when manufactured by people, may have some fine ideas and principles built in, but they don't get the job done. They distract us and sidetrack us from the only bridge that can get us back to our Creator.

Oddly enough, Jesus was embroiled in conflict with some of the most religious people from the very beginning of His public speaking ministry. Matthew 23 contains a scathing rebuke of the whole mentality behind the religious traditionalism of the Pharisees. Jesus said,

> "Everything they do is done for men to see: They make their phylacteries wide and the tassels on their garments long; they love the place of honor at banquets and the most important seats in the synagogues; they love to be greeted in the marketplaces and to have men call them 'Rabbi.'
>
> "But you are not to be called 'Rabbi,' for you have only one Master and you are all brothers. And do not call anyone on earth 'father,' for you have one Father, and he is in heaven. Nor are you to be called 'teacher,' for you have one Teacher, the Christ. The greatest among you will be your servant. For whoever exalts himself will be humbled, and whoever humbles himself will be exalted." (verses 5-12)

Jesus took a baseball bat of truth to egoism—which, in this case, masqueraded as superior righteousness. The Jewish fundamentalism of His day had deteriorated into a charade of professional piety. Appearances were everything; looking morally and ethically superior was the name of the game. These religious leaders were meeting their own inflated ego needs at the expense of the people they were manipulating. Now, do you think it was appropriate for Jesus to attack them with such withering scorn?

> "Woe to you, teachers of the law and Pharisees, you hypocrites! You are like whitewashed tombs, which look beautiful on the outside but on the inside are full of dead men's bones and everything unclean. In the same way, on the outside you appear to

people as righteous but on the inside you are full of hypocrisy and wickedness." (Matthew 23:27-28)

"You snakes! You brood of vipers! How will you escape being condemned to hell?" (Matthew 23:33)

Is this merely a name-calling tirade and an outburst of pent-up frustration, or is Jesus doing something important here? Perhaps we could phrase the question this way: *Is it right to call a religious spade a spade?* The point Jesus dramatically emphasizes is that there is nothing sacred about the realm of religion per se. Nor are religious leaders above accountability for distorting truth and behaving despicably. As was the case in Jesus' day, religion can be the perfect dodge, the ideal setup for a personal power trip. Clever, dominant personalities have always found organized religion to be a terrific base for self-aggrandizement.

> *Clever, dominant personalities have always found organized religion to be a terrific base for self-aggrandizement.*

Jesus revealed that the true Creator God does not condone what we do in His name to try to buy off His claim over us. God clearly comes out against all religious pretentiousness, no matter who is doing it. The fine-tooth comb of just judgment must first begin with those who make God-is-my-boss claims. Second Peter 2 takes God's disdain for false religion and those who exploit willingly gullible people even further.

> These men are springs without water and mists driven by a storm. Blackest darkness is reserved for them. For they mouth empty, boastful words and, by appealing to the lustful desires of sinful human nature, they entice people who are just escaping from those who live in error. They promise them freedom, while they themselves are slaves of depravity—for a man is a slave to whatever has mastered him. (verses 17-19)

Talk about pungent analysis. The Holy Spirit clearly has a problem with religious impostors and charlatans. Men and women who massage the egos of their constituents with phony concoctions of "pop truth" are ruthlessly exposed. Their inferior motives are never covered up in the

Word of God. The amazing thing about the Bible is that God operates without partiality; He has no favorites that He holds to a less strict standard than others. The world of religion enjoys no special breaks from God. So, why should it get a special break from the rest of us?

AN UNEXAMINED BELIEF SYSTEM IS NOT WORTH HOLDING

Why don't we admit the obvious? All religion is not the same, just as all cures for warts are not equal. Some religious ideas are dead wrong. They are in total denial of reality. Many religious philosophies are a mixture of truth and error. Our idea of faith *can* be examined. Truth must be separated from error.

It is unreasonable and anti-intellectual *not* to carefully examine the content of your faith. I'm *not* a Christian because my parents were or because my culture was saturated with Christianity—I'm a Christian and follower of Christ because I have done careful research and found no other life that can hold a candle to it.

How about you? It is likely that you are reading this book because you are either a serious seeker or follower of God. Plato was right when he said, "An unexamined life is not worth living." I'd like to take that a step further and suggest that an unexamined belief system is not worth holding.

> *Plato was right when he said, "An unexamined life is not worth living." I'd like to take that a step further and suggest that an unexamined belief system is not worth holding.*

If you are attempting to find and follow the true God, I applaud your journey. Think. Study. Search carefully. The Spirit of God will come alongside any honest seeker. He can be relied upon to guide each of us into all truth (John 14:17,26; 16:13).

In *The Velvet Covered Brick*, Howard Butt encapsulates how to escape from mere religion disguising itself as Christianity, and find new life in God. "You were made to be good. But you cannot be good on your own. Your efforts to be good only reinforce your pride. Religious riches keep you away from God more completely than any other kind. So relax, quit trying so hard, and start trusting . . . your Leader."[1]

✠

In this second part of the book I've attempted to answer the question, What's wrong with us? The evidence is overwhelming that we live in a dangerous world because we have universally chosen to live for ourselves. We make choices based on what we think will be best for our own self-interest. What will maximize my pleasure, fun, adventure, and satisfaction? What will make me look good? What will give me more control? What will give me more wealth, possessions, and prominence? And in our determination to get what we want and think we need, we hurt and take advantage of each other. Earth is a bloody and violent place because we are proud, selfish egotists.

Some religious ideas are dead wrong. They are in total denial of reality.

In his book *With Willful Intent—A Theology of Sin*, David L. Smith comes to this same conclusion.

> Egocentricity may be seen in a wide spectrum of sin—indeed in all sin. Kierkegaard hit the nail on the head when he argued that disobedience to God and His commands is self-assertion (or, ego-centricity). Such disobedience may yield itself in the well-known kinds of sin such as vice and willfulness or in the lesser-noticed types such as legal righteousness and resulting despair. But all are examples of the rebellion of the ego or self against God.[2]

We've focused long enough on what's wrong with us. It's time we moved on to God's solution. The next section will concentrate on Jesus' gospel of the kingdom.

We'll begin by trying to understand why the kingdom message has been largely missing in our churches. Then we'll carefully examine what Jesus taught and how we can escape the hellish conflicts of our own self-centeredness; how we can walk out of spiritual darkness and live more at home in God's kingdom of light.

NOTES

1. Howard Butt, *The Velvet Covered Brick* (New York: HarperCollins, 1973), p. 87.
2. David L. Smith, *With Willful Intent—A Theology of Sin* (Wheaton, Ill.: Scripture Press/Victor Books, 1994), p. 553.

TAKING ANOTHER STEP—
QUESTIONS FOR MEDITATION

1. How has the selfishness of other people affected your life? Who do you avoid because their selfishness irritates you?

2. Has your pursuit of "rights" and "freedom" led you into any enslaving habits or obsessions?

3. What choices have you made that have hurt others and adversely affected your own life?

4. Do you see the various definitions of sin being used by the people in your world? Have you favored one or more of them yourself?

5. Does God's assessment of our sinful behavior anger you? Why, or why not?

6. If God can't tell us the truth about ourselves, who can?

7. Can you identify any example of where sin became its own punishment in your life?

8. If you're a Christian and have been welcomed into God's kingdom, why go back to controlling your own life? Isn't it apparent by now that selfish egoism creates "hell" in our churches, just as it does in the world?

PART THREE

THE SAFE FOLLOWER AND REPENTANCE

→ T H I R T E E N ←
From Religion to Relationship

I was three years into pastoral ministry and closing the service had become my specialty. I gave an appeal for salvation three times a week—Sunday morning, Sunday evening, and Wednesday evening—because conventional wisdom had it that if even one unbeliever might be present, it would be dereliction of duty to end without presenting the gospel. Conventional wisdom also had it that convincing people to make a decision for Christ was best done with the altar call formula.

People did respond to my appeals, and when a person complied with the evangelistic procedure, we considered him converted, saved, or born again. And without a doubt many actually did find salvation and a new life in Christ in this manner.

But gradually, the fallout began to haunt me. Of the respondents, more fell away than followed through. At first, in my personal insecurity, I assumed that it must be me. I must not be dedicated enough, praying enough, filled with the Spirit enough, morally clean enough for God to give me *lasting fruit*. There followed an extended period of self-doubt and introspection. I began to entertain thoughts of leaving the ministry. The results of my harvesting just didn't stack up to the reports I was hearing of what God was doing elsewhere.

At a pastors' retreat I spilled out my frustration and told a group of my peers what I was experiencing. They seemed surprised that I was so hard on myself. An older pastor I respected attempted to encourage me.

"The best evangelists," he said, "have a success ratio of 10 to 15

102 The Safe Follower and Repentance

percent. Every 'soul-winning' pastor has a similar experience to what you've been describing. Be glad for the 10 percent or so that stick. You've been faithful to preach the gospel and ask for a response. God will determine who is really sincere and who isn't." Somehow, I wasn't encouraged by this attempt to reassure me.

Others thought my follow-up procedure probably needed work. After listening to what several of them were doing, I could see that they had a much more thorough "new believers" course than I did. I returned home with lowered expectations and higher resolve.

For two years I tried even harder with "new Christian" training materials and methods. Despite the best training and materials available, all too often when my coaching and instruction were removed at the completion of the beginner course, the new Christians didn't take it any further.

Next, I started reading books about discipleship. Believing one-on-one mentoring to be the missing key, I trained a team of laypeople in my church to do discipling ministry. The results were considerably better but still frustrating and, overall, still disappointing. Some who made salvation decisions responded well and went on to become faithful, contributing, even contagious Christians. The majority, though, did not grow as I had hoped. As soon as my motivation, my initiative, and my elbow grease were no longer present, they tended to find some creative way to self-destruct.

Finally, some of the best disciple makers I knew encouraged me to be more selective in choosing new believers to disciple. "Go with the 'goers,'" they said. "Find the most faithful and motivated individuals and stick with them." And that bit of advice served as a wake-up call.

What about the 85 percent that never continued on in the faith? What about the fickleness and lack of motivation in the 15 percent that did initially follow through? At last I admitted to myself that, at best, the evangelism efforts in my church were bearing about 6 to 7 percent good fruit. In cold, hard facts that meant that for every 100 individuals who prayed to receive Christ, only 6 or 7 became self-motivated, productive, long-haul Christians.

My friends in ministry all thought my numbers were far too low. Of course, they didn't keep track of their own results statistically, but they were sure their bottom lines were better than mine. Some accepted my challenge to keep track of the people with whom they were working, and before long they admitted we were all in about the same percentile. So, what was left to examine? Methods had helped to some extent, but there had to be a better way. In desperation I began to read the New Testament. Ironic, huh? This time I deliberately set aside my perceptions of what ministry was and even what the gospel itself was. The pages flew by and my eyes began to widen. For years I had brought my own preconceived assumptions to the Scriptures and interpreted the Bible to fit my point of view. I saw what I "knew" was there, not what was really there.

> *In our attempts to standardize and simplify the gospel for mass consumption, we changed the message.*

It began to dawn on me that the message Jesus called the "gospel" and the message I thought was the gospel were two different messages. At this point my reexamination of the text grew feverish. How could I have missed the fact that Jesus never used the same approach with any two people? And what was this big emphasis on the "kingdom of God" all about?

The more I pored over the New Testament, the more I became convinced that the problem with frustrating results in my ministry was really a misunderstanding of the message of the gospel itself! What shook me to my boots was not so much that I had been off target but that everybody else in the evangelical world seemed to be off target as well.

THE MESSAGE MATTERS

One thing became obvious. In our attempts to standardize and simplify the gospel for mass consumption, we changed the message. I made a list of the words and phrases that I and my evangelical colleagues were using to tell people how to become Christians.

- "Believe on the Lord Jesus Christ."
- "Call upon the name of the Lord."
- "Receive the gift of eternal life."
- "Accept the pardon from sin paid for at the cross."
- "Ask Jesus to come into your heart."
- "Pray the sinner's prayer, 'Lord, be merciful to me, the sinner, and save me for Christ's sake.'"

- ■ "Make your decision to receive Christ as your Savior."
- ■ "Raise your hand. Now those who raised their hands come forward to the front of the auditorium and pray to receive Christ with a counselor."
- ■ "Make sure you know where you are going if you should die today; place your faith and trust in Jesus Christ as Savior and Lord."
- ■ "Give your life to Jesus."
- ■ "Close the distance between you and God. Accept His offer of forgiveness, and an eternal love relationship with Him is yours for the asking."

Anyone who has spent any amount of time in evangelical circles has heard those phrases or combinations thereof over and over again. This is how we *close the deal*, whether in evangelistic preaching services or personal witnessing.

What was now glaringly obvious to me was that the gospel of Jesus was clearly different from these phrases. He consistently called His message the gospel of the kingdom and He asked people to repent. I determined to find out what the Lord meant.

AN ADEQUATE RESPONSE

I was born at the end of World War II, in 1945. As a boy I heard many stories about the war from uncles, cousins, and neighbors who had been in uniform. Elementary school teachers taught me an organized history of the war and, in fifth grade, I first remember hearing a detailed account of the Japanese surrender.

General Douglas MacArthur was the official representative of the United States, and a highly decorated Japanese admiral represented the Japanese Imperial Forces. The two men met on the deck of the battleship *Missouri*. As the ceremony came to the actual moment of surrender, the Japanese admiral extended his hand in the familiar gesture of friendship and peace, but General MacArthur refused to take it. He kept his right hand at his side. Sternly he said, "Sir, your sword first, please." Then when the defeated admiral handed over his sword, he extended his hand and grasped the Japanese officer's hand.

Why did MacArthur ask for the sword first? Because the formal disarming of the enemy was the symbol of surrender. Until the weapon was handed over, the hostilities had not formally ceased.

God is after a similar response. He calls it *repentance,* a word that is largely misunderstood these days. Biblical repentance is much more than merely feeling sorry about what you've done. We have the mistaken idea that if someone is repentant it means that person expresses regret, perhaps with tears, for what he or she has done wrong. That may very well be a part of true repentance, but the word belongs with the arrival of God's kingdom. Ultimate authority has arrived. It's surrender time. The moment of truth is here. Will you give up your resistance and bow to the conquering King of heaven? Will you give up your sword?

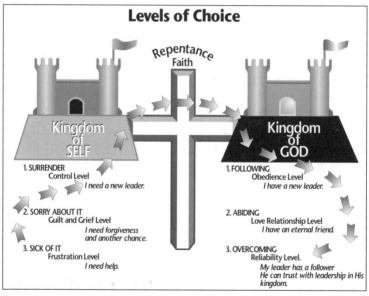

Diagram 13.1

The above "Levels of Choice" diagram is an attempt to visualize the journey from the kingdom of self to the kingdom of God. The "sick of it" and the "sorry about it" levels are intended to show the kinds of decisions that don't deal with the control issue that lies at the heart of our kingdoms of self. It isn't until the heart "gives up the sword" and by faith steps out on the sacrifice of Christ that entrance to the kingdom of God is granted by grace.

In the kingdom of God followers of Jesus obey their Lord as a way of life. The indwelling Spirit provides enabling grace that sustains the ongoing love relationship with Christ. Consistent obedience and love produce faithfulness and reliable service in spite of adverse circumstances. A rebel has been thus transformed into a follower God can trust and depend on for all eternity.

TRUE REPENTANCE

Have you ever noticed how common it is for people to be sorry, to cry, to act out grief, and yet not repent? That kind of superficial token repentance is not at all reassuring to the one receiving the apology.

If a husband and wife are embroiled in a battle of the wills, painful things can happen. Let's consider a couple engaged in a serious power struggle. He wants his way and she wants hers. A relatively minor issue triggers an explosive battle—the checkbook, the discipline of the children, a thoughtlessly insensitive comment. Suddenly they are at each other's throats, their colliding egos sending sparks of anger through the house.

Extremely unpleasant things can and do happen in these kinds of domestic conflicts. Husbands and wives say terrible things to each other. You've heard the expression "all's fair in love and war." The danger is intensified when it becomes the love of war. It may come right down to intense confrontation. Violent anger often erupts into words that strike like a club and cut like a knife.

Immediately after the fight you may regret what you did and said. You may feel very sorry. You may think, *That was low! How could I be involved in something so ugly and tacky? That was beneath me.* You go back to your spouse and say, "Honey, I'm sorry, I guess I got out of line." You cry a little bit and make up. But does your partner trust your sorrow? Not necessarily . . . and for good reason. Being sorry doesn't address the real issue.

What the husband or wife is waiting to hear goes something like this: "Sweetheart, I am so strong-willed. I get way out of line sometimes when I'm insisting on my own way. I said some terrible things and acted like a monster because I was trying to intimidate you and crush your resistance to my will. I have been wrong in my need to win. I want to give up my stubborn, bullheaded need to be in control. Will you forgive me?"

As soon as one of the combatants begins to talk like that, you can be sure that his or her partner will be all ears. "This is new! You really mean it? You don't want to fight anymore? You're giving up the battle and want to work on . . . harmony? Darling, that is what I've been waiting and longing to hear for years. I want to stop fighting too. I'll join you."

Sorrow over relational conflict is never enough, nor is grief over the consequences of wrong behavior. Submission to each other is the only appropriate resolution. Sorrow cannot be trusted, but fresh choices of voluntary humility can.

> *He is not impressed with tears of sorrow. He is not even moved by admission of guilt. He is always impressed with repentance.*

This is exactly the thing God is waiting and longing to hear. He is not impressed with tears of sorrow. He is not even moved by admission of guilt. He is always impressed with repentance. God inevitably says to each sinner, "Your sword first, please." Give up. Lay down your weapons. Stop the resistance and the hostilities and He'll grace you with a new beginning.

If you're having trouble with this emphasis on repentance, be careful to examine the Scripture for yourself. There are some fascinating discoveries to be made. For instance, it is important to recognize that the baptism of Jesus was a baptism of repentance (Matthew 3:11; Mark 1:4,9). Jesus said it was necessary for Him to do this in order "to fulfill all righteousness." Now, why did Jesus lead the way in repentance? After all, He was sinless. He was already holy and righteous. So, what was this all about?

The answer is absolutely consistent with His kingdom message. He was demonstrating His own humble submission to His heavenly Father. He was repenting! Not *from* sin but *to* the rule of His leader. Repentance is first yielding oneself to God's kingdom. It revealed the righteousness of Christ's obedience to the Father. In us it also involves repentance from self-rule and its accompanying sinful acts and choices.

God intends to solve the problem that has made earth such a dangerous place—dangerous even for Him. His salvation saves us from His judgment and saves Him from our rebellion. His love for us has made Him vulnerable. We all have learned from hard experience that love is risky. God is too wise to allow selfish rebellion into His kingdom. He has no intention of putting up with the pain of perpetual resistance to His will. He wants sons and daughters He can trust, not spoiled brats and juvenile delinquents in His family.

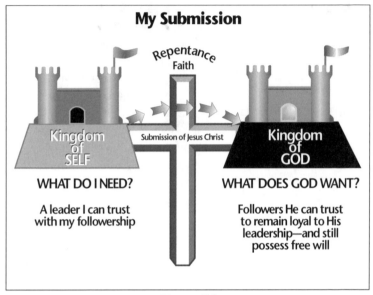

Diagram 13.2

So, He invites me to the ego-testing device—the cross. There I see His humility and find the Leader I can trust. And there He asks for my humility and submission. He seeks my safe, ego-proofed followership, and only the cross can produce it. If I am a cross-disarmed, cross-slain, cross-bearing follower—God can trust me. "I have been crucified with Christ and I no longer live, but Christ lives in me" (Galations 2:20)—a life transformed at the deepest levels of my personhood. This is not some "new slant" on the gospel. This is the central message of Jesus and His band of courageous disciples.

FIRST-CENTURY IMPACT
How does this compare to the message of the early church? What were the early Christians preaching and teaching that so powerfully impacted and changed people's lives? Let's take a look at the first sermon preached by Peter on the Day of Pentecost and recorded in Acts 2, picking it up at verse 25 where Peter is quoting Psalm 16:8-11:

David said about him:
> "I saw *the Lord* always before me.
> Because *he is at my right hand,*
> I will not be shaken.
> Therefore my heart is glad and my tongue rejoices;
>> my body also will live in hope,
> because you will not abandon me to the grave,
>> nor will you let *your Holy One* see decay.
> You have made known to me the paths of life;
>> you will fill me with joy in your presence."

Brothers, I can tell you confidently that the patriarch David died and was buried, and his tomb is here to this day. But he was a prophet and knew that God had promised him on oath that he would place *one of his descendants on his throne.* Seeing what was ahead, he spoke of the resurrection of the Christ, that he was not abandoned to the grave, nor did his body see decay. God has raised this Jesus to life, and we are all witnesses of the fact. *Exalted to the right hand of God,* he has received from the Father the promised Holy Spirit and has poured out what you now see and hear. For David did not ascend to heaven, and yet he said,

> "*The Lord said to my Lord:*
>> '*Sit at my right hand*
> until I make your enemies
>> a footstool for your feet.'"
>> (Acts 2:25-35, emphasis added)

Did you notice how Peter presented the gospel of salvation? First he reviewed the events of the crucifixion and resurrection, but superimposed on the cross was the crown! He identified the Savior as the royal successor not only of David's throne but also of heaven's throne!

It was when the enormity of what they had done to the Sovereign Lord of the cosmos hit them that the people were overcome. Ashen-faced and in hushed tones they asked, "What shall we do?" It was dawning on them that they had assassinated the Lord of glory, who had conquered death and was now back at His place of supreme authority at the right hand of God. "We're toast! Is there anything we can do to avoid His wrath?"

Peter's immediate Spirit-led response was, "Repent [change sides] and take a public stand with Him through baptism. Take up His name and His cause and you will receive the gift of the Holy Spirit to let you know you are off the hook of God's judgment." (See Acts 2:38.)

Repentance was foundational to the gospel of the early church. It was the code word for the act of taking sides with God. What would happen in today's churches if we asked for such a response? Wouldn't this be the precondition for the revival we are seeking?

⇢ F O U R T E E N ⇠
Getting Back on Track

I live in the Pacific Northwest, an area currently known for its nonchurched population. Since moving to Seattle in 1979, I've run into nearly as many people who claim they *used* to be born-again Christians as I have people who say they *still are* born again. Let me explain why this has been bewildering for me.

I was raised in the Upper Midwest, an area of the country where evangelical Christians were very much in the minority. For instance, I pastored a church in Green Bay, Wisconsin, where at the time 85 percent of the community was Roman Catholic and most of the remainder was part of mainline Protestant denominations. The evangelical churches were small and struggling to survive. We often heard people say they had been raised in a church—baptized as an infant, confirmed, and married there—but hadn't attended services in years.

We evangelicals looked at the majority of the Christian community and said: "Well, what do you expect? People are bound to fall away if they aren't being fed the Word of God. Why, these people probably aren't even *saved*." We prided ourselves in the fact that most of our people who had been converted or born again stuck with their faith and their church. Since many of us believed in eternal security and "once saved always saved," we were confident that God would keep His own by His power and faithfulness. Although we allowed for periods of backsliding, falling away, or carnality, we were convinced that real Christians were disciplined by the Lord and brought back to active obedience.

FORMERLY BORN AGAIN?

Then I moved to the Northwest, where I noticed that nearly everybody was a fellow transplant. They were from the East, the Midwest, the South, California, Alaska. And surprisingly, a large number of them had Christian backgrounds. A significant percentage of unchurched people I've talked to were raised in Sunday school, attended church and youth group, Christian camps, vacation Bible school, Awana, and even Christian colleges. They prayed the prayer, made the decision, walked the aisle, raised their hands for prayer, and considered themselves born again.

But when they moved to the Northwest, they never connected with a church. Now, after a few years of living without the influence of a local church, they calmly say, "I used to be a born-again Christian. I tried it. It's okay. I just don't have a compelling need for that kind of thing right now." They're busy with boating, skiing, backpacking, camping, or just fixing up their house and caring for their yard on weekends. They say they don't have time for church and frankly don't really miss it. As I talk with active Christians and church leaders around the country, I hear similar reports. The fact is, "former evangelicals" are becoming quite common in our culture.

What's going on? Doesn't the gospel work anymore? Is conservative evangelicalism just like any other brand of Christian religion? Can you dabble in it for a while and then walk away?

True Christianity is something that grips your life, radically changes you and transforms you into a new person in Christ. It is a way of life, an all-encompassing lifestyle that affects everything you are and everything you do. When we welcome Jesus Christ into our souls as Savior and Lord, an eternal union takes place. Dropping out or changing your mind and discarding your relationship with Christ hasn't figured into my view of how Christianity works. Obviously, many former or inactive Christians have a different way of looking at it.

PREVIOUSLY CHURCHED

I've noticed a pattern in these church dropouts who still consider themselves born again. They claim that their personal relationship with Christ is just that—personal. They don't see a need for other Christians or organized Christianity.

✠

Ginger sat in my office nervously balling up a tissue. She was there out of concern for her oldest son, whom she confessed was a handful. "I haven't been inside a church in twelve years," she said as she opened the conversation. "Do you still use the *King James Version* here?" When I said we used a much more readable translation, she was not reassured. She went on to tell me a familiar story of the self-destruction of the Bible-teaching church of her youth.

"The issue," she said, with fire in her eyes, "was which translation was the true Word of God and which ones were perversions."

She had not been back to church in over a decade — and yet she was ready to take me to task for having led my church into inexcusable error! It did not take a rocket scientist to figure out which side her family had been on.

When I asked if she was planning to return to church for the sake of her teenagers, she frowned and shook her head. "All three of my kids have 'prayed the prayer,' so I know they're saved. There's no way I'll risk having them go through the pain I experienced at their age."

"How do you maintain your growth as a Christian?" I asked.

"I listen to Christian radio and watch Christian television occasionally," she replied.

Ginger's concept of a relationship with God was based on making a one-time "decision," then reminding herself that the decision was the right one.

✠

Floyd plays noon-hour basketball with me. He has a pretty fair jump shot and a hot temper.

One day we were both sitting out a game and we got to talking. I was startled to find out that he was a born-again Christian.

"Yup," he said. "I gave my heart to Jesus my junior year in college. Got pinned down by Campus Crusade."

"What church do you attend?" I asked.

"I don't," he said. "I work a second job on weekends. Have for almost ten years now. Sometimes I miss it, but my wife has gotten into soccer and her team plays on Sunday mornings. So . . ."

Floyd came to Christ through a parachurch ministry and has never connected with a local church. He says he feels no need for worship, Bible study, or prayer with other believers. His faith is private and he likes it that way.

✠

Mary is a waitress at a restaurant I frequent. She usually exchanges pleasantries with a degree of closeness. She once confided to me that she made a decision for Christ in high school at a Young Life meeting.

"What's happened since then?" I asked.

"Well, I kinda messed up," she said, shrugging. "I fell in love with a guy who wasn't a Christian."

"Then what?" I prompted.

"We lived together for a couple of years, then I got pregnant, so we got married. Since then, he hasn't liked it when I've gone to church. I go to Bible Study Fellowship with a friend once in a while on Monday nights when he's at work."

I sympathized with her dilemma as she refilled my coffee cup. But my mind was adding up another chalk mark in the already-crowded column of unconnected "believers."

THE AMAZING GRACE ESCAPE CLAUSE

One other frustrating pattern that concerns me is the number of conservative evangelicals who have walked away from the Lord in pursuit of something or someone they wanted more than being obedient to Christ. A very common situation occurring with increasing regularity is married Christians who fall in love with someone other than their partner. They then disappear from their church, get a divorce, remarry, and eventually resurface a year or two later in another evangelical church, most likely of a different denomination or a megachurch where questions are unlikely to be asked. I've made it a point to ask those that fit this profile who have started attending my church how they justify their behavior.

One man recently said, "Oh, Pastor, I know what I did was sin, but I was trapped in such a terribly unhappy marriage. My first wife and I were wrong for each other right from the start. I don't think I ever really loved her. I don't believe in divorce, but once I met my new wife I finally admitted to myself that I'd made a mistake with my first marriage."

When I suggested that he had made an even bigger mistake with his second marriage, he emphatically disagreed.

"I've never been happier in my life. Besides, nobody's perfect, you know. And we all make mistakes. I'm sure there are things in your past you wouldn't want people to know about."

While I was reeling from this telling shot, he proceeded to give me a theological lesson on the grace of God and God's infinite ability to forgive sinners.

A few weeks later a young mother of two told me she had recently divorced her husband of seven years in order to marry a wonderful Christian man she met at her office.

"I'm curious," I asked. "How did you work this whole thing out in your thinking? You've told me you knew divorce was sin. You said your first husband was also a Christian. He didn't abuse you and wasn't unfaithful to you. So, how did you justify leaving him to marry another man?"

"That's a good question," she said. (I felt affirmed — briefly.) "Certainly, I don't have to tell you about the grace of God."

It was apparent that I was in for more postgraduate instruction. Then, she said something that I've often suspected but never actually heard a Christian admit.

"I intended to ask for forgiveness and come back to the Lord even before I began the affair. It was unthinkable to live my life without Ken. I know my divorce was wrong in God's eyes, but it seemed like the best decision at the time. And I haven't committed the unpardonable sin, you know. Besides, I'm so-o-o happy with my new husband. He's turning out to be a real man of God. We pray and read the Word together every night, and we just love your church!"

Like the others, her story was deeply troubling to me. Professing faith but not following in obedience is a pattern that suggests there is no understanding of the centrality of Christ's kingdom.

THE COST FOR LEAVING OUT THE KINGDOM

Where does this kind of thinking come from? Has God changed the way He connects with people? No! Rather, we've forgotten how to follow Him. Perhaps we've even substituted our version for the message Jesus gave us. The kinds of misaligned Christian behavior I've been describing are, by and large, the consequences of changing the message of Jesus

Christ. In my judgment, we are paying huge consequences for leaving out of our gospel message the essential fact that Jesus called us to come into a "kingdom"—the kingdom of God. George Barna, in *Evangelism That Works*, wrote the following:

> I am convinced that much of the difficulty of church-based evangelism is that we seek *decisions* for Christ rather than *conversions*. A decision may be as simple as repeating the "Sinner's Prayer" with no real follow-through after that act. A conversion, on the other hand, is a total life transformation in which the decision to follow Christ results in a new lifestyle, a new heart for people and for God, and a determination to live for totally different ends.
>
> *Most of the cutting-edge evangelistic churches have major problems with low retention of converts.* This was the most disturbing revelation of all. The conclusion I have come to is that churches are so focused on obtaining decisions that they ignore conversions. It is one thing for a person to assent to follow Christ. It is another to then pick up his cross and bear it after making the decision.[1]

The New Testament opens with a kingdom gospel. John the Baptist, in Matthew 3:2, announced his powerful message in the desert: "Repent, for the kingdom of heaven is near." There was a tremendous response to his preaching. Huge crowds traveled into the desert to hear him and to be baptized.

Then Jesus began His public ministry. Matthew summarizes His message in 4:17: "From that time on Jesus began to preach, 'Repent, for the kingdom of heaven is near.'"

After many kingdom parables, each revealing additional truth about the value of the kingdom or how to access the kingdom, Jesus makes this remarkable statement in Matthew 24:14: "And this gospel of the kingdom will be preached in the whole world as a testimony to all nations, and then the end will come." (Jesus' message is examined in more detail in chapter 16.)

The biblical gospel *is* the gospel of the kingdom. It implies a sovereign leader. A kingdom has laws that govern behavior and penalties for breaking them. Following Jesus means buying into a realm of jurisdiction and authority that puts God at the controls of your life. So, where did we get permission in this modern era to eliminate the kingdom from the gospel? If Jesus Himself said it was His plan to have the gospel of the kingdom preached throughout the church age until His second coming, shouldn't that be the defining mandate? Part of the explanation for the missing kingdom can be found in the historical and cultural changes that have influenced our thinking.

BACK BEFORE A MONARCH WAS A BUTTERFLY

The changing of the guard at Buckingham Palace in London has to be one of the most photographed rituals of the camera age. Kodak should be required to kick-back a percentage of all the film used to record the royal family. But the English monarchy is a symbol only; the queen of the commonwealth is, in reality, a mere public relations expert.

> *We are paying huge consequences for leaving out of our gospel message the essential fact that Jesus called us to come into a "kingdom"—the kingdom of God.*

For the most part, the kings and queens of today are powerless curiosities. Their role is the preservation of national identity and a connection with the glories of the past. This is in stark contrast to the rulers of history. When Jesus began His earthly visit no one would have had difficulty understanding His references to a kingdom. It would have been impossible to find a place in the Roman Empire where the throne and authority of Caesar were not a constant reality. Everyone who heard Jesus speak in kingdom language knew that respect and obedience to the ruling leader were appropriate and, in fact, required.

In America and the rest of the modernized Western world it is not easy for people to identify with the jurisdiction and dominion concepts inherent in a kingdom model of government. Today we are only familiar with the rights of the people, the freedom and liberty of the citizens. When our politicians fail to satisfy the majority of their constituents, they are turned out of office at the next election. In this environment of independence and autonomy for the individual, it is difficult to be understood when explaining the biblical concepts of the kingdom of God.

Perhaps this is one of the reasons the kingdom message of Jesus and the apostles has all but disappeared in the twentieth century.

But we must come back to the fact that the King of heaven and earth insists on being recognized for who He is. He will not permit His dominion to be avoided. This is the leadership priority of God. By leadership priority I mean all the clear kingdom emphasis we find in both the Old and the New Testaments. The kingdom message addresses the leadership and followership issues of sin, salvation, and sanctification. It provides the frame of reference for standardizing the definitions and methodologies of evangelism. It is the intellectual bedrock for interpreting the applications of discipleship. It is thus imperative that we start where Jesus started. To try to explain the message and mission of Jesus without the kingdom is to rewrite the gospel.

THE KINGDOM DRUMBEAT

It is rare in today's churches to hear reference made to the kingdom theme of Scripture. An affluent democratic society receives kingdom thinking about as enthusiastically as a rock-concert crowd would hear classical music. Concepts like the authority, power, and glory of God and the reasonable submission and obedience of humankind have an unfamiliar beat. E. Stanley Jones, a man who loved the kingdom, wrote:

> Jesus put at the center of the prayer which He taught His disciples this petition: "Thy Kingdom come, Thy will be done." He put it at the center of this prayer because it was at the center of His purpose, and He wanted it to be at the center of theirs. This is in keeping with the rest of His teaching, for the Kingdom was central in all He said and did.[2]

His leadership must become "our song" again. The melody of the gospel of the kingdom must once more sweep over the church.

But what about this "kingdom"? The all-important question is: Is the kingdom an illustration or a reality?

The Holy Spirit has some favorite illustrations that are intended to reveal truth about God's relationship with His people. His repeated use of familiar word pictures keeps jumping out at thoughtful readers of the Bible. Many of these vivid images are found in both the Old and New Testaments.

- The shepherd and his sheep
- The gardener and his vineyard
- The water of life and the thirsty
- The potter and the clay
- The father and his children
- The builder and the living stones
- The commander and his warriors
- The head and the body
- The heavenly bridegroom and his earthly bride
- The vine and his branches
- The high priest and his royal priesthood
- The light and the seeker of light
- The master and his servants

There is vital truth to be discovered in each of these illustrations. But the Holy Spirit uses one powerful word picture that is quite different from these: the revelation that God Himself is *the King of the universe* and all that is willingly in subjection to His leadership is regarded as *His kingdom*. This is not an illustration, a picture of something else. The kingdom is reality. It is the reason the "leadership issue" is at the heart of the written Word of God.

THE FINAL AGENDA

What a difference the kingdom message of Jesus makes when it is understood and embraced! We learn that our God is the authority over every area of our lives. Our Day-Timers are His. Our checkbooks are His. He is our leader in everything — all aspects of the Christian life begin to function smoothly when He is in first place.

Followers of Christ don't drop out or disappear into self-absorbed lifestyles. Nor do they invent a convenient "grace escape clause" for going their own way. They follow — and God's Spirit empowers them by His grace to make God's agenda the governing passion of their hearts.

You may recognize your heart in diagram 14.1 (page 120) and realize that you are still heavy on the "My Agenda" side of the repentance process. If so, this may be a good time to offer fresh followership to your Lord. The best way to do this is through agenda-swapping prayer. Eugene Peterson's delightful book on the Psalms called *Where Your Treasure Is* would make a strong contribution to keeping God's agenda growing in your heart. He refers to prayer as the primary means God has given us for "unselfing ourselves" (repenting). I give you this sample to whet your appetite.

The Process of Letting God Lead

Diagram 14.1

These people who pray know what most around them either don't know or choose to ignore: centering life in the insatiable demands of the ego is the sure path to doom. They know that life confined to the self is a prison, a joy-killing, neurosis-producing, disease-fomenting prison. Out of a sheer sense of survival they are committed to a way of life that is "unselfed."[3]

Here is the heart attitude behind natural, spontaneous comunication with God. Prayer is "taking off" my will and "putting on" His. It is embracing His loving leadership as a constant process.

THE SAFEST PLACE TO UNSELF YOURSELF
In order to explain how powerful and attractive the unselfing prayer process is, let me offer Jeremiah's "oasis in the desert" illustration. It is intended to show us how desperately dependent on God we really are. There are some surprises waiting.

"But blessed is the man who trusts in the LORD,
    whose confidence is in him.
He will be like a tree planted by the water
    that sends out its roots by the stream.
It does not fear when heat comes;
    its leaves are always green.
It has no worries in a year of drought
    and never fails to bear fruit." (Jeremiah 17:7-8)

From the tree image, the prophet then moves to the source of the stream of living water—the throne room of the universe! There's an incredible gem of motivational truth waiting to be discovered here.

A glorious throne, exalted from the beginning,
    is the place of our sanctuary. (17:12)

This is the throne of grace—the very focus of prayer that we have been invited to approach with confidence, so that we may receive mercy and find grace to help us in our time of need (Hebrews 4:16). When we pray and bow before the throne, as is appropriate in the presence of our Sovereign, there, flowing from under the throne, a wondrous discovery awaits us. "Then the angel showed me the river of the water of life, as clear as crystal, flowing from the throne of God and of the Lamb" (Revelation 22:1).

In prayer before His throne, the unselfing of my self-sufficiency is met with the "fount of every blessing." My fear of losing is washed away in the flood of His goodness. The more I bow in prayer, the more I come in contact with the river of His inexhaustible kingdom provisions! Unselfing myself in such a glorious place is not at all the process I dreaded at first. Rather, it is with sheer delight that I go from sipping to swimming in His bountiful love for me. In His presence, where I was afraid I would be diminished, I am treated with great respect and affection. In prayer I am assured that He intends to maximize my potential and productivity. "What have I to dread? What have I to fear? Leaning on the everlasting arms." Unselfing myself in prayer is exposing myself to light but also to love and life. What an awesome God we serve!

Lord, it's me again. I'm here before Your throne to consciously be with You. I love it here. I delight in belonging . . . in being at home with You. Search me, O God, and know my heart, try me and know my thoughts. See if there is any remnant of self-in-control in me. Show it to me and I will cooperate with You in getting rid of it. Lead me today. My heart is full of gratitude. You have been so tender and patient with me. Thank You for the water of life. As I bathe in it and drink my fill, I am utterly content. You are my source! Amen.

NOTES

1. George Barna, *Evangelism That Works* (Ventura, Calif.: Gospel Light, 1995), pp. 100-101, 131, emphasis added.

2. E. Stanley Jones, *Is the Kingdom of God Realism?* (New York: Abingdon-Cokesbury Press, 1940), p. 71.

3. Eugene Peterson, *Where Your Treasure Is* (Grand Rapids, Mich.: Eerdmans, 1993), p. 12.

The "Slice" I Want

Three days after the tragic bombing of the Murrah Federal Building in Oklahoma City, President Clinton laid the blame for this outrage at the door of conservative talk radio. The administration "spin doctors" had decided that it was to their political advantage to "frame the issue" as incitement to rage and hate by right-wing extremists.

We live at a time in history when framing the issue has risen nearly to an art form. Bright and clever people are hired by newspapers, radio stations, television networks, and politicians to use words as tools. Words are powerful levers. They don't just communicate information; they shape information and as a result mold the way events and issues are perceived.

Take abortion, for instance. For a variety of reasons, abortion supporters have decided it's to their advantage to frame the issue as "a woman's right to choose." Abortion opponents are reluctant to allow the debate to focus on the mother's reproductive freedom and prefer to target the baby's right to life as the central issue. This makes the discussion a confrontation of rights.

The party that frames the issue controls the direction and content of the debate. It is an ancient and effective way to produce a desired outcome or accomplish a preferred agenda. For example, let's look at the personal issue of differences and conflict between marriage partners. More and more people who are unhappy with the degree of discomfort in their relationships are calling them abusive relationships. Women, particularly, are learning that there is a huge pool of resources and options available in this culture for women who frame their relationships in terms of abuse. Such claims become a means of developing a support system for leaving their husbands.

Men, on the other hand, create running room for their agenda by utilizing the "stressed-out/burned-out" language of today's business environment. Their favorite recreational pastime is framed as necessary in order to let down and relax. When the self-centered use of their free time is given this twist, it takes on a kind of a sacred inevitability. Who can argue with maintaining your health and sanity?

Framing the issue is a way of life for us. We all do it, whether consciously or unconsciously. It can be used honestly or dishonestly, for good or for evil purposes.

HOW DID JESUS DO IT?

The most important information in the world is the message Jesus Christ came to communicate. He called it the "good news" or "gospel of the kingdom." Over the past two thousand years the essential message of Jesus has been sliced and diced in a great variety of ways.

I've selected what I think are the six most common configurations of gospel truth that I see within the evangelical church today and arranged them in the following chart. Each "set" of definitions is logically connected: the diagnosis matches the prognosis and the prescribed process of recovery. I'm including this comprehensive overview to acknowledge that the Christian gospel contains a rich layering of truth upon truth. To someone just starting out in the Christian life, this breakdown of the various categories may seem complex. On the other hand, to a lifelong follower of Christ, each piece is precious but has been appreciated over time in a process of understanding and growth.

The crucial question is this: Where should we start in communicating such a rich smorgasbord of ideas? Which flavor of good news is the first course, according to the chef's design, in the six-course meal? I'll answer that question by the end of the chapter. First, let's take a closer look at the six layers of ingredients.

Some pastors and teachers systematically and intentionally include all of these categories in order to give balanced, comprehensive understanding to their hearers. Much more common are Bible teachers who develop a preference, and then consistently frame the issues from that preference. This tendency is difficult to avoid because our minds naturally try to bring order and simplicity out of complexity. Let's briefly examine the layers separately.

INGREDIENTS OF THE GOSPEL

DIAGNOSIS	PROGNOSIS	RECOVERY PROCESS
SIN IS:	SALVATION IS:	SANCTIFICATION IS:
Alienation Spiritually dead (Separated from God)	**1. Love (grace)** By faith receive unconditional acceptance and forgiveness —**Reconciliation**	**Walk in Love** With God and each other—embrace grace, fruits, and gifts
Darkness Blinded minds Ignorance of God	**2. Light (grace)** By faith knowing, understanding, and believing essential gospel —**Illumination**	**Walk in the Light** Educate, train, and equip with biblical truth brought home to the heart by the Holy Spirit
Deadness Inability Depravity	**3. Life (grace)** By faith receive the life-activating work of the Holy Spirit and be born again —**Regeneration**	**Walk in Newness of Life** Appropriate supernatural ability and resurrection power
Captivity In bondage to sin and Satan	**4. Liberty (grace)** By faith set free from sin's penalty and power —**Redemption**	**Walk in Victory** Learn to function as an emancipated servant of God in the power of the Spirit
Unrighteousness Missing the mark of God's character and revealed law	**5. Legality (grace)** By faith receive pardon; God's justice is satisfied and the righteousness of Christ is imputed —**Justification**	**Walk of Faith** Understand positional righteousness and cooperate with the Spirit in a process of developing practical righteousness
Rebellion Defiant egoism Self-enthronement Independence	**6. Leadership (grace)** By faith surrender to Christ's kingdom; repent—give up control and come under the rule of God —**Transformation**	**Walk in Obedience** Learning followership through a process of submission to God's Word and dependence upon the Spirit

Gospel as love. Perhaps the most widely used salvation model in the evangelical world is the gospel as *love.* Sin is defined as wrong choices and behavior that have alienated the sinner from God. The separation of a holy God from sinful humanity can be bridged by the forgiveness offered by Jesus through the cross. The appeal is for the seeker to draw near to God and receive the free gift of His love and grace. At the moment people accept the offer of entry into the family of God, they receive the assurance of sins forgiven and a home in heaven when they die. This emphasis works quite well with people who feel distant from God. It tends to produce relatively strong immediate response but then tends to fade quickly under the expectations and commitments of discipleship.

Gospel as light. The gospel as *light* has been popular for a long time. Churches that emphasize expository Bible teaching usually prefer to major on this layer. The unbeliever is assumed to be ignorant and in need of accurate information or truth. Complicating the lack of knowledge is a spiritual blindness that cloaks minds so the light of truth doesn't shine through. Proclaiming the essential facts of the gospel of the cross and the resurrection enables the Holy Spirit to illuminate the mind with truth. Believing and having faith in that truth brings about salvation. The transformation process is then seen as renewing your mind in Bible study. "You can't do what you don't know" conveys the sentiment.

Gospel as life. Another popular emphasis is the gospel as *life.* This group of teachers is most comfortable presenting sin as an absence of spiritual life. The focus is on emptiness and meaninglessness. Depravity is seen as the inability to respond to God. This is the fallen condition into which every person is born. What is necessary to correct the problem is the drawing of the Holy Spirit, culminating in regeneration to newness of life. The spiritual growth process is visualized as entering the enjoyment of the abundant life by learning to make use of the inexhaustible provisions and privileges God has given. This model is dependent on a miraculous supernatural infusion of Christ's resurrection life and power that is the result of God's sovereign initiative.

Gospel as liberty. The warfare approach to the gospel specializes in *liberty* from the bondage and captivity of sin. The Devil is identified as a slave master duping sinners into obsessive, compulsive, and addictive behaviors. The captive is bound and held hostage by God's adversary and must be released from Satan's grip. The work of Christ is regarded as setting prisoners free, providing liberty to the captives. In Christ the believer finds a new master and the Christian life is seen as a life of freedom under the lordship of Christ. Redemption from slavery to sin provides deliverance from sin's penalty and power. The Christian recovery movement utilizes this model, as do ministries that specialize in deliverance.

Gospel as legal issue. Some, whose roots are still strongly connected to the Reformation, prefer to present the gospel as a *legal issue.* Because of the Protestant rediscovery of justification by faith, the focus tends to be on the judicial acts of God in removing the guilt and judgment that holy justice demanded through the cross. Those who accept the Judge's grace-offer by faith receive pardon for the judgment they deserve. In addition, they receive the righteousness of Jesus, which they do not deserve. In this configuration of the gospel, sin produces legal guilt for violation of God's standard of holiness, technically defined as "missing the mark." Sanctification is the process of walking in the righteousness of Christ by the energizing of the Spirit and learning how to appropriate the resources provided in Him. This is sometimes referred to as "the exchanged life."

All of these levels of the gospel message address valid nuances of God's revelation of salvation; they all address felt needs and offer salvation from a legitimate perspective. Think of them as floors at which the elevator of truth can stop, each floor offering an effective entry point. My suggestion is that the floor we will now examine is the "ground floor," which is the best place to start.

Gospel of the kingdom. The one remaining layer of truth on our chart focuses on the leadership issue. This is the *gospel of the kingdom* and the way Jesus chose to frame the issue of sin, salvation, and sanctification.

Sin is defined as independence or rebellion. It originates in rejection of the authority and leadership of the Creator. Salvation is reentry into the kingdom of God, also called the kingdom of heaven and the kingdom of Christ. It focuses on a faith response through surrender or repentance to trustworthy leadership. The self-enthroned sinner is asked to give up his or her resistance and come under the dominion of Jesus Christ. This reestablishes the intended order of the universe. It changes a one-time enemy of God into a son or daughter in the family of God destined to inherit the kingdom of God. The sanctification process is a lifestyle of repentance and humility. The believer develops a life of obedience and followership under the supervision of the Holy Spirit and the Word of God.

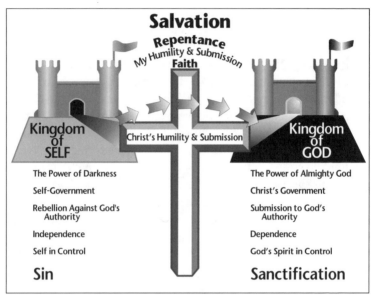

Diagram 15.1

WHY THE KINGDOM EMPHASIS?

All of these different slices of the gospel message can be substantiated by the Word of God. Reconciliation, illumination, regeneration, redemption, justification, and transformation are all part of the saving work of Christ Jesus and can be separated and examined in detail. Where the dissecting of truth goes astray is when our human preferences get involved. Those who consistently study and communicate the Word of God tend to develop a simplified explanation of the gospel. Including all aspects gets too complicated. What we choose to include or exclude in our "stripped-down" version usually fits into one of the levels of ingredients described in this chapter. Some Christians wisely use all of these approaches at different times for different purposes or for different audiences. But many of the communicators I've talked with on this subject had never thought about how they had arrived at their preferred emphasis. It had just happened over the course of their ministry. What follows is an attempt to persuade all of us to get our cue on where to start from Jesus.

THE FOCUS ON FOLLOWING

Jesus "framed the issues" of sin, salvation, and sanctification as a *kingdom* or *leadership* matter. He deliberately led with this issue throughout His earthly ministry. If the Master of the universe chose this approach, it would be wise to assume that He had a good reason. What could it be? Why would He focus His message on the leadership issue when there were obviously other important aspects involved as well?

I've pondered that question and come up with two reasons. First, He is clearly following His job description as revealed in the Great Mandate (1 Corinthians 15:24-28). He understood His earthly ministry as the key element in a strategy to defeat all rebellion against the throne of God. Therefore, He deliberately chose to focus on an invitation for humankind to access the kingdom through repentance or unconditional surrender. The gate swung open. The purchase price of redemption was paid. A new and living way was made for those willing to return to heaven's leadership. The kingdom choice was built upon the temple, the priesthood, and the sacrificial system of the Old Covenant. A new deal was cut — the final blood covenant.

The second reason has to do with the outcome Jesus intended. He was not merely after souls, refugees, or converts. He was clearly seeking disciples. His definition of a disciple started with followership. "Follow Me" was His invitation, His question, and His command. It involved learning and becoming; but first and foremost, it was the breaking up of independent self-rule. The Godhead had decided to salvage all human beings who would choose to surrender. The everlasting King was intent on turning defiant, hostile opponents into loving, loyal subjects. David Swartz is a pastor who has caught on to this purpose of Jesus. In his book *The Magnificent Obsession*, he writes:

> Does Jesus really lay this deep claim on every life? Viewed through the lenses of what western Christianity has become, you wouldn't think so — not if what we see around us is normative. But Jesus' absolute claim to rule over the hearts of men was part of things from the beginning. He commonly allowed others to address Him as "Lord"—a word meaning "master" and a covenant title in the Old Testament for God. He taught that obedience was the only proper response to His demanding teaching — not negotiation or a dash for the commentaries to get a

second opinion. His command — "Follow me" — challenged people to risk abandoning their most cherished dreams for the sake of His Kingdom.[1]

Stonewall Jackson was a Confederate leader of outstanding ability. His military campaign in the Shenandoah Valley during the Civil War was brilliantly planned and executed. But great as he was in his own right, he was far more confident in the leadership of General Robert E. Lee. Jackson once said he was so sure of Lee's leadership, he would follow him into battle blindfolded. What a follower!

THE HEART OF THE DISCIPLE — THE REAL ISSUE

A disciple is a trustworthy follower. God will not subject Himself or His kingdom to an everlasting power struggle. Disciples have chosen their permanent Master and are committed to obeying Him. For disciples of Jesus Christ, God is first their leader, then their love, life, light, liberty, and legal justifier. Starting with the kingdom forces the issues that make believers into followers right from the initial repentance/faith transaction.

The words of Jesus on the subject of discipleship or followership are provocative. They operate as a kind of sorting device. They offend egoists. They are welcomed by humble, servant-hearted followers. Let's examine a few of the Master's lessons on what it means to follow Him.

TOUGH CHALLENGES TO THE KINGDOM PRIORITY

Then a teacher of the law came to him and said, "Teacher, I will follow you wherever you go."

Jesus replied, "Foxes have holes and birds of the air have nests, but the Son of Man has no place to lay his head."

Another disciple said to him, "Lord, first let me go and bury my father."

But Jesus told him, "Follow me, and let the dead bury their own dead." (Matthew 8:19-22)

"I will follow you wherever you go," promised the first potential disciple. Jesus responded by reminding the man that he would be entering a life of hardship and difficulty. He was saying, "This is no lark, no glamour job. If you follow Me you will pay a price. The full paycheck comes later when the final form of the kingdom arrives. Until then following Me will be sacrificial. So count the cost now. I'm not looking for fair-weather followers who don't finish what they start."

Stark, isn't it? But also clear. Jesus didn't make following Him easy or as attractive as possible. We do that. He made it clear that it would be a life of costly surrender. Salvation is the free gift that costs the recipient everything.

The second candidate for serious discipleship said, "Lord, I've got a family emergency. My father just died. I feel responsible to my family. I'm sure You'll understand the importance of supporting my loved ones at this time of grief and loss. I'll be back to follow You after the funeral."

> *Salvation is the free gift that costs the recipient everything.*

Jesus shocked this would-be disciple with his response: "Follow Me, and let the dead bury the dead." Upon superficial examination this statement seems to be the height of calloused insensitivity. It certainly violates current grief-recovery guidelines. On top of that, it seems in direct violation of the fifth commandment, to honor your father and your mother. So, why would God in human flesh contradict His own principle?

The purpose of Jesus was to underline for all His disciples, then and now, the surpassing priority of followership. Jesus was saying, "Family does not come first. If I am your Lord and Master, then My concerns come ahead of your most pressing personal concerns." In Luke's version of this conversation an enlightening phrase is added. "Let the dead bury their own dead, but you go and proclaim the kingdom of God" (Luke 9:60). This addresses the same issue as wealth and riches. Some people don't follow well because they have a lot of money and material possessions to care for. Wealth has an extremely strong tendency to become a rival kingdom to God's kingdom. "You cannot serve two masters. One or the other will prevail, so make your choice," says Jesus (see Matthew 6:24).

Family relationships are another form of wealth. Some families are tight-knit units of love relationships. The family can be the most powerful influence and the deciding factor in a person's life. Family priorities and pressures can rule a person's life, making it impossible to let God reign and accomplish His purposes. On another occasion Jesus made an equally radical demand.Consider Matthew 10:34-39:

"Do not suppose that I have come to bring peace to the earth. I did not come to bring peace, but a sword. For I have come to turn

"'a man against his father,

a daughter against her mother,

a daughter-in-law against her mother-in-law—

a man's enemies will be the members of his own household.'

"Anyone who loves his father or mother more than me is not worthy of me; anyone who loves his son or daughter more than me is not worthy of me; and anyone who does not take his cross and follow me is not worthy of me. Whoever finds his life will lose it, and whoever loses his life for my sake will find it."

Two kingdoms are colliding. Two kinds of wealth and two sets of priorities are competing for loyalty. The expectations of the King of kings is that our love, commitment, and obedience to Him be above every other love relationship. As much as we may love, honor, and respect our parents, this must not alter our followership of Christ. As much as we love and are committed to our spouses, our love and responsibility to our Lord is higher. If we organize our lives and priorities around the needs and desires of our family, we are not following Jesus. Marriage, children, parents, and extended family can compete with God's kingdom. There should be no conflict of interests for a true disciple.

DEATH TO DISTRACTION

The cross we are to take up as we follow our Lord is a relational cross. The first concern is, What does my sovereign Lord want? Jesus tells us in John 12:24-26 (emphasis added):

"I tell you the truth, unless a kernel of wheat falls to the ground and dies, it remains only a single seed. But if it dies, it produces many seeds. The man who loves his life will lose it, while the man who hates his life in this world will keep it for eternal life. *Whoever serves me must follow me;* and where I am, my servant also will be. My Father will honor the one who serves me."

If what my spouse, parents, or children want shapes my choices more than Jesus does, I am not a follower of Jesus. If I shrug off the call of

God to go to the mission field because I don't want to lose any advantages for my family, I am a follower of my family. If I make my family the center of my life, according to Jesus, I will lose my family! Imagine that. They will not catch the overriding cause of God. They will likely live for their own cause. Focusing on a lesser priority than God's kingdom is a sure way to destroy that lesser kingdom.

Do you want a strong marriage, a successful family? Then seek the kingdom of God first. It may feel like you're going to louse up your family life for the sake of Jesus, but there is no other way to develop lasting family health and happiness. Jesus' kingdom is the safest, healthiest, and most desirable place for any family.

Be careful with this principle, though. Jesus is not advocating the abandonment of the important roles and responsibilities of the family. He's stressing the importance of putting every other priority behind the first-priority kingdom commitment. Balance is critical here. This is not either/or, it's both/and—with the kingdom in the top spot. There are plenty of horror stories about radical followers who have neglected their families and turned them off to the kingdom. Unfortunately, these can be used to justify a "saving one's life" style of discipleship. We must stay alert to the needs of our families, but even more alert to the danger of favoring our own kingdom.

> *Focusing on a lesser priority than God's kingdom is a sure way to destroy that lesser kingdom.*

The ultimate priority of the kingdom of God becomes the cross every genuine follower of Jesus shoulders daily. It means death to distraction and interference from lesser gods, lesser kingdoms, or lesser loves. The reason Jesus consistently "framed the issue" of salvation in leadership/followership language is abundantly clear. He was seeking followers who were as relaxed and ego-free as little children—as He was Himself. He was after followers who would trust themselves to God completely.

NOTE
1. David Swartz, *The Magnificent Obsession* (Colorado Springs, Colo.: NavPress, 1990), pp. 22-23.

What Jesus Called Good News

Jesus Christ was a master communicator. He was the Living Word, the self-disclosure of the eternal, invisible Creator. Hebrews 1:3 informs us that "the Son is the radiance of God's glory and the exact representation of his being." Jesus Himself said, "Anyone who has seen me has seen the Father" (John 14:9).

He did a superb job of revealing truth in language and word pictures that His hearers could understand. The response of the people was dramatic. "Never has a man spoken as this man does!" "He speaks with authority, not like the scribes." "Where else could we go, You have the words of eternal life." The crowds thronged around Him, eager to hear Him speak.

What was Jesus sent by the Father to communicate? The Gospels contain several summary statements that give us an overview of Christ's message. We often state it as, "Believe and receive, you're forgiven, you're going to heaven, welcome to God's family!" But after Jesus' baptism and temptation in the desert, He began to explain the true beginning of discipleship: "From that time on Jesus began to preach, 'Repent, for the kingdom of heaven is near'" (Matthew 4:17). And after that, "Jesus went throughout Galilee, teaching in their synagogues, preaching *the good news of the kingdom*, and healing every disease and sickness among the people" (4:23, emphasis added).

His message did not change in three years of public ministry.

But he said, "I must preach *the good news of the kingdom of God* to the other towns also, because that is why I was sent." (Luke 4:43, emphasis added)

Jesus went through all the towns and villages, teaching in their synagogues, preaching *the good news of the kingdom* and healing every disease and sickness. (Matthew 9:35, emphasis added)

After this, Jesus traveled about from one town and village to another, proclaiming *the good news of the kingdom of God.* (Luke 8:1, emphasis added)

When Jesus prophesied that the same gospel would be preached until the end of the age, He removed any question that the gospel might lose its kingdom overtones. "And *this gospel of the kingdom* will be preached in the whole world as a testimony to all nations, and then the end will come" (Matthew 24:14, emphasis added).

Why am I emphasizing this point? I assure you it's not some academic exercise. At stake is appreciating the full content of the gospel. If we don't include the kingdom, repentance, and growth in kingdom living in the good news we preach today, we reduce and alter the message of Jesus and are guilty of devising a different gospel. The gospel *is* "the kingdom." I didn't say that, Jesus did! The good news is that the dominion of God can be reestablished over human hearts. A way has been made. There is a door of entry—none other than Jesus Himself!

LOOKING THROUGH THE DOOR

Jesus' mission on earth was to provide access to the kingdom of God for all who would repent of their insurrection and revolt against the Creator. He did this by substituting Himself as the lightning rod for God's righteous indignation and justice. Without question, God's offer of reentry into the realm of His eternal kingdom is only available through the work of the cross.

Yet Jesus did not call the cross or His death and resurrection the good news. For Jesus, the kingdom was the good news. The magnificent work of the cross is the beginning. Atonement, reconciliation, redemption, justification, and propitiation are all essential ingredients of the gospel, but the theme of the good news is the rest, freedom, peace, and high investment value of living life under the leadership of the Sovereign Lord of heaven and earth.

The message of the Christian gospel over the past fifty years has increasingly emphasized the access door to the kingdom instead of what is behind the door. Jesus certainly did say, "I am the door." But we've overemphasized the door imagery as though "getting saved" is all there is to it. Christian evangelists and missionaries have worked so hard at marketing the entrance that it has itself become the gospel. Now, getting through the door of opportunity produced by Calvary's costly love is crucial and should never be minimized. But the "pearl of great price" is living in and inheriting the kingdom of God, not merely entering it. The focus of the ticket of salvation is the eternal party going on behind the gate inside the King's palace.

What this overemphasis has produced is a generation of believers who think the issue is getting in and getting others in. Recruiting. Not training. Not much attention is paid to what they are getting into — a whole new way of life! Getting in on eternal life in heaven is vastly different from welcoming heaven's reign here and now. What we are saved from is a big deal, but more important is what we are saved unto. Christ is our "door," but He is also our life beyond the door. When the eternal kingdom is welcomed, appreciated, treasured, and enjoyed, salvation has accomplished its intended purpose. God's human creatures have been restored to following their loving Leader.

WHAT THE APOSTLE PAUL CALLED GOOD NEWS

Those who insist on a gospel of grace minus the kingdom and repentance believe that they get their model from Paul, the Apostle to the Gentiles. They assume that the gospel of Jesus and the disciples went through a transition during the early days of the church; that as the gospel to the Jews moved to a worldwide audience, the ingredients changed from kingdom language to relational-reconciliation language. Without question, the end result is that the kingdom and repentance are forgotten, or else viewed by many evangelicals today as unnecessary in explaining the gospel.

This is a serious mistake. It is a misunderstanding of the key role of the kingdom and repentance in the pattern that Jesus gave us. And there are significant consequences. *The transformation process is severely weakened in those who accept salvation without understanding the significance of the kingdom component.* We now have a gospel that changes us only a little, or not at all. It's no secret that we have a gigantic problem with non-following believers inside and outside our churches.

Is this assertion about Paul true? Did he discontinue using the kingdom emphasis of Jesus? Now, there is no question that the apostle Paul championed the revelation of the grace of God that he had received. He certainly clarified and defined the gift basis of salvation. He was strong on the fact that good works, religious practice, and keeping the law are not ways to earn favor with God. Through Paul, the Holy Spirit made it clear that acceptance and inclusion in the kingdom is without question a gift of God received by faith.

The big question is, What *else* did Paul teach about salvation? The best summary is found in Acts 20:20-27, which is in the middle of his farewell address to the elders of the church in Ephesus. He knows he is likely to be imprisoned in Jerusalem, and doesn't expect to see this group of friends and fellow workers again. In wrapping up his ministry with them he summarizes what he has done there and elsewhere.

Paul's self-analysis contains three ways of saying the same thing. (The emphasis in the passages is mine.)

- Verse 21: "I have declared to both Jews and Greeks that *they must turn to God in repentance* and have faith in our Lord Jesus."
- Verse 24: "If only I may finish the race and complete the task the Lord Jesus has given me — the task of *testifying to the gospel of God's grace.*"
- Verse 25: "Now I know that none of you among whom *I have gone about preaching the kingdom* will ever see me again."

I am convinced that if we could ask Paul if he preached a gospel of grace, he would answer with an emphatic yes. If we asked him, "Did you preach a gospel of the kingdom?" he would answer, "Of course." If we asked him, "Did you preach a gospel of repentance?" he would answer, "Certainly." He would have no problem affirming all gospel ingredients because he saw them as three ways of describing the same message.

In another summary statement, Paul attempted to put his ministry into a nutshell for King Agrippa. In Acts 26:17-20, he describes his commission from Christ on the road to Damascus.

> "'I am sending you to them [the Gentiles] to open their eyes and turn them from darkness to light, and from the power of Satan to God, *so that they may receive forgiveness of sins and a place among those who are sanctified by faith in me.'*
>
> "So then, King Agrippa, I was not disobedient to the vision from heaven. First to those in Damascus, then to those in Jerusalem and in all Judea, and to the Gentiles also, *I preached that they should repent and turn to God and prove their repentance by their deeds.*" (emphasis added)

Once again the message of faith and forgiveness is set alongside the kingdom message of repentance in a way that makes it clear that Paul saw no distinction between the two.

At the end of his life, under guard in Rome, Paul was still preaching this combination. In Acts 28:23 and again in 28:30-31 the Scripture affirms that he was a kingdom teacher. "From morning till evening he explained and *declared to them the kingdom of God and tried to convince them about Jesus*" (Acts 28:23, emphasis added).

The significance of this is huge. The gospel of Jesus and the gospel of Paul were identical. Paul's message contained a further clarification on the distinction between law and grace, or salvation by works and salvation by grace through faith. Yet, he never left the kingdom theme of Jesus.

What happens to the gospel if the key ingredients of the kingdom and repentance are eliminated? If salvation is presented as only a gift to be received, or an offer of forgiveness to be accepted, or a relationship to be reconciled, what is the result?

When the kingdom is dropped out of the gospel message, repentance ceases to make sense. Instead of being forced to deal with the issue of control and leadership (that is, my kingdom versus God's kingdom), I am only asked to accept the work of Christ on my behalf. Repentance without the kingdom becomes an awkward idea and is usually dropped out of the mix. If included, it is defined as grief over sin and turning around or changing one's mind. Believing, receiving, or accepting Jesus and His redemptive reconciling work on the cross is partial language. It is essential but incomplete.

If I want the benefit of salvation, it will cost me my personal sovereignty, my independent autonomy, my own agenda, my "throne." Why? *Because that is exactly what I must be saved from in the first place!*

WHAT WE ACCEPT IN PLACE OF THE ORIGINAL GOOD NEWS

During the twentieth century, science and technology have affected our world and our lives in an accelerating process of change. The church of Jesus Christ has been influenced along with everything else on our planet. One significant change in ministry has come as the science of marketing has been applied to packaging the gospel presentation. Sales training called Personal Evangelism Classes has become standard procedure for any outreach-oriented church, as well it should be. Millions of believers are now "trained witnesses." Memorized proof texts, linear logic, convincing arguments, and closing techniques are all practiced and firmly in place. Most sincere Christians are equipped to make the offer of eternal life to their lost neighbors and friends.

> *If I want the benefit of salvation, it will cost me my personal sovereignty, my independent autonomy, my own agenda, my "throne."*

On the surface, we appear to be effective. At least one-half—some researchers say more like 60 percent—of the American people have prayed a salvation prayer and made a decision to receive Christ. They, therefore, are considered to fit the general category of having been evangelized or "born again." And here we must face a troubling and uncomfortable reality. A. W. Tozer, in the introduction of his book *The Knowledge of the Holy*, tells it like it is:

> The *loss of the concept of majesty* has come just when the forces of religion are making dramatic gains and the churches are more prosperous than at any time within the past several hundred years. But the alarming thing is that our gains are mostly external and our losses wholly internal; and since it is the *quality* of our religion that is affected by internal conditions,

it may be that our supposed gains are but losses spread over a wider field.[1]

We have discovered, to our dismay, that the majority of these supposed converts are no different after they bought our gospel than they were before.

In fact, many who show up in Bible-believing churches exhibit scant evidence of more than superficial subculture adaptation. They learn the evangelical jargon, become comfortable in the church society, listen to Christian radio, but in reality remain very much like their nonChristian neighbors in values, moral conduct, and lifestyle.

How can this be? *Where is the supernatural process of transformation?* Why are professing believers so often closed to the life-changing presence and power of the Holy Spirit? I ask you to consider with me the possibility that the application of marketing and sales expertise to evangelism has actually changed the content of the good news. Tweaking and massaging the gospel for ease of mass consumption has gradually changed the content—and killed its original *power.*

THE EFFECTS OF MARKETING

The cardinal rule of salesmanship is to concentrate on the attractive features, the advantages, and the benefits of the product. The lion's share of good sales technique is "hyping" the value and the reasons why customers owe it to themselves to become proud owners or proud members. The intent of this portion of the persuasion process is to create a desire for the product.

What piece of information is held back until "the close"? The price! And then the cost is minimized and customers are encouraged to think they're getting a great deal at an extraordinarily low price.

When this approach is applied to the gospel of Jesus Christ, modifications to the biblical model are inevitable. For instance, the benefits are easy to promote.

"What's your felt need?" a presenter may ask. "You say your life is in turmoil and you're stressed out? Well, if you let Jesus come into your life, He'll give you peace and inner tranquility." Then he or she might say, "Are you discouraged? Oh, you say you've really been down and blue? Let me assure you that when you open your heart to Christ, He'll give you the most fantastic joy imaginable!"

Then, of course, the "offer you simply can't refuse" comes into play. "It's free! It's a gift! There's nothing you can do to earn salvation. You can't pay for it even if you want to. Jesus already paid the price. He took the consequences of your sin upon the cross. All you have to do is receive the forgiveness and love of God and enter into the abundant life!"

The presenter continues. "Now, why wouldn't you want to have eternal life? You do want to go to heaven when you die, don't you? Is there any reason why you couldn't receive God's offer of love and forgiveness right now? Let me explain the prayer."

The typical Christian sales/witness approach is highly effective in getting the prospective believer to go along with the momentum of the technique and "pray the prayer."

The problem lies in the substantial modifications that have been made to Jesus' message. The effect of using marketing and sales techniques in evangelism is that they change the message. And when the message is altered, what the message produces is also changed. Salespeople do not make good evangelists if they depend on their craft. We must all depend on our Leader and His example for success. Our message must be His authentic kingdom gospel of grace in its entirety if we want to see its original life-changing power.

You may be one of those who, without realizing it, received an incomplete gospel. You assumed that the doorkeepers who stood at the entrance and introduced you to Christ knew what they were doing and you complied. You believed, prayed a prayer of accepting or receiving Christ, asked for forgiveness, and invited Christ into your heart and life. You have waited, but so far you've experienced disappointment, frustration, inability to change, and finally boredom. You may actually have come to the point of despair, thinking that you are somehow an exception and that it just doesn't work for you.

If so, what's happened to you is most likely a consequence of a gospel that has been altered. This is not your fault. The version you were led to believe would accomplish your salvation simply did not have the essential component of humble surrender in repentance. Since the heart of our sin problem is our self-centered need to be in control, unless that is addressed in salvation, and the back of our resistance is broken through repentance, nothing really changes.

Grace, the supernatural forgiving love and transforming power of God, is released through the deliberate act of giving up the kingdom of self. Giving up is not a "work." It is a cessation of resistance. It is the losing wrestler surrendering to the winner. God repeatedly makes it clear that He resists the proud (those who are full of their own egoism) but gladly gives grace to the humble (Psalm 18:27, James 4:6-10, 1 Peter 5:5-6). The faucet that turns on the pipeline of saving grace is the voluntary choice of humility. This is the heart of repentance. The event of salvation then immediately becomes the process of humble obedience. And enabling grace keeps on flowing.

If the conflict over control has not yet been resolved in God's favor in the core of your heart, now would be a good time to settle it.

Here's a suggested prayer:

Heavenly Father, You are right about what is keeping us apart. I have been resisting You and avoiding You because I've been insisting on holding on to the control of my life. I realize that my obsession with having my own way has been the cause of the distance between us.

Thank You for providing the way back under Your leadership through Jesus and what He accomplished for me at the cross. I accept Your forgiveness and I now surrender to Your leadership and Your love. I want to be part of Your kingdom now and forever. Amen.

That is repentant faith. It is giving God permission to make your turf part of His dominion. It is welcoming His will. It is embracing His leadership and embarking on a life of followership.

That kind of prayer is the beginning of true worship. It's beautiful music to God's ears and a lovely fragrance to His nose. It contains the essence of what He has been waiting to hear from each person born on this planet.

When *His* kingdom comes—what a difference! When salvation embraces the kingdom a new government arrives. True, you will have to learn to live *under new management* in all areas. You are no longer an entrepreneurial independent. You have joined the corporate kingdom of the most high God. The ultimate issue of *who* is in control is the focus of all your choices from now on, day by day, for the rest of your life. He is your Leader. You are His follower.

But there is mystery about the kingdom as well. We have eyes to see the kingdom vision and ears to hear the kingdom song, but all too often, our eyes don't see and our ears don't hear. Let's see how Jesus explains our problem.

NOTE
1. A. W. Tozer, *The Knowledge of the Holy* (San Francisco: HarperCollins, 1978), from the preface.

→ SEVENTEEN ←
The Mystery of the Kingdom

If the kingdom of God is such a big deal, why doesn't everyone want to get in on it? If it's the ultimate treasure, the perfect pearl of great price, the highest reward a person can seek, why do so few see and comprehend its value?

The whole world is pursuing alternatives to the kingdom of God: money, pleasure, power, prestige, possessions. It has been well said, "What you sacrifice for, you sacrifice to. What tops your value system wears the crown of your heart." "Where your treasure is, there your heart will be also" (see Matthew 6:21).

The effect of resisting the kingdom of God is that God's rule is obscured. The eye stops seeing it, the ear stops hearing it, and the heart stops treasuring it. When we fix our eyes and our hearts on other things, we act as if the King and His kingdom are irrelevant.

CUTTING THROUGH THE FOG OF SELF-DECEPTION

"So, okay, run that past me again. I'm not sure I see what's so important about this kingdom thing. Let me see if I'm making sense of it." Jerry was talking. He'd been meeting with me for early morning breakfasts for a month.

"You know I believe in God and the Bible," he continued. "I told you I gave my heart to Jesus as a twelve-year-old at summer camp. So, I'm a Christian, right? I know I've messed up my life—the booze, the two divorces, the gambling debts, and all that. But, I've always been a Christian in my heart." His eyes were pleading for me to affirm his fantasy.

"I've been listening to your story for a month, Jerry. You've been down a pretty rough road. Frankly, I'm surprised that you seem so convinced that you're a Christian. From what you've been telling me, it doesn't look like Christ has figured in your decision-making process at all. Is that a fair assessment?"

> *The effect of resisting the kingdom of God is that God's rule is obscured. The eye stops seeing it, the ear stops hearing it, and the heart stops treasuring it.*

"No!" He was showing signs of angry desperation. "I've always wanted to go to heaven. I love Jesus." He teared up.

"Jerry, I don't doubt that you love Jesus, and your ex-wives, and your kids whom you can't see because of restraining orders — but your back trail reveals that you love yourself a whole lot more than any of them."

I braced for an explosion, knowing that I was waving the needle of truth close to his balloons of cherished self-deception. Instead, his eyes took on a haunted look and he nodded. "Well, Preacher, you sound just like my exes — and my current live-in too, for that matter. Maybe you're on to something there."

Encouraged by his partial recognition of his personal priorities, I asked, "Where is the evidence that you love Jesus or have ever loved Jesus?"

He flared immediately. "Wait a minute! How can you play God and tell me what's in my heart? I know what I feel, and that's what matters to me." Red-faced and furious, he rose to leave.

"Sit down, Jerry. I'm the only friend you've got. You told me so when we got here this morning. Why don't you just relax and think about the question I asked. You're just reacting again, and you know you can't afford to burn any more bridges."

He stood there clenching and unclenching his fists, glaring down at me. Then an indifferent look came over his face and he dropped back into the booth. His eyes refused to meet mine — he was clearly tuned out.

With nothing left to lose, I told him the truth. Gently and with compassion I recounted to him the long, nightmarish list of disastrous, self-indulgent choices he had made. "Where in all of this tangled mess is there any sign that God, the Bible, or Jesus meant anything at all to you? Sure, you may have had a sentimental soft spot in your emotions for Jesus. But it had to be on about the same level as what you felt for a favorite childhood teddy bear.

"Think about what you're saying. You insist that you believe in God and the Bible, but you act as if *you* are in the driver's seat of your life. God is a word that evokes a warm feeling. You get emotional when you hear 'Just as I Am' sung. But you have no allegiance to God. Jesus makes no difference in your decision-making process. He hasn't been allowed to change your behavior. You've missed the whole effect that believing in Him produces."

His body language was still stiff and indifferent, but I sensed that Jerry was listening intently. I plunged on. "My friend, God isn't interested in having you believe in Him in some technical or emotional way. He simply wants to be God. He wants to be your Leader. He designed you to function best under His direction. That's what the kingdom is all about. It's the catchall word for the Ruler of the universe taking charge and being in control of your life."

There was a long pause. Jerry was sitting with his head down, but now I heard a sniffle. He dabbed at his face with a napkin.

"What if you were to give Jesus complete control of your life? What if you totally surrendered to Him? What if you began to follow Him as your Leader? What do you sense would happen?"

He raised his head and stared at me with a faraway look in his eye and slowly recited a list that sounded almost memorized. "I suppose I'd have to make my child-support payments and I wouldn't be able to make the card game at the poker club tonight, and I'd have to dump the bottle I've got stashed in the car, and I'd have to move out of Carol's place today. How's that for openers?"

We sat in silence. Jerry was counting the cost of repentance. He had obviously been acutely aware of his "kingdom issues" all along. It was a breathless magic moment where time and eternity were being reconfigured. The Holy Spirit was giving gracious germination to the kingdom mustard seed of faith. The loving rule of God was being considered by a man long used to going his own way.

Softly he asked, "What do I say? What prayer will make it work this time?"

"Do you know the Lord's Prayer?" I asked.

"Yup." He nodded. "Well, I'm a little rusty."

"That's okay. Let's say it together. It's a kind of special way of saying 'I give up' to the Lord. Ready? 'Our Father, who art in heaven, hallowed be Thy name. Thy kingdom come, Thy will be done, on earth as it is in heaven . . .'"

After we finished we sat in silence for a minute or two. A big smile slid across his face. "Thanks," he said. "I think I'm finally catching on to that kingdom thing you've been talking about. Wanna help me move?"

For three years now Jerry has followed through on his surrender to the Lord Jesus. He is a radically changed man with a growing reputation for integrity and generosity. Everything about his life is influenced by his ongoing process of following Jesus in the kingdom of God. His life is a miracle of transformation.

WHY ALL THE FUZZINESS?

I rejoice to see the kingdom coming in the lives of others. It's what I live for. And my greatest joy is to see it coming in my own life, challenging as it is. But what has long puzzled me is why it is so difficult for us to see the kingdom reign of God. It is clearly desirable, sane, and healthy. Yet, the fuzziness and strange interference in my own heart and the hearts of those with whom I work have both alarmed and astonished me. How can something like God's obvious right to rule our lives as His creatures be so hard a life principle to hang on to? Why does it slip away so fast? Why do we waste so much creative energy trying to work out new ways of getting around it? Especially when taking back formerly surrendered territory is so predictably disastrous.

The answer to those questions was given by Jesus in Matthew 13, in the passage we know as the parable of the sower. You know the story. A farmer sowed seed in four different areas, with varied results. The birds ate the seed that fell on the path; the seed landing in rocky terrain sprouted quickly but died for lack of soil; the seed falling among thorns was choked off shortly after germination. Only the seed that fell on good soil bore a bountiful harvest.

The disciples had heard many parables by the time Jesus told this one. They were finally to the point where they decided to come to Him with the obvious question: "Why? Why the tricky little stories with the double meanings? Why keep people guessing about what You really mean? Why do You speak to the people in these parables? You could get a whole lot more accomplished by making things clear."

Jesus replied,

> "*The knowledge of the secrets of the kingdom of heaven* has been given to you, but not to them. Whoever has will be given more, and he will have an abundance. Whoever does not have, even what he has will be taken from him. This is why I speak to them in parables:
>
> > "Though seeing, they do not see;
> > though hearing, they do not hear or understand.
>
> In them is fulfilled the prophecy of Isaiah:
>
> > "'You will be ever hearing but never understanding;
> > you will be ever seeing but never perceiving.
> > For this people's heart has become calloused;
> > they hardly hear with their ears,
> > and they have closed their eyes.
> > Otherwise they might see with their eyes,
> > hear with their ears,
> > understand with their hearts
> > and turn, and I would heal them.'
>
> But blessed are your eyes because they see, and your ears because they hear. For I tell you the truth, many prophets and righteous men longed to see what you see but did not see it, and to hear what you hear but did not hear it." (Matthew 13:11-17, emphasis added)

Jesus was saying, "You see, My followers, this is all about the secrets of the kingdom of heaven. Those precious secrets have been given to you but not to them. You have something they don't. As a result, when you gain knowledge and understanding of My kingdom, you keep on acquiring more ownership of the kingdom. They, on the other hand, aren't yet receptive to the kingdom. So, kingdom talk doesn't register with them. The longer they stubbornly stay out of the kingdom, the less they are capable of even beginning to comprehend it."

A POSSIBLE SCENARIO

I had some fun with this next portion. I created an imaginary conversation between Jesus and His disciples that is faithful to the content of the recorded exchange. My impression is that the actual text is a shorthand version of extensive dialogue. Jesus was explaining where the fog in our thinking about His kingdom comes from. He went back to the message of the Old Testament prophets for His explanation. It may have gone something like this:

Jesus scanned their puzzled expressions. "I see you're having trouble tracking with Me. It will help you catch on if I take you to some of the best-known Old Testament material. Remember Jeremiah 5:21 and Ezekiel 12:2? They both say approximately the same thing that is found in the classic passage I just quoted from Isaiah 6:9-10. Now, think. Think hard. Why are their eyes and ears not working properly?"

Jesus paused, then continued. "Do you remember what led up to each of those prophetic descriptions of hardheartedness? A certain type of behavior sets up this blockage. How did the prophets scope it out? Let's start with Jeremiah. What did he say was wrong with our nation? Let's have a discussion of this. Everybody participate. I know you learned this in your early synagogue school training."

Peter jumped right in. "Do you mean Jeremiah 2, Lord, where the prophet accuses Israel of exchanging God's glory for worthless idols, where he castigates his people for forsaking God, the spring of living water, and digging their own cisterns?"

"Excellent." Jesus was pleased. "You're right on target. Any more assessment passages come to mind?"

Andrew spoke next. "As I remember it, Jeremiah also told the people, in that same chapter, that their own wickedness will punish them, their own backsliding will rebuke them. So they should realize the consequences of forsaking the Lord."

"Jeremiah 2:27 has always stuck in my mind," said Matthew.

> "'They say to wood, "You are my father,"
>   and to stone, "You gave me birth."
> They have turned their backs to me

> and not their faces;
> yet when they are in trouble, they say,
> "Come and save us!'"

"Let's see, I'm stuck," Matthew said. "What comes next?" James finished it:

> "'"Why do you bring charges against me?
> You have *all rebelled against me*," declares the Lord.'"

Judas, not to be outdone, cited Jeremiah 5:3, which tells how, regardless of God's correction, the people made their faces harder than stone and *refused to repent*. "Now that explains why people don't get it!" he said.

UNDERSTANDING BLINDNESS AND DEAFNESS

"Good," Jesus said. "Each of those quotes helps explain why people don't catch on. But let's examine this subject further. How about Ezekiel? What does he think produces blindness and deafness to truth? Anyone remember the context of my reference to the prophet Ezekiel?"

"That's an easy one, Lord," said John. "The passage you refer to starts with Ezekiel saying the word of the Lord came to him, telling him he was living among a rebellious people. Then he's told to act out a dramatic parable by packing for exile right out in public so all the people can watch."

Andrew interjected, "God was using parables in the times of the prophets too, wasn't He? I mean, He had Ezekiel dig through the wall and stuff his suitcases through it, then crawl through himself and disappear into the dusk of evening. All the while he was to cover his eyes as if he couldn't bear to look at what he was leaving behind. Hey, that was good stuff. But . . . it didn't do any good, did it? They still didn't turn from their rebellious ways."

Jesus punched Andrew playfully on the arm. "Bravo, you go to the head of the class. I couldn't have put it better Myself, and I was there when it happened!"

The disciples got a chuckle out of the Master's humor.

Then Jesus said, "Now, with Jeremiah and Ezekiel fresh in our minds, let's think about Isaiah. What do you remember about the Scripture that precedes that quote I gave you from Isaiah 6? What was the provocation that prompted the blind-eyes and deaf-ears evaluation of the Father?"

"Oh," exclaimed Peter, "much the same kind of thing that we just cited from Jeremiah. Let me see if I can remember that famous vineyard passage from chapter 5. I ought to, it was one of my rabbi's favorites.

"The vineyard of the LORD Almighty
    is the house of Israel,
and the men of Judah
    are the garden of his delight.
And he looked for justice, but saw bloodshed;
    for righteousness, but heard cries of distress. [Isaiah 5:7]"

"Lord," James broke in, "it gets pretty strong.

"Woe to those who call evil good
    and good evil,
who put darkness for light
    and light for darkness,
who put bitter for sweet
    and sweet for bitter.

"Woe to those who are wise in their own eyes
    and clever in their own sight. . . . [Isaiah 5:20-21]"

"Okay, that's enough." Jesus cut him off. "Now, do you see what I'm getting at? I'm not being arbitrary or unfair with the crowds by speaking to them in parables. Rather, I'm employing a kind of sorting device. What people hear in a parable is determined by the kingdom sensitivity of their heart. If they're preoccupied with their own kingdom, the truth of the kingdom of God is deflected. It's like they have a mental shield up. Rebellion shrouds a person's ability to see the kingdom. Self-centered preoccupations are like ear plugs to the good news of the kingdom. The clearer I make the message, the deeper their guilt will be, but there will be no variation in the response."

Thomas put two and two together. "You meant it when You said the poor in spirit would inherit the kingdom of heaven, didn't You? I've thought about Your Sermon on the Mount a lot, but that sentence You started it off with really stuck with me. Would it be accurate to say that to the degree that a person is full of himself—his plans, his dreams, his pleasures, his ambitions, and his wealth—he is not open to or interested in the kingdom?"

Jesus smiled with approval. "You've nailed it, Thomas. That's excellent thinking. Those who empty themselves in the sense of their own need or desire to control their lives are entranced, mesmerized, and consumed with desire for the kingdom of God. When you're poor in spirit you have little competitive resistance to God's leadership. You delight to follow. Therefore the Spirit can quickly fill you with God's agenda. When God's will is embraced, His heart is engaged in the love relationship each of you was created to enjoy. He is the most important and valuable part of His kingdom. There's absolutely nothing like His love, take it from me. I know there's no treasure in heaven or on earth that's worthy of comparison with the generous love of our heavenly Father."

> *When you're poor in spirit you have little competitive resistance to God's leadership. You delight to follow.*

"Master, run through the meaning of the different responses to the message of the kingdom again, will You?" asked Matthew. He was still having trouble with the idea of each person filtering what he hears and sees.

Jesus recognized that Matthew was hung up on a technical point. "Matthew, this is the way the human mind works. There are always grids, filters, or sorting mechanisms in place to one degree or another. If you have no interest in something, you probably won't pick up on it when it surfaces inside your audiovisual reception range. Horse breeders are preoccupied with horses; fishermen are constantly immersed in catching fish. Right, Peter? Lumberjacks see trees very differently than the rest of us do. You get the point. Now let's go back to the parable that started this discussion."

THE CRITICAL FACTOR

Jesus continued. "Here's what it means. The human heart is like soil. The message of the kingdom is like seed. The sower is the Spirit of God.

"At its worst the heart can be closed and hardened to the point of zero penetration of kingdom truth. This is easy picking for the enemies of God. They swoop in with their philosophies and self-serving world-views to sweep away even the beginning of understanding. The people in this category are completely self-absorbed. Their own little worlds and their own little minds are all there is as far as they're concerned.

"The next type of heart soil is initially enthusiastic and receptive. At first glance the benefits of the kingdom are seen as desirable. But, when they begin to feel the demands of God's leadership and see the potential damage to their own self-centered, pleasure-seeking agenda, they begin to backtrack. When persecution and trouble get thrown at them by God's enemies, they quickly abandon all interest in the heavenly kingdom. They were in it for themselves, and they get out of it because they think they'll be better off.

"The third type comes from those who have a lot to lose. They're consumed with the need to care for and protect their wealth. The kingdom of God is choked out by the demands and concerns of their own personal pursuits and preferences. In the competition for attention, God's interests and plans lose out in favor of their own. The weeds of self-interest grow faster and stronger than the wheat of kingdom commitment.

"The fourth heart is called the good soil. Here the kingdom bears fruit. Yet, even here there are varying degrees of cooperation with God's kingdom. Once again the effects of mixed loyalties can be seen. Some permit the supervision of God to produce thirty, some sixty, and some one hundred times what was sown. The extent of cooperation and yield-edness to God's leadership determines the amount of productivity. Following consistently is the critical factor!

"Gentlemen," Jesus concluded, "you are incredible. I'm tremendously impressed with the fact that you've caught on. Your eyes are blessed because they see the kingdom, and your ears are blessed because they hear it. You've made the kingdom your first priority and therefore you are being given the keys to unlock its secrets, its treasures, and its privileges. Listen, guys, the 'greats' of the past figured out that something fantastic was coming. They saw it in shadowy images. They picked up enough impressions that it created longings in them to get in on it. But it wasn't time yet. You are the privileged ones. Consider yourselves among the most fortunate of men. You're getting in on the fabulous kingdom of God at the ground floor."

✠

Yes, I've taken some liberties with the text, but this fictional Bible study between Jesus and His disciples could easily have taken place. I think it's safe to assume that the Master loved the give-and-take of interaction, that He utilized the advantages of animated discussion to teach effectively. There are plenty of examples in the Gospels when He did just that. In spite of my elaboration, I've stayed true to the message and meaning of the parable and its interpretation by Jesus.

THE REASON FOR KINGDOM OBSCURITY

The point of the parable is hard hitting in its accuracy. Our response or lack of response to the seed of the kingdom of God is definitely determined by our willingness to let go of our own kingdom. The shrouding of the kingdom of heaven in our minds is produced by commitment to alternative kingdoms. It varies from person to person. Total commitment and surrender to the kingdom is rare but possible. The most common thing we see in evangelical churches is the choking out of the kingdom by the preoccupying pressure and stress of trying to have it all. A church that is producing even thirty times itself is exceedingly rare.

In fact, any believer producing kingdom fruit the way Jesus describes it in the good soil category would be regarded as a sold-out, radically committed, on-fire fanatic. Wilted followership and a choking drivenness are what appear to be normal among us.

As a result the kingdom is a mystery. The kingdom is dimly seen, kingdom truth is distorted and kingdom fruit is scarce. Imagine what full-blown consistent followership would do when it comes to reversing kingdom deafness and blindness. Followers of Jesus hear and see the clarion call and the glorious vista of the coming kingdom of God. And, according to Jesus, if you are among those with eyes to see the kingdom vision and ears to hear its song, more and more seeing and hearing will be given to you. This is renewal and revival. When individuals and churches get into the "good ground" of fresh surrender to their Leader, the fabulous productivity of the kingdom flourishes in the church and in the community.

⇢ EIGHTEEN ⇠
No Formula

I remember the day it dawned on me that Jesus never used the same approach with any two people. It was a shock. I had always assumed there was a standard formula to the gospel. I always heard it preached that way, and I always preached it that way. I had seen "four steps" pamphlets in the tract racks, on pay-phone shelves, and on the top of toilet tanks all my life. All the seminars and classes on witnessing taught a simplified, basic pattern. A one-size-fits-all approach to presenting the gospel seemed to be the accepted procedure.

John 3 and the conversation between Jesus and Nicodemus was the topic of my next sermon. As I got into the text, I began to cross-reference, looking for other passages that say the same thing or something similar. After searching through the four Gospels, I sat in my study with only the following sentence on paper: "Nicodemus was the only person who was instructed to be born again by Jesus. Why?" At the time I didn't know the answer.

I studied every recorded interaction that Jesus had with people. He seemed to have no single method or standardized approach. Each time His gospel presentation was unique. Each person was handled as a special case.

Eventually I realized there were no classic witnessing encounters intended to be "*the* pattern" in the recorded ministry of Jesus. There was no evidence of a formula. It was only to Nicodemus that Jesus said, "You must be born again." It was only to the rich young ruler that the

Master said, "Go, sell what you have, give to the poor, and come follow Me." It was only the woman at the well who was offered the Living Water that quenches the thirst of the soul.

By now I was confused. Which approach should be used with which type of person? Why had the Nicodemus encounter been selected as the standard formula by most of the evangelical world for working with serious seekers? Why not the woman at the well or the thief on the cross?

The more I studied, thought, and prayed, the more I became convinced that I was on to something important. The standardized, simplified Christian sales formulas I had assumed to be necessary now began to seem suspect. If Jesus had wanted His disciples to use a three-, four-, or five-step approach with every unbeliever, why hadn't He demonstrated such a methodology Himself?

By now some of you may be suspecting that I have slipped out of the mainstream of orthodox evangelicalism. How can anyone raise questions about so sacrosanct a matter as the tools we use for leading people to Christ? The issue, of course, is the obvious fact that Jesus didn't use them. Perhaps we should try to understand why not.

THE THEME

Was there any connection between the vastly different ways Jesus approached the hearts and minds of lost people? At first I didn't see any rhyme or reason to the different subjects Jesus addressed. Maybe Jesus could make up a different way of communicating the gospel for each person. After all, He was God in the flesh and could bring people to Himself any old way He felt like. Or could He? I was certainly understanding the compelling reasons why people like myself had attempted to come up with a clear, concise gospel presentation. It was just plain easier that way.

Finally, I began to notice the preoccupation Jesus had with the kingdom. By the time I had studied everything our Lord had to say about His kingdom and how to enter it, I was beginning to understand His lack of a sales formula. It became apparent that He wasn't trying to recruit or even "close a deal."

When I realized that He was announcing terms of surrender to each individual, it began to make sense. He was confronting the issue that was keeping each one of these people out of His kingdom. If you don't factor in Christ's preoccupation with the kingdom, His lack of a standardized approach is puzzling. But when His way of framing the issue as a God's-kingdom-versus-our-kingdom confrontation is understood, each distinctly individualized conversation begins to fall into a discernible pattern.

When we attempt to determine what the kingdom issue was in each case, the answer is revealing. Like every one of us, these people had developed their own kingdoms. There were things they felt compelled to retain control over. These control and ego issues are part of every human life. When the King offers to rule and reign in us, our preferred options are suddenly in the spotlight.

THE RICH AND POWERFUL

In the rich young ruler's case (Luke 18:18-30), the alternative kingdom issue is easy to identify. When this sincere, young seeker asked Jesus what he should do to inherit eternal life, Jesus *did not* say, "You don't have to do anything. Salvation isn't a matter of your good works. It's a gift. All the work is accomplished by Myself as your Savior."

He first checked out whether or not the seeker considered Him good in the sense that God is good. "Do you think I am God?" He asked. Second, He probed the man's compliance with revealed truth. "Do you take God's Word seriously? Have you obeyed the basic commandments?" The rich man seemed to pass these first two tests.

Jesus then went to the heart of this man's personal kingdom. "One thing you lack: go sell your possessions and give the proceeds to the poor, then come follow Me. And by the way, you will have treasure in My kingdom, heaven itself."

The man went away sad, because he had great wealth. Then Jesus commented to His disciples, "Isn't it so true that rich people find it hard to enter the kingdom of heaven? I tell you, it's easier for a camel to go through the eye of a needle than for a rich man to enter the kingdom of God."

Jesus zeroed in on the control issue in this man's life. He couldn't give God control of his life because he thought he had so much to lose. Central to the man's value system was a personal kingdom that had to be protected and preserved—not given up.

He was confronted with entrance into the kingdom of God. At issue was the surrender of everything that formed the walls of his own kingdom. It proved to be too much to ask. Even the disciples initially saw this exchange as unfair. "Who then can be saved?" they asked in great astonishment.

They were asking, "Lord, isn't the price too steep? Are You serious? Do You really expect people to give up the owner/operator role in their lives? If You keep holding this kind of standard up, nobody is going to be willing to respond! You're simply asking for too much."

Jesus cryptically replied, "With man this *is* impossible, but with God all things are possible."

The apostle Paul later decoded that statement. It was revealed to him by the Spirit that God not only gives us opportunities to access His kingdom, He also gives an ability to respond in the affirmative in spite of our kingdom issues (Ephesians 2:8-10). This is the grace of God making possible the "impossibility" of breaking down our walls of independence and self-sufficiency. Yet grace does not force the choice. It is activated by the humility of a willing heart (Matthew 18:3-4).

What did this man have to lose? His position. He was a prominent person in the community, a ruler. If he gave up his wealth, he would undoubtedly give up his power base as well. Power, influence, and wealth usually go hand in hand.

Wealth Has Many Forms

This brings me to a discovery I've made about wealth. It isn't only measured in money. For some people wealth is gauged in family position and connections. In most communities certain families have controlled the local politics for a long time. For instance, in the time of Christ the family of Annas controlled the priesthood. Caiaphas, the high priest at the time Jesus was crucified, was the son-in-law of Annas. Caiaphas could well be described as possessing a wealth of valuable connections through the family dynasty. It's really not surprising that when this powerful high priest was confronted with the one perfect sacrifice for sin, he rejected the very Lamb of God that all other sacrifices pointed toward. His religious and family "wealth" was threatened, and he found himself involved in a murder plot in order to protect his self-interest.

For others, wealth is measured in physical appearance. Some people are gifted with beautiful or handsome bodies and faces. Their attractive good looks become their kingdom power base. Doors are opened and people offer favor through this advantage.

For some it is unusual ability. Athletic, artistic, or musical abilities can all become the claim to fame and prominence that becomes a substitute for the kingdom of God. Perhaps the most powerful distraction from the kingdom of heaven in modern times is intellectual ability. Smart or brilliant people are strongly tempted to live independently of God. Having a high IQ and educational achievement can be a kingdom that fiercely opposes God's kingdom. Unusually capable people find it easy to build a do-it-yourself life that leaves little or no room for God.

The ordinary, working-class good ol' boy has a kingdom of friends and acquaintances. His buddies and the crowd he hangs out with at the bar or plays softball with are his riches. Belonging and fitting into their irreverent, self-made-man camaraderie seems necessary. They take care of him, keep him company, and without them he would feel lost and alone. When Jesus offers to lead him and love him, it feels like a threat to all he already holds dear.

I surmise that similar observations were behind the disciples' question, "Who then can be saved?" Giving up and losing what we consider essential to our personal happiness, security, power, and control is a fearful thing to all of us. In our old-nature condition it is unthinkable to risk control of our personal assets by someone else. The irrational fear of losing what we are convinced we must have is the motivation behind refusing God's kingdom supervision in our hearts.

"If I give my whole life to Jesus Christ, He might take away favorite things I like and ask me to do things I really don't want to do. If you'll permit me to add Jesus and a free ticket to heaven to my possessions, I'll be happy to sign up. But please don't ask me to give up my personal sovereignty. I don't want to run the risk of having God assign me to the mission field in Africa or some third-world slum!"

Jesus never lets up on rich-young-ruler types. He insists on undistracted followership. Becoming His disciple has always meant the surrender of every form of wealth to His control.

NICODEMUS

The story of Nicodemus is perhaps the most used story to "lead people to Christ." But do we even understand what it means? What was the kingdom issue for this renowned authority and highly placed teacher in Israel? Isn't it a tipoff that he chose to visit Jesus at night? He was very aware of his peers among the Pharisees and what was "politically correct" among the ruling council, called the Sanhedrin. What they and the rest of the people thought of him was something he had to factor in constantly. He was a man of prominence and reputation. He had arrived at the pinnacle of power and prestige in his Jewish world. How does Jesus present the kingdom gospel to this sophisticated, highly educated leader?

John 3:1-16 is a kingdom discussion. Nicodemus confessed that he already believed that Jesus was a teacher who had come from God. Jesus knew He had a man before him who was seeking to understand His message. He began by going right to the heart of the matter: "No one can see the kingdom of God unless he is born again" (verse 3). This statement is similar to those Jesus made whenever He saw children in proximity to human pretentiousness. Whenever he saw adults taking themselves too seriously, he used children as an object lesson in humility to set them straight (Matthew 18:1-4, Luke 18:17).

Jesus was letting Nicodemus know that all the credentials he had accumulated over a long life would not help him enter the kingdom. All of his carefully constructed accomplishments and his reputation were effectively shutting out the King of kings. The ladder he had climbed was leaning against the wrong wall. He must be willing to start from scratch, like a newborn, and receive a spiritual rebirth that didn't depend on his own efforts or achievements. This new birth required the same kind of faith that dying people placed in the bronze snake set on a pole in the wilderness (Numbers 21:6-9). Only this time the object of faith was the Son of God. The pole was to be the cross of Calvary.

Jesus was clearly saying to Nicodemus, "You need Me. I am essential to your entrance into the kingdom. In order for you to be willing to put the weight of your deepest trust down on Me, you must be willing to abandon your 'power base' and 'claim to fame.' The new start will be accomplished in you by the power of the Holy Spirit."

The illustration of being born again was Christ's way of getting at the kingdom issue of Nicodemus's impressive achievements. Why didn't Jesus use this same "born-again" language with others? I think the answer is obvious. Jesus was asking for Nicodemus's wealth in exactly the same fashion that He asked for the material possessions of the rich young ruler, only in different words. Both men were confronted with the implications of their own castles and asked to abandon them.

The new birth language is used again in the Epistles. Paul (Titus

3:5), James (James 1:18), and Peter (1 Peter 1:3,23) all refer to the life-producing work of the Spirit and the word as a birth event. But there is no indication given that it would or should replace the kingdom language of Jesus.

THE WOMAN AT THE WELL

Here is an entirely different approach. It all starts with a request for a drink of water.

> When a Samaritan woman came to draw water, Jesus said to her, "Will you give me a drink?" . . .
> The Samaritan woman said to him, "You are a Jew and I am a Samaritan woman. How can you ask me for a drink?" (For Jews do not associate with Samaritans.)
> Jesus answered her, "If you knew the gift of God and who it is that asks you for a drink, you would have asked him and he would have given you living water." (John 4:7,9-10)

Although the Samaritan woman didn't know it, Jesus was closing in on what she thought she had to have in order to satisfy her inner thirst. She had consistently been turning to men to find fulfillment.

When Jesus asked her to call her husband, He put the kingdom issue on the table. She had no husband at the time, but she had five previous husbands and was then living with a man. She had already drawn from at least six masculine wells trying to find satisfaction. Now a seventh man was mysteriously offering her living water that would permanently quench her heart's thirsty longing for satisfaction, security, and love.

She was embarrassed and tried to throw Jesus off her trail by bringing up an old controversy between the Jews and the Samaritans regarding divinely sanctioned places of worship, but Jesus didn't bite. God was interested in the heart, not the geographic location.

Then she tried again by bringing up the Messiah. "When he comes," she said, "he will explain everything [about worship] to us" (John 4:25). Imagine her shock when Jesus looked her in the eye and said, "I who speak to you am he" (verse 26)!

The rich young ruler had his alternative kingdom of wealth. Nicodemus had his kingdom of influence, prominence, and power. This

Samaritan woman had her kingdom of masculine strength to lean on. All were asked to let go of their own self-made kingdoms in different words and in different ways, but the central concern of the Master was the same.

He was asking, "What do you think you must have more than My kingdom? Whatever keeps you preoccupied and distracted keeps you from entering the kingdom of heaven. Give it up. Surrender to My leadership, and I will take responsibility for all the things you need. Seek My kingdom first, and all these other things will be added unto you." *This is the connecting theme of the gospel message.*

Leading people to Christ will take as many approaches as there are people.

To use a "sell all and follow me" approach, a "you must be born again" approach, or a "take a drink of living water" approach exclusively as a one-size-fits-all formula misses God's objective of setting up His kingdom in our hearts. Leading people to Christ will take as many approaches as there are people. Certainly there will be similarity among our gospel presentations. The kingdom itself will appear as our standard reference point, but each individual's anti-kingdom bias will take different forms and must be dealt with differently.

THIS RINGS TRUE

This interpretation of the variety of approaches Jesus used to get at the barrier issue in each individual life is true to reality. In my personal witness I constantly run into the same kind of kingdom confrontations in the hearts and lives of individuals.

Mack is a plant manager for one of the largest companies in the paper products industry. He has risen rapidly through the ranks and now enjoys a national reputation as a successful leader. He visited the church where I was pastoring one Sunday morning and, after hearing the message, asked if he could meet with me during the week.

A few minutes into that meeting I found out that he had recently begun an affair and had moved out of his home and into an apartment with his mistress. He insisted that he still loved his wife and children and did not intend to leave them permanently.

His question was this: "Pastor, I've arrived at the top of the heap, but my heart is still restless and unsatisfied. I know I need to become religious and develop my spiritual life, but where do I start?"

I took him through a discussion of sin and salvation that clarified why he was distant from God and what it would take to access the kingdom. I shared the incredible forgiveness and pardon provided through the self-sacrifice of Christ at the cross.

He understood that the way back to God's kingdom had been provided. He also understood the implications of repentance and surrender to Christ's leadership. When I finally asked him if he was ready to come into the kingdom and begin following Jesus, he immediately shook his head no.

"Everything you've said makes sense. It answered my questions, and I have the strong impression that it's all true. I want to become a Christian and I will as soon as I get some things sorted out."

"Like what?" I asked.

"Like my mistress. Right now I can't imagine living life without her. I am so totally alive and happy when I'm with her, I can't give her up just yet."

This successful but thirsty man was a combination of the rich young ruler and the woman at the well. He controlled a material kingdom and a sexual kingdom that kept him from entering God's kingdom.

THE DYING THIEF

"All this kingdom way of looking at the gospel makes some sense, Pastor. But what about the thief on the cross? Didn't he just exercise faith?"

That question has been put to me several times through the years. Behind it is the mistaken conviction that a stripped-down, minimal version of the gospel is available. The assumption is made that the dying thief didn't have to repent but "only believe." I always answer it the same way. I go to the Scripture.

One of the criminals who hung there hurled insults at him: "Aren't you the Christ? Save yourself and us!"

But the other criminal rebuked him. "Don't you fear God," he said, "since you are under the same sentence? We are punished justly, for we are getting what our deeds deserve. But this man has done nothing wrong."

Then he said, "Jesus, remember me when you come into your kingdom."

Jesus answered him, "I tell you the truth, today you will be with me in paradise." (Luke 23:39-43)

Death row is not such a strange place to find a God-fearer. This man knew he was guilty and deserved his punishment. He also had heard enough about the deeds and words of the Master to conclude that He was who He claimed to be, the Son of God and promised Messiah, and certainly not deserving of execution.

He was humble and totally dependent on mercy from Jesus. "Remember me when You come into Your kingdom," he said. He was abandoning his tough-guy image, his pride, his anger, and his bitterness, and was putting all his hopes on the one he recognized as the Lord of glory. He was asking for inclusion in Christ's kingdom!

And Jesus accepted his repentant faith. A transaction took place there on the cross. You know there was a smile on Jesus' battered face when He said, "Today, you will be with Me in paradise!"

Death-bed conversions can be genuine. They can also be an intentional manipulation of God's grace. To deliberately hold out on God and live your life for yourself and then try to get your ticket to heaven punched at the last possible moment is a complete misunderstanding of what God is after. He is not interested in clever operators who play games with His grace. The thief on the cross disregarded his own kingdom and embraced the kingdom of Jesus, just as everyone else is asked to do.

God is seeking people who follow Him, fear Him, worship Him, obey Him, and love Him. Such people are safe citizens. They can be trusted to protect the new community of faith from the deadly subversion of unresolved rebellion. He is after nothing less. There are no "cheap seats" for those unwilling to follow Jesus.

AN ADEQUATE RESPONSE

This chapter begs that the obvious question be asked: Have you heard and responded to the good news that entrance into God's kingdom is available to you through repentance and faith? If you must admit that you've never really faced the kingdom "issues" in your life but still consider yourself a Christian, this would be a good time to revisit salvation. It's likely that you've continued to build a kingdom of your own that competes constantly with Christ's. In such a life Christianity becomes a veneer, a facade behind which our ancient nemesis of self-in-control still thrives.

Why would God make an exception of you? Why would He let you into His family without dealing with what makes you untrustworthy? It is obvious that God intends to let you keep the precious gift of freedom of choice. He clearly doesn't want to make robots out of us. The question is: Can God trust you with freedom of choice? Has your "right to yourself" felt the ax? That's what salvation is designed to accomplish.

True repentance and faith ego-proof us. Our independent self-rule is broken at the cross. We are now happily living in an eternal kingdom where *one safe will* reigns and harmony is normal.

> *Have you heard and responded to the good news that entrance into God's kingdom is available to you through repentance and faith?*

The saving work of Jesus doesn't just keep you and me out of hell. It keeps our hell-producing self-centeredness out of the church and out of heaven. So, don't look for a bargain-basement entry pass. It doesn't exist. Anything less than a kingdom encounter at the point of salvation merely sets up a pseudoform of religiosity. A Christianity that fails to make you an obedient follower of Jesus is not the real thing. But it can inoculate you against catching true "kingdom fever."

If you are still getting stuck on what may seem to be a departure from a "faith alone" gospel, read on. The next chapter is an examination of the *kind of faith* Jesus was after. I think it will remove any remaining reservations that you may have about the response God is expecting from each of us.

→ N I N E T E E N ←
The Best Example of Faith

The highest praise from the lips of Jesus for a Jew went to John the Baptist. "I tell you the truth: Among those born of women there has not risen anyone greater than John the Baptist" (Matthew 11:11).

The greatest honor Jesus paid to a Gentile went to a Roman centurion. The story is told in Matthew 8:5-13 and Luke 7:1-10. A centurion was a career officer in charge of 100 soldiers. As a Roman soldier in Israel, normally he would have been treated with hostility as a foreign invader. Surprisingly, this man had won the respect and friendship of the community of Capernaum where he was stationed. Read the words of great honor he received from the Master.

> The centurion replied, "Lord, I do not deserve to have you come under my roof. But just say the word, and my servant will be healed." . . . When Jesus heard this, he was astonished and said to those following him, "I tell you the truth, I have not found anyone in Israel with *such great faith*." (Matthew 8:8,10, emphasis added)

Luke's version of the story is equally inspired but significantly different. He clarifies that the centurion did not speak to Jesus in person but rather through intermediaries. What at first appears to be a discrepancy between the two writers is quickly explained by some historical research.

In those days, if you sent an emissary on your behalf, it was considered the same as delivering the message yourself. That is particularly true in this setting where the foreigner is treating Jesus as if He were royalty. He approached Jesus through intermediaries in the way you would approach a king—going up the line of authority. Matthew observes that the centurion spoke to Jesus. Luke clarifies exactly how he did it. He did speak to Jesus, but he spoke through others.

Now, let's take a closer look at the centurion. What did he do that caused such a strong response from Jesus? Why did Jesus declare, "This man has greater faith than anyone else living in the land of Israel"?

APPEALING TO AUTHORITY

The centurion came with his need just as so many others had. Whether with leprosy, blindness, palsy, demon possession, or an empty but sophisticated heart like Nicodemus in John 3, they all carried their own expectations and agendas to Jesus. But the centurion came on behalf of another. Clearly he loved and highly valued a servant in his household. He was a man who cared about the people he led.

But did you notice how he approached Jesus? He appealed to Him as if He were the King of kings and the Lord of lords. Respect and honor are clearly visible as the encounter progresses.

Jesus responded favorably. Apparently someone must have run ahead with the news that the Master was coming, because the centurion was so overwhelmed by the thought of heaven's commander in chief coming to his home that he sent friends out to meet Jesus. They were instructed to say, "Our friend does not consider himself worthy to have You go out of Your way for him. He says he doesn't deserve to have You come under his roof. Don't trouble Yourself further. Our friend, the centurion, recognizes Your authority. He himself is a man under authority and an authority to the soldiers under him. He tells this one, 'Go,' and he goes; and that one, 'Come,' and he comes. He says to his servant, 'Do this,' and he does it. So, You see, he understands that You don't need to go out of Your way. Just say the word because clearly You have the authority to handle this matter."

Jesus stopped in His tracks, stunned. "This is incredible! This man gets it. Here's a man who understands who I am and how to respond to Me appropriately."

Now, would you call what the centurion did and said *faith?* It doesn't sound like faith, does it? Yet obviously, it was exactly the kind of full-bodied faith for which Jesus was looking. He said, "I have not seen such great faith in all of Israel!"

This Gentile God-seeker understood the issue. He lived in a world of designated authority. As a Roman soldier the world revolved around who was in charge. His commanding officer reported to the generals in Rome, and they reported to the emperor, Caesar. In Jesus, he recognized ultimate authority. He sensed that if Jesus was who He claimed to be, He would have the power of life and death. He would be able to *say the word* and anyone anywhere could be healed. *Faith!*

Jesus' enthusiastic approval of the centurion's respect and submission tells us something extremely vital. Jesus held this Roman soldier up before His disciples and the crowd following Him and said, "This is what I'm after. This is the appropriate way for humans to treat Me. This is what I'm looking for in every human heart. This is great faith!"

Jesus is after followership. He is not merely interested in saving our souls, meeting our needs, and healing our hurts. Oh, He does that too, but His first concern is that we become kingdom players. He intends that we operate under His authority for the rest of our lives and for all eternity.

NO EXCEPTIONS!

What I observe in Jesus astonishes me even more than these observations about the centurion. I find it both thrilling and baffling. *Jesus Himself was a man under authority!* Consider the incredible humility that He exhibited toward His leader, the heavenly Father. This further clarifies the attitude behind His baptism of repentance mentioned in chapter 13. The following scriptures, all words of Jesus, further affirm His humility toward His Father.

> "My food . . . is to do the will of him who sent me and to finish his work." (John 4:34)

> "By myself I can do nothing; I judge only as I hear, and my judgment is just, for I seek not to please myself but him who sent me." (John 5:30)

> "I have come down from heaven not to do my will but to do the will of him who sent me." (John 6:38)

"My teaching is not my own. It comes from him who sent me. If anyone chooses to do God's will, he will find out whether my teaching comes from God or whether I speak on my own." (John 7:16)

"I am not here on my own, but he who sent me is true. . . . I am from him and he sent me." (John 7:28-29)

"I do nothing on my own but speak just what the Father has taught me. . . . He has not left me alone, for I always do what pleases him." (John 8:28-29)

"For I did not speak of my own accord, but the Father who sent me commanded me what to say and how to say it. I know that his command leads to eternal life. So whatever I say is just what the Father has told me to say." (John 12:49-50)

This is only a portion of Jesus' statements clearly avowing His submission to the Father. As God-man, He was operating under a deliberate obedience. What that means is that God Himself functions in an authority framework. Within the Trinity, the Father, Son, and Holy Spirit practice voluntary humility, submission, and obedience (John 3:35, 16:13-15).

The implications are enormous. First of all, God has subjected Himself to the same principles of humility and submission that He asks of His creatures. This assures me that He insists on leading me because He loves me, not because He can't handle my being in control.

God is a credible, worthy, respectable Supreme Leader because He practices the same qualities, standards, character traits, and values He expects of His creation. Jesus, God in human flesh, was showing us by example how to walk by obedient faith. God was obeying God. Divinity was subjected to divinity. A willingly compliant Jesus voluntarily followed His leader. Therefore, He was not operating in super-egoism when He turned to His disciples and said, "Follow Me." He was leading by following and following by leading.

SETTING UP THE MODEL

This has wonderful implications for all areas of life. Those of you who are parents will see a superb model for your strategically important role here.

Children must learn to be followers before they can be trusted with leadership. If their leaders are autocratic, egocentric, self-asserting, and domineering, they will learn to emulate self-centeredness. If, on the other hand, their parents are humble, servant-hearted, and obedient to their leader, Jesus Christ, the children have the best chance to learn the supreme value of an ego-proofing submission to God.

God is a credible, worthy, respectable Supreme Leader because He practices the same qualities, standards, character traits, and values He expects of His creation.

The apostle Paul self-consciously said it like this: "Follow my example, as I follow the example of Christ" (1 Corinthians 11:1). Worthy leadership flows out of faithful followership. A godly wife will gladly follow a husband whom she knows is following his Lord and Master. Children will embrace the authority of parents who live under the authority of heaven as a way of life. When adults live as if there really is a God in the driver's seat of the universe and of their home, it is tremendously reassuring and instructive to the children.

The same principle is operative in churches. Congregations emulate their pastors. A spiritual leader who constantly waves his authority and position in the faces of his people is creating the very threat he is attempting to ward off. Motivated by his own insecurities, he doesn't realize that his flock will develop what they see in him. When a leader demands submission but is not humbly submitting himself, he creates non-followers after his own kind. They too will become manipulators and power brokers.

If leaders say there is a God yet act like they are in control of their lives, they cancel out the perception of a legitimate authority structure in the universe. God is then perceived as a fabrication of leaders who are using the God-idea as a way of manipulating those they want to keep in line. It isn't surprising that Karl Marx saw religion, particularly the Judeo-Christian teachings, as a device used by the establishment to keep ordinary people in subjection. He was a casualty of adults who lived as if they were in control. He saw hypocrisy and power mongering and assumed all religious authorities were operating the same way.

To follow Jesus is to become like Him. To be conformed to His likeness is to develop into the same kind of follower/leader He is. A person under authority is a person of great faith. The Bible affirms that such faith pleases God and attracts His reward.

THE "FIX" IN CRUCIFIXION

Are you a man or woman under authority? I'm not asking if you believe in Jesus or have received His gift of salvation. Genuine faith restores God to His place as your supreme authority. If you've attempted to get in on the salvation of Christ without resolving the kingdom issue of who governs your life, you've misunderstood saving faith. The purpose of the cross was to provide for our entrance into the kingdom of God, not just onto its doorstep. It was the method God chose to restore non-followers to active follower status.

The Lord of all has no intention of perpetuating the rebellion that cost Him the death of His Son. If you've truly experienced salvation, you've been transformed from a hostile competitor to a team player. This is the "fix" in the Crucifixion. The life and death of Christ is intended by God to resolve the authority problem with which each of us was born. If this is not true for you and if you are still running your own life, please don't quibble over some theoretical possibility of a non-follower's salvation. In the kingdom of God every citizen, child of God, and servant of God is a "person under authority" in process. If you're not under authority, don't hesitate. Bow before the Maker of heaven and earth.

Welcome His leadership and love as He turns your life into part of His kingdom.

TAKING ANOTHER STEP—
QUESTIONS FOR MEDITATION

1. Do you remember the moment you surrendered your sword and let Jesus take control of your life?

2. *Repentance* means giving up your kingdom and switching sides. It's the turnaround and the change of mind that allows God's Spirit to take control and rule in our hearts. Have you understood the kingdom dimension of repentance? Have you repented?

3. Where has the Holy Spirit been asking you for fresh repentance?
   - Control of time?
   - Control of money?
   - Control of entertainment or pleasure?
   - Control of sex?
   - Control of possessions?
   - Control of your tongue?
   - Control of moods or attitudes?

4. Which of the six slices of gospel truth have you personally preferred? How was the issue framed when you first heard the good news?

5. What "wealth" may be distracting you from following Jesus?

6. The prayer on page 122 is an example of a beginning place for surrender to Christ. Add your own words of invitation for Christ to come into your life and become your leader.

7. Think about the circumstances of your life—the good ones and the tough ones. If Jesus was your manager in the good circumstances, what would it look like? In the difficult circumstances?

8. In the parable of the sower, with what type of "ground" do you most closely identify?

9. What's the "big dream" in your heart? Do you feel you have to protect it from God's ownership and supervision? If so, what does that tell you about your dream?

10. The "great faith" of the centurion is an adequate response to Christ's kingdom message. Are you under Jesus' authority? Do you go when He says, "Go," and come when He says, "Come"?

PART FOUR

THE SAFE FOLLOWER
AND SANCTIFICATION

→ TWENTY ←
The Process Begins

Wes took the first steps of repentance at our church's Christmas Dessert Theatre outreach, an annual event where our entire congregation mobilizes to share the good news with our friends. Both he and his wife, Cyndi, were apprehensive about what to expect at a Baptist church function. They had this image of us as strict, straight-laced people who—for some sick reason—enjoyed being yelled at by red-faced, hellfire preachers. What they experienced, however, was so unlike what they had expected that they were not just pleasantly surprised—they were blown away!

The drama and music were intentionally designed to meet them where they were. They knew about the religious roots of Christmas, but Christmas had never made much sense to them. By the end of the evening they had been treated with great dignity and courtesy and were thinking seriously about the meaning of Christ's birth. Wes decided to sign up for a "just looking" class we call Discovery.

Efforts were made to meet him at entry level—or as Wes put it later, "The cookies were on the bottom shelf where even a nonreligious type like myself could reach them!"—and four months later he realized he believed it. He believed there was a Creator God, that the Bible was His message to humankind, that God had come to earth in a human body in the person of Jesus Christ, and that when Jesus submitted to crucifixion He created the only available entrance to God's kingdom.

But his inner resistance surprised him. Wes had assumed becoming a Christian was an intellectual matter. It was a big breakthrough for him when he admitted to himself that he was reluctant to repent. He liked being in control. He stalled, dropped out of the class for a few weeks, but could not shake off the conviction that surrender to Christ was the right thing to do. One April morning, on his way to work, he began to talk to God out loud right there in his car.

He said, "Lord, this is Wes and I'm ready to let You be my God. Please forgive me for ignoring You and avoiding You for so long. You've been more than patient with me. I'm coming to You because I understand Your Son made it possible for me to come back. I know He died in my place and took on Himself the consequences of my stubborn obsession with wanting my own way. You can have what's left of my life. Just take over and lead me, okay?"

That day marked an eternal transaction for Wes. He became a man under kingdom authority. And immediately his life began to change. Cyndi had been watching him like a hawk throughout this whole process. She thought he might just be going through a phase. But then he changed. He was humble and gentle, when before he had always tended to be arrogant and sure of himself. He treated her with a kindness that she liked but was sure wouldn't last. The most obvious initial change was that he stopped swearing. He still got angry, but he handled it as if God were present in the room. The graphic expletives faded into the dim past.

Cyndi started accompanying Wes to Discovery class and, within a month, she also decided to follow Jesus as her Lord and Master. Both of them had now repented and entered the kingdom of God. A process of surrender to the control of God's Spirit had begun.

THE GROWTH OF THE KINGDOM

Wes and Cyndi have been remarkably obedient Christians right from the start. Their commitment to Jesus Christ has reflected the fact that they counted the cost and yielded to His leadership. But they've both struggled with the ongoing process of daily following through. Every true believer knows the frustration of finding out that the old self-in-control nature is alive and well. It soon became obvious to Wes that repentance was a way of life. He found himself making many choices on a daily basis to follow Christ and live in obedience to His Word.

Now, three years later, he knows that this is the normal Christian life. All other believers are involved in the same process. His small group and accountability partners have been a source of great encouragement. Cyndi has struggled with the same control issues, and together they've prayed for and supported each other. Gradually the kingdom reign of their Sovereign Lord and Savior has been growing stronger in their lives.

THE USUAL MISCONCEPTION
It is common for new Christians to assume that repentance from the old kingdom of self-in-control into the kingdom of God is a one-time deal. It just seems like the old life should be completely gone and the new life fully in place. Adding to their confusion is the fact that some preachers teach it that way.

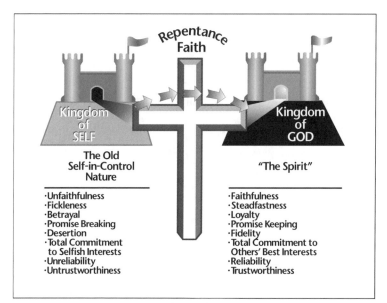

Diagram 20.1

This diagram reflects a black-and-white, all-or-nothing, one-side-or-the-other model of the Christian life. It looks good in theory and accurately depicts the stark contrast between the two kingdoms, but it isn't true to life experience.

The fact is, the ego doesn't die when Christ is invited in to set up His kingdom. The old self-reliant, self-centered sin nature attempts to regain the territory it lost to the Spirit of Christ. This sets up the need for a lifelong process of ongoing repentance. Each believer must learn how to cooperate with the indwelling Holy Spirit. His main concern is our growth in availability and obedience to our King. He never lets up on that objective.

THE SPIRIT'S JOB

Surrendered believers may intend to give every part of their lives over to kingdom control, but very quickly the conflict described in Galatians 5:16-17 becomes an ongoing reality.

> So I say, live by the Spirit, and you will not gratify the desires of the sinful nature. For the sinful nature desires what is contrary to the Spirit, and the Spirit what is contrary to the sinful nature. They are in conflict with each other, so that you do not do what you want.

Diagram 20.2 (page 179) depicts the fact that human beings compartmentalize their lives. We might call these categories "comfort zones," "fortified treasure chambers," or just identifiable sections that we tend to manage as separate entities. For instance, we can easily separate our church life from our home life or work life. When we leave one area and move into another, we're quite capable of closing the door to the compartment we've just been in. We can act as though the first area was God's territory, but now that we're in this other compartment, we're in control and can do as we please. The Holy Spirit's assignment is to force the issue of control in each and every segment of our lives.

One of the common inconsistencies of Christian teenagers can be explained by this diagram. Ben is a young person who sincerely loves the Lord. When he's with his family and around the church youth group, he finds it easy to live for Christ. Then Monday comes and he is back in the public school environment, where peer pressure and the politically correct social agenda are at odds with his faith. The way he copes with this is by segregating his worlds. When he's at church he acts like a Christian. But when he's in the secular compartment of his life — in the football locker room, at a school dance, or at a postgame party — he blends in so well that nobody would guess he is a Christian.

This same uncanny ability to separate our lives into sections plagues Christian adults as well. Wendy works for a computer software firm that is pushing hard to be number one in its field. Management expects the employees to make work their life. It is not uncommon for Wendy to work fourteen hours a day, seven days a week. She is frequently asked to do things that violate her conscience. But she goes along and gets along, and her career has been going fantastically. She is rising fast and is now being paid big bucks. The work compartment of her life is not integrated with her Christian faith. She has managed to keep them neatly sealed off from each other.

Diagram 20.2

The human capacity to compartmentalize explains why Mafia gangsters can sell drugs and run houses of prostitution, then go home to their families in nice neighborhoods and seem like fine, upstanding citizens. They can even be members of churches and do good and charitable deeds.

Closer to home is the tendency among Christians to leave significant chunks of their lives out of the Holy Spirit's management contract. We give our finances to God, but keep for ourselves our fear of failure. We yield our devotional life to the Spirit's control, but our entertainment might still include R-rated movies and spicy novels. We remain consistent in our church attendance, and yet our inner struggle with disappointment or grief may wall us off from God.

Repentance is the lifelong process that keeps on breaking through the maze of compartments in our inner world. The Holy Spirit is patiently relentless in His determination to take over the property promised to Him. In street language, He "puts out a contract" on our remaining points of resistance. We must be careful to allow for no confusion about how this happens.

PROCESS REPENTANCE BRINGS CONTINUAL REVIVAL

There have been incredible outpourings of spiritual life and power throughout history that we have chosen to call revival. Mighty works of God were done that reversed the direction of whole nations. I am 110 percent in favor of revival. But I'd like to make a suggestion in the face of strongly held sentiment to the contrary.

What if there is absolutely nothing mysterious or hard to understand about the phenomenon called revival? What if it's more than prevailing in prayer and waiting for God to surprise us with a special, occasional visitation of His presence? What if God intends for revival to be normal for all His people all the time? I bring up these questions because I've observed that Christians who subscribe to "visitation revivalism" act like their problems will be over if they can just get to where the fires of the Spirit are burning the brightest or the hottest. I personally know of pastors and laypeople who will hop on a plane and go wherever they hear that revival has broken out. They are constantly on a quest for unusual fervency and sensational "outpouring" phenomena.

What is revival? It is an event *and* a process! In both instances it is nothing more or less than fresh repentance. Personal revival occurs whenever the Holy Spirit is allowed to expand His supervision in our lives. Each breakthrough produces all the symptoms of revival—fresh and passionate worship, a release of new power and grace for victory over sin, a new enthusiasm for witness, and a renewed release of the fruit of the Spirit into our relationships. As He gets more of us, we get more of Him. It's that simple!

When a church or large group of churches embrace repentance as a way of life, operating in a "spiritually revived" state becomes the normal way of life for that group. There are no mysterious preconditions to meet, no "revivalists" to consult. *Revival* is a word Christians have historically used to describe the way God pours out His Spirit and His power wherever His kingdom is allowed to take over turf we have been holding onto ourselves. Taking sides with God in the maze of interconnected compartments of our lives is amazingly dynamic. The ongoing lifestyle of repentance keeps the transformation process moving. It carries out the intent of the original kingdom transaction that made us not only citizens of the heavenly kingdom, but children of the King Himself.

WHERE ARE THE SAINTS?

There's a reason revival is usually so short-lived. It's the same reason great churches rarely last more than fifty years in their prime. That reason is this: The old self-in-control sin nature never gets any better than it was when we first came to faith in Christ. If allowed to creep back into control, it does the same thing in the church that it did in the world.

We can try to control the process of God being in control. We can even attempt to quantify, formulate, and market revival. We can simulate the sound and feel of genuine worship. We can keep our churches familiar, comfortable, and within our preferences. After all, God blessed these forms, methods, and programs in the past, so why not in the future?

Here's my point: If the older, more experienced Christians don't keep showing the new believers how to continue in repentance, the momentum of the church breaks down. The most humble, the most selfless, the most sacrificial, the most flexibly submissive people in our churches should be those who have been at it the longest. But you and I know that just the opposite is what is consistently happening.

The new Christians, who have just discovered submission and obedience to the Spirit and the Word of God, tend to be the most spiritually powerful and productive. Their lives are changing. Their impact is felt inside and outside their personal circles of influence.

Many of us "older" Christians forget the need for continuous submission in all things. We tend to lapse back into attempts to control our lives and our churches. The old guard, the "pillars" of the church, the "powers that be" all too often behave like classic power brokers. They use constitutions, Robert's Rules of Order, and parliamentary procedure to control their churches and maintain their influence. When that fails there's always the "rumor mill" and the telephone campaigns behind the scenes that can be used to regain control or influence decisions. When the most experienced and tenured among us are setting the example of going back to the self-enthronement of the old sin nature in order to preserve the status quo, God's life, power, and presence are pushed out.

The evangelical landscape is covered with dead and dying churches. Congregations that were thriving twenty-five years ago, twenty years ago, ten years ago, five years ago—even one year ago—are now sick and self-destructing. Why? At the risk of oversimplifying, here's my argument: Submission is an event, and then a *lifetime process*. Once we start kingdom living, we must keep submitting our wills to our King. That's what repentance means—turning from our way to God's way, as a *lifestyle*. When we stop repenting we start regressing. The reason this happens seems elusive but it isn't. When we stop humbling ourselves, we shut off the free flow of the supernatural ability that God calls grace. James gives us the means of maintaining churches God can keep on blessing. He is describing what puts out the fire of the tongue and settles the quarrels and conflicts among us. More strength is provided when more humility is offered.

> *Submission is an event, and then a lifetime process. Once we start kingdom living, we must keep submitting our wills to our King.*

> Or do you think Scripture says without reason that the spirit he caused to live in us envies intensely? But *he gives us more grace.* That is why Scripture says:

> > "God opposes the proud
> > but *gives grace to the humble.*"

> Submit yourselves, then, to God. Resist the devil, and he will flee from you. Come near to God and he will come near to you. Wash your hands, you sinners, and purify your hearts, you double-minded. Grieve, mourn and wail. Change your laughter to mourning and your joy to gloom. Humble yourselves before the Lord, and he will lift you up. (James 4:5-10, emphasis added)

This is a passage for longtime believers. This is what makes the saints, the genuine articles, the twenty-four-carat treasures of the church. This is what makes bomb-proof, bullet-proof, ego-proof kingdom warriors. *God* resists the proud. God removes Himself from ego-saturated churches and they self-destruct.

Satan loves proud, self-sufficient, self-centered Christians. He does everything he can to encourage them to continue their sabotage of God's kingdom. But if he succeeds, it is God who pulls the plug on power politics and control games among His people. The glory departs.

Mature and consistently faithful believers are the hope of the church. They alone can use their vantage point of experience to show us the way into deeper repentance. They are necessary. They are valuable. And they are desperately needed. Are you willing to be one? Will you step out beside the apostle and say, "Follow me, as I follow Christ"?

THE SINS OF "OLD AGE"

Churches die when the seasoned veterans revert to pre-repentance behavior. I'm fifty-one years old. I have discovered, to my dismay, that the temptations of late middle age are worse than the temptations of youth! I was hoping to outgrow lust, greed, and covetousness, but they're still there and stronger than ever. What they did was switch categories: Now there's a *lust* for comfort and convenience, a *greed* for recognition, and a *covetousness* for security. The Christian life of yielding to the control of the Spirit has not become easier as I've gotten older. And what frustrates me is that in my world, at least, there are so pitifully few tested and true old-timers to show me the way. Retirement-age Christians who have stuck with the process of repentance long enough to have become "great souls" are largely missing.

Churches stagnate when the longtime Christians no longer humble themselves. The young ones are left to the trial-and-error school of hard knocks. We should be surprised and incensed when the winsomeness of early repentance turns back to the kingdom of self. If the Word of God is allowed to set the standard, baby Christians should logically be the ones with the most self-enthronement. On the other hand, believers of forty or fifty years should be profoundly humble and selfless as they near the end of a life of repentance.

Much more needs to be said about this. I'm convinced that fresh repentance among the ranks of silver-haired believers would utterly transform the face of the Western church. Would that be revival? You bet it would! Repentance is always the centerpiece of revival. But how much better if repentance was a way of life, not merely an occasional binge? Bathing daily is a lifestyle. Living in the bathtub for weeks once every fifty years may clean things up, but it doesn't make up for the years of dirt and grime.

Repentance is the beginning of the Christian life. It transfers the deed of the life to its rightful owner. It's the middle of the Christian life also, as we appropriate the resources God's grace provides to the humble who are following through with the leadership contract we made with our Lord. And it is the end. Throughout our lives we must never stop choosing to stay under the control of our Sovereign Savior.

True revival doesn't need to come and go. It's the blessing God pours out on lifestyle repentance. Revival is the normal experience of followers of Jesus. But how can we get unstuck if we're bogged down, or back on track if we've lost our bearings? The next chapter offers insight into maintaining momentum over the long haul in spite of outbreaks of internal sabotage. The fact that surrender isn't finished in one point-in-time decision is apparent to all of us. So what makes progress possible over the course of a lifetime?

TWENTY-ONE

Strongholds and Blind Spots

Even after we've invited Jesus Christ into the "mission control center" of our lives, we still struggle periodically with the leadership of the Holy Spirit. New control issues surface that surprise us. If not fore-warned, we may conclude that we're an unusual case. Frustration can give way to disappointment and despair if we're not alert to what's going on.

"Let me get this straight. You're saying that when I permitted God to take over, my life then became part of His kingdom?" Mary had come to faith in Christ in the past year and was working hard to figure out just how the Christian life functions.

"The part that puzzles me," she continued, "is the fact that I still have struggles over control of specific things that are important to me."

"Why does that confuse you?" I asked.

"Well, when I surrendered to Jesus, I meant it. I gave Him every-thing and expected that He would take charge and that the battle would be over. But it hasn't happened that way. Apparently He only rules where He has my voluntary consent. It amazes me that there are layers of resistance that I never dreamed were there. I hit a nasty little pocket of rebellion just this past week. I couldn't believe that I could be so stubborn with the One I love and have long since chosen as my Leader. Is there something I'm missing? Am I unusual? Sometimes I wonder if I'm really saved."

"Mary," I replied, "you are without question a sincere follower of our Savior and Lord. I've watched many people come to Christ, and you have all the life signs of the Holy Spirit's presence. I can see that you have the best of intentions when it comes to cooperating with your new Master. There is no valid reason to question your sincerity. His kingdom is within you. You now belong to Him."

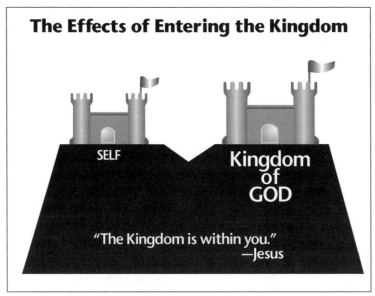

Diagram 21.1

I drew her the diagram above and explained that she was still a separate self with her identity and individuality intact. God doesn't absorb us. He completes us. He makes us the perfect person He created and intended us to be. What changes is the jurisdiction issue. He is now our authority and we are His loyal subjects.

"But that's just it," Mary protested. "I'm not a very loyal subject. I feel like there's a traitor within me."

"There is a traitor giving you trouble," I agreed, "but it's a common frustration that all Christians face. It's the same old sin nature that had the audacity to challenge God for control to begin with. Your new nature has enthusiastically embraced the ongoing privilege of taking sides with God. That process goes on hour by hour and day by day as you follow through on your initial commitment. Here's a portion of

Scripture that explains some of what your struggle is about." I then read 2 Corinthians 10:3-5 (emphasis added).

> For though we live in the world, we do not wage war as the world does. The weapons we fight with are not the weapons of the world. On the contrary, they have divine power to demolish *strongholds.* We demolish arguments and every pretension that sets itself up against the knowledge of God, and we take captive every thought to make it obedient to Christ.

THE LIES THAT BIND

I drew her another picture to help her visualize the little castles of sovereign selfhood that still exist in every Christian's life.

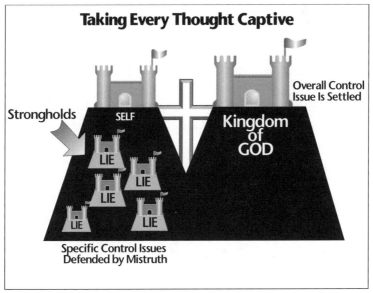

Diagram 21.2

"Mary, these strongholds tend to be built on some pretentious fiction that was constructed by the egoism of our past. Strongholds are always built around a lie—something that seems true to us but is really a clever falsehood that serves as an excuse to sustain control. We can also refer to them as blind spots. As you're finding out, they can be difficult to identify and remove, even with the help of the Holy Spirit and other obedient believers."

I went on to share several examples of lie-based strongholds that the Holy Spirit had torn down in my own life. She was reassured. Later she reported that it helped her a great deal to visualize the mop-up campaign that the Spirit of God is carrying out in each follower of Christ.

THE LAST BASTION

Several years ago my wife, Scharme, and I visited some castles in England and Scotland. Almost every castle we saw had at least one strong tower or final citadel. It was, in reality, a miniature castle within the larger fortification, with defensive turrets built into the top for firing arrows, dropping rocks, or pouring boiling oil on attackers. If an enemy breached the moat and got over the outer walls, the surviving defenders would flee to the final stronghold, where they had a chance to hold out until reinforcements could arrive. The castle could be captured and still have unsurrendered strongholds.

> *The lie is this: I cannot be expected to function like other Christians.*

That gave me the idea for this next diagram. This is a top view of a typical stronghold. The thick walls are the layers of defensive rationalizations, justifications, and protective excuses that surround the lie within.

The lie is this: I cannot be expected to function like other Christians. My life situation is so different that the truth that applies to other people and works for them doesn't work for me. I'm different. I'm an exception. My case is unique.

It's not easy to expand the kingdom in our lives when dealing with a stronghold like this, but it is possible. It will take moment-by-moment cooperation with the Holy Spirit and a willingness to let the truth set us free.

Here's the truth about you: You are special. You are unique. You are one of a kind. Your individuality is something God designed and something He treasures. The Creator sees your distinctive differences and loves you for your custom-made personhood.

Calvary and the atonement of Jesus declares to us that we are each incredibly valuable to the Father. We have the capacity to know God, to love Him, to obey Him, and to serve Him. We were each designed for significance and greatness in His eternal family and kingdom.

But *no one is an exception* to the patterns and principles of kingdom living. You're special and unique, but you're not an exception. All the truth of Scripture will work for you as well as other followers of Christ. You cannot, nor should you, be excused from obedience on the basis of some special-case scenario. Everything God can do for others He'll do for you. God has no favorites. He singles out no one for special treatment. So if this is an issue for you, face the lie of exceptionism and stop giving it sanctuary.

Diagram 21.3

Bombard the disinformation with Scripture. Insist that the old nature's propaganda tapes of the pathetic, victimized, dysfunctional self are exposed to the light of God's Word. Invite the truth-telling accountability of fellow kingdom freedom fighters. You can demolish exception thinking and any other misconception that has become a stronghold. The process of continual surrender will work for you. God's power is at work within you. Your part is to follow directions and follow through.

PROTECTING THE HEART OF GOD

Scharme's miniature Yorkshire terrier, Little Anne, loves dried pigs' ears. She prances around the house with these things in her mouth, and the look on her face as she gnaws away suggests that she thinks she's died and gone to heaven.

One night, unable to sleep, I was prowling the house in the dark, barefooted, and happened to step on a slimy, saliva-soaked, frayed, and well-chewed pig's ear. My reaction was immediate and spontaneous—I jumped sideways, cracked my shin on the forgotten coffee table, danced backwards, and fell over the rocking chair. That ear felt . . . *alive!*

The shock of encountering horror in the dark is familiar to all of us. I'm referring to the unpleasant sensation of making contact with a pig's ear remnant of the old sin nature. It's a memorable experience to discover a previously unnoticed stronghold. Let's take a look at another common blind spot.

For some of us the stronghold of exceptionism looks like diagram 21.4.

Diagram 21.4

POCKETS OF PRIDE

I have a distinct distaste for human pride. It doesn't surprise me that God gets heartburn over it.

There are six things the LORD hates,
   seven that are detestable to him:
      haughty eyes [pride],
      a lying tongue,
      hands that shed innocent blood,
      a heart that devises wicked schemes,
      feet that are quick to rush into evil,
      a false witness who pours out lies
      and a man who stirs up dissension among brothers.
             (Proverbs 6:16-19)

Sometimes when God speaks it's like the lid of a septic tank is lifted. His word reveals slithering residents of previously sealed sections of my heart. Often I had no clue they were even there. You see, I react with disgust and revulsion whenever I see creepy, crawly arrogance in others. Vanity, narcissism, and conceit never fail to turn me off. Bragging, boasting, name dropping, cockiness, and disdainful superiority grind me faster than any other kind of behavior.

At the same time I must reluctantly confess that I have an extremely difficult time seeing it in myself. It has been well said that our blind spots lie in the shadow of our egos. I can *smell* pride even before I can see it — in you. But when it comes to identifying it in myself, I seem to lose my five senses. The good news is that whenever I permit God to sensitize me, His Spirit quickly becomes my infrared night vision goggles. When I see myself through His eyes, the blind spots of my well-camouflaged pride stand out in bold relief.

My pride has come in many forms. Here are a few that my faithful friend, the Spirit, has helped me identify and do battle with:

- An assumption of superiority.
- The need to be more right than anyone else.
- The impulse to prove and promote myself.
- The tendency to take credit for things that were really the ideas or the work of others.
- Hypersensitivity to criticism.
- The attractiveness of self-pity when I've been hurt or offended by others.
- The strong need to defend myself and even retaliate.

■ The ease with which I can hold a grudge over slights that I've been guilty of committing myself.

■ My uncanny ability to rationalize, justify, and excuse what I do and say while at the same time, and even over the same issues, being unsympathetic and judgmental with others.

■ Leveling behavior; that is, building up myself by tearing others down.

As I reread this list, I'm embarrassed. I find myself extremely reluctant to reveal to you these evidences of stronghold activity in my life. Yet I'm glad to admit that I'm allowing the Holy Spirit to tear down the remnants of my rebellion in the hope that it will encourage you to do the same. Covering up and pretending we have our followership of Christ all together isn't the answer. We've all tried that with disastrous consequences.

WELCOMING EXPOSURE

It is in our own best interest to agree with Jesus about this cover-up tendency that lies within all of us.

This is the verdict: Light has come into the world, but men loved darkness instead of light because their deeds were evil. Everyone who does evil hates the light . . . for fear that his deeds will be exposed. (John 3:19-20)

Besides the fact that most crime and violence take place between sunset and sunrise, this scripture is addressing our universal *denial instinct*. Oh, how I wish hiding from the light had ended with the salvation transaction. But before I realize it, there I go again, protesting my innocence. "Me? Oh no, not me. I wouldn't think of doing something like that!"

We can see this knee-jerk reaction to the searchlight of truth early in the lives of children. They don't have to be taught to cover, hide, or deny. It comes naturally. In adults, the ability to evade the truth about our motives and behavior becomes highly skilled. Honest Christians admit, brokenly and with great sorrow, the battle they personally have with staying in the light. It seems that the further maturing believers go in their walk with the Spirit of God, the more sensitive they must become to the subtleties of stronghold pockets of resistance.

At the Holy Spirit's insistence, I committed myself long ago to being an honest man. In the beginning it seemed that the Lord and I made tremendous progress. The overt lying stopped. The dishonest manipulation of situations for selfish advantage slowed way down. I was fast becoming a man of God externally. Then the bell rang for round two and my opponent came out of his corner with newly grown muscle and fresh energy. The fact is, it has become more difficult to make progress with internal honesty than it was with the external type. Consistent growth and ongoing maturity have not come easily for me. The transformation process ebbs and flows. This has not made me doubt the new creation power of the Spirit, but it has helped me understand the seriousness of the stronghold problem.

I now accept the battle for truth in my inward parts as a constant in my life. If you're committed to conforming to the humble, God-submitted likeness of Christ for the rest of your life, you know what I mean. The kingdom reign of God in the castle of my heart is only enjoyed when I harbor a holy hatred of every selfish holdout. Pride, exceptionism, and any other form of self-deception must go.

I've even discovered a difference between passive and active surrender. With passive surrender, I wait for Him to take the initiative and put His finger on a holdout. With active surrender, I rest in the love of God and remain alert — watching as He creates circumstances that will expose those cockroach-sized "pigs' ears" that hide in the crannies of my heart. They breed fast and die hard. Their extermination demands constant vigilance.

OTHER STRONGHOLDS

Here are some other strongholds you might want to be wary of:

- I need to stay in control because I'm so shy and sensitive.
- I can't give God complete control because my marriage partner would take advantage of my submission.
- I'm oversexed. God's rules are too restrictive.
- I'm a fearful person. Losing control scares me most of all.
- God understands why I can't surrender.
- Security and comfort have always been big issues with me. I can't risk having God take away my support system.

- My children need my full attention. God can have my life after I get them raised.
- I like to eat. I can understand why the Israelites complained about the manna. I suspect that if I gave my appetite to God, my life would be boring.
- In order to "reach my friends" I have to be with them doing the things they enjoy.
- I'm basically honest. I don't need help with transparency, integrity, and accountability.
- My church or parachurch circle is more right, more blessed, and more spiritually powerful than others. I'm *okay* because I'm with a superior group.

A LABOR OF LOVE

After confessing my own ongoing internal struggle in the relentless pursuit of a safe ego, I should add that there is tremendous satisfaction in protecting those I love from the residue of my old, prideful nature. Without a doubt, the one person who can hurt my wife the most is me. The one person who can damage the respect and love of my children is me. Because I'm regarded as a spiritual leader, the one person who can most discourage and destroy my church is me. My first responsibility in the area of protective leadership is to cooperate with the "safe self" program of the Holy Spirit so that those who mean the world to me are not placed in harm's way. The fruit of the Spirit-controlled life—although hard on my pride—is easy to live with for others.

Last, the overarching concern of my heart is that I no longer contribute to the abuse that my magnificent Savior puts up with. I think one of the greatest fears of a self-aware follower of Jesus is the terrifying potential we have to crucify the Son of God afresh. I have found Bill Bright's insight immensely helpful: "When Christ is on the throne, self is on the cross. When self is on the throne, Christ is on the cross." When Christians are so in love with the Lover of their soul that they are passionately committed to not hurting Him again, they are gaining rapidly on the goal of maturity.

✠

Strongholds, with their obnoxious holdout hostility against God, cannot be tolerated. If allowed a toehold, they quickly produce spreading resentment against His gracious rule. A loving child of the King is ruthless with each discovery of previously unnoticed or hidden points of resistance. When one of the mini-strongholds is allowed to spring up around a convenient self-serving lie, it inevitably brings pain to the Father's heart. Those who love God with all their heart are fiercely protective of His feelings. That's the way true love works.

This stage of growth when we are motivated by tender love for our matchless Lord is the place of holy freedom. His name, His honor, His reputation, His glory, and His feelings have been placed in our hands. Thrill with me to the extreme joy of protecting His humility from the remnants of our rebellious egoism.

→ TWENTY-TWO ←
The Mixed-Bag Situation

There is a corporate blind spot in the conservative Christian culture that's so potentially troublesome that we need to examine it carefully. But before we do that, I want to give it some "big picture" perspective.

Our God is in control even when we think we are. He "raises up" and "puts down" as it pleases Him. His kingdom is producing a mighty harvest even though it is sometimes difficult to distinguish between the "wheat" and the "weeds." I'm not content with the tension of this mixed-bag situation, but I recognize that our Master predicted it would be this way. I can wait for the final sorting that He promised. I remember His advice, "Who are you to judge another man's servant? To his own master he is approved or disapproved." (See Romans 14:4.) And that cautions my Don-Quixote–like tendency to quest and become an "attack sheep." Yet I am compelled at least to "bleat" a warning.

In the last thirty years many evangelical enterprises and ministries have become moneymaking businesses. Christian publishing, Christian bookstores, Christian music companies, Christian radio and television stations, and megachurches have become highly successful. What used to be a self-sacrificing labor of love now creates wealth and celebrity status with astonishing regularity.

Much of this is clear evidence of the blessing of God. Obviously when God raises up and bestows honor upon an individual or ministry, it will prosper. Christian entertainment, art, and literature are not wrong. Widespread acceptance is not an indictment. The accountability question is not so much what is popular or what is selling, but rather what is missing? And why is following Jesus in faithful obedience so rare among us? Is it possible that the cash registers are drowning out the voice of our Great Shepherd?

Money talks in every arena of our world today. If the work of the kingdom is handed over to market-driven forces, who is leading and where will we be led? In my opinion, this financial factor is weakening the message. As can be expected, it's making a big deal out of financially lucrative aspects of truth. At the same time it's minimizing what is arbitrarily considered financially nonviable. "It won't sell" is the death knell.

> *If the work of the kingdom is handed over to market-driven forces, who is leading and where will we be led?*

What parts of the gospel message do *you* think receive the most attention? The answer I would give is this: the portions that seem to provide the most immediate benefit. Surprised? Probably not. Predictably, people buy what makes them feel good and avoid what makes them uncomfortable. Christian bookstores are full of books about God's love and grace, God's acceptance and forgiveness, God's goodness and promises, God's blessings and rewards. Whole sections of material address the biblical response to specific felt needs such as marriage, parenting, friendship, and curiosity about the prophetic future. Getting God working for you, solving your problems, making your life happier and more successful tends to be the focus.

What doesn't get much attention are those parts of the Bible's message that people don't like to hear. For instance, the messages of the Old Testament prophets have never been best-sellers when taken in their entirety. They're only well received if the sensational elements of future predictions are the focus. Books that hit too close to home on the subject of sin have rarely moved off the shelves. When the size of the crowd, broadcast audience, or budget is the criterion for determining success, we get off balance. The subjects of sin, righteousness, and judgment that, according to Jesus, were to be *the* focus of the Holy Spirit's work in the world during the church era are simply not getting much attention.

I know this is starting to sound a bit strident and perhaps even harsh, but I'm alarmed. Why haven't we been more alert and taken more precautions, especially in the face of the tremendous temptations arising from the hundreds of millions of dollars being made? If I'm right and what's good for business is shaping the very gospel we believe and preach, then perhaps it's time to do some serious housecleaning. If we allow profit margins to determine what gets heard and read, we will soon die out. God will be forced to judge those who adulterate His Word for the purposes of selfish advantage. (The further I go with this wake-up call, the more uncomfortable I'm becoming. "Who am I to bring this warning?" keeps ringing in my ears. Yet, I'm compelled to finish this.)

MONEY, MARKETING, AND THE MESSAGE

Why are there so many ideological and theological fads in the evangelical world? Each year the newest rage hits the Christian bookstores, promising to solve readers' personal problems or their churches' problems.

New waves of material are being churned out in order to keep business booming. The financial machine we've created needs new products and fresh buying surges to survive. So, just as the fashion industry keeps rearranging design and color to affect the latest style in order to sell new clothing, the Christian publishing and broadcasting world must create new spiritual menus. It's simply good for business. Are we really this crass? Probably not intentionally. But it's high time we faced the fact that market pressures do shape the message.

If you recognize at least some truth in what I'm saying, please stay with me a little longer. The recovery of the power and vitality of the first-century church is a longing that rises from deep within every sincere church leader and committed Christian. Revival or revitalization has been talked about, prayed for, and at times experienced, yet never codified or systematized. Contemporary Christian fads capitalize on the feeling that something is missing, that there's got to be more than what we are currently experiencing. Each proposed solution creates a new flurry of purchasing that eventually becomes standardized as a new section on the retail shelves. Here are some of the emphases that I've watched sweep through the evangelical culture in recent years.

- Returning to the gifts of the Spirit.
- Returning to signs, wonders, and miracles.

- Returning to the systematic teaching and expository preaching of the Word.
- Returning to a focus on discipleship.
- Returning to aggressive evangelism.
- Returning to concentrating on church growth.
- Retooling our strategy of church planting.
- Returning the ministry to the laity.
- Returning to house churches and small groups.
- Returning to ministries of mercy, servanthood, and meeting needs.
- Recapturing worship.
- Rediscovering prayer.
- Refocusing on unity, oneness, and harmony.
- Reaching unreached people groups.
- Resisting the Devil and rearming for spiritual warfare.
- Rediscovering the significance of women.
- Rediscovering men's ministry.
- Recapturing national morality through social activism.
- Rediscovering personal piety and the devotional disciplines.
- Rebuilding marriage.
- Repairing the family.
- Renewing our focus on the end times and the return of Christ.
- Restoring health, physical fitness, and emotional wholeness.
- Returning to simplicity and a nonconsumer lifestyle.

Now, which of these deserve our attention? Is the answer all of the above? If so, how are we to cope with such complexity? And how are we ever going to experience unity when we're chronically divided over which emphasis is most needed?

Almost all of the above emphases have developed into "movements," complete with entrepreneurial, parachurch corporations; headquarters; mailing lists; fund-raising campaigns; and training seminars. All claim to be either the missing piece or essential ingredient that, if emphasized sufficiently, will restore the church or the individual. All have good people, good material, good intentions, and a sympathetic following behind them.

It takes only a few moments of sober reflection to recognize that these movements have not improved our spiritual health. Slowly but surely the evangelical church is settling into stagnation despite our efforts. One-third of our churches are growing; but one-third are plateaued and one-third are declining.

Even with the efforts of countless experts, consultants, analysts, and communicators — and in spite of reams of materials, calendars crowded with resourcing opportunities, and homes full of Christian products — the evangelical world is tired, ineffective, and for the most part, powerless. The only people who benefit consistently from all the confusing and competing ads and fads are the Christian industries. The business of selling to the conservative Christian market is thriving. So much so that huge secular corporations have been buying up Christian publishing, recording, and broadcasting companies one by one. Many of the most trusted brand names in Christendom are now owned by nonChristians. Huge amounts of money are being made, yet few seem willing to discuss what this commercialization of ministry is doing to the message and to the church. How could such a development not create blind spots and strongholds?

In my judgment, the complexity of panaceas is confusing average Christians. They're aimlessly milling in circles instead of following their Lord. They mistakenly assume that they must stay on top of the latest products and attend the current seminars and conferences in order to be in the know and in the flow. Since all the top names seem to be encouraging and endorsing the latest offerings, they must be good for you. But are they? What if what is going on is to a large extent not of God? What if much of this is human kingdom building that is actually using the things of God to further personal agendas? What if it amounts to the same kind of commercial clutter that so offended Jesus when He furiously cleansed the temple?

I see some hopeful signs. A rediscovery of the lost kingdom of God is at long last beginning to emerge. People want more than a constant diet of what "popular" churches are doing, what celebrity Christian broadcasters are saying, and what the top Christian publishers are releasing. They want to know, "What is God doing? Where is God at work? How can I invest my life in that which is eternal?"

The protest could be made that "they don't buy the good books when they're published." Can publishers help it if Christians don't seem interested in substance? If the demand is for fast food, it amounts to a financial death wish to insist on serving up health food. (Do I hear an echo of the television networks' rationalizations here?)

The fact is, Christians *are* buying what's good for them. The publishing phenomenon that swept Henry Blackaby to uncomfortable fame—for *Experiencing God*—is a prime example. Simple yet profound, solid yet powerfully effective, this book is changing lives and churches all over the world. Is this just a fluke? No, rather it is a signal that there is a huge market for deeper, "good for you" evangelical material.

THE OBVIOUS QUESTION

Since I've spoken up, how about us turning the searchlight on me? Fair enough. Is the *kingdom* just another fad? I've given considerable thought to that possibility. It's certainly conceivable that I could be guilty of the same things I'm warning others about. After all, I'm subject to the same temptations as everyone else. But as far as I can tell right now, my motivation for promoting the kingdom message isn't coming from what remains of my egoism. In fact, I'm absolutely convinced that rediscovering the kingdom is the only safe way out of our situation.

> *The one thing I'm passionately sure of is that the kingdom emphasis restores the leadership of the Sovereign Savior to His church.*

The one thing I'm passionately sure of is that the kingdom emphasis restores the leadership of the Sovereign Savior to His church. I long with all my heart to see "His kingdom come and His will be done on earth, today, as it is in heaven." All other issues and concerns sort themselves out when the restoration of Christ's kingdom is moved to top priority in our hearts. All other kingdoms crumble when our King reigns supreme.

Jeremiah's warning weeps from the pages of God's Word:

> From the least to the greatest,
>   all are greedy for gain;
> prophets and priests alike,
>   all practice deceit.

They dress the wound of my people
    as though it were not serious.
"Peace, peace," they say,
    when there is no peace. (Jeremiah 8:10-11)

Safe followers of Christ must be supersensitive to all that massages the ego. Money, power, material possessions, prominence, influence, and privilege all regularly tempt the most successful among us. Even Solomon in all his wisdom was not able to stand up successfully to such powerful distractions. So why would we think we could handle it without God's leadership?

What a tragedy it would be if Revelation 3:17 was written to the Christian leaders in the churches and in the world of evangelical ministry businesses at this time in history—and we refused to listen. "You say, 'I am rich; I have acquired wealth and do not need a thing.' But you do not realize that you are wretched, pitiful, poor, blind and naked."

Humble self-evaluation and voluntary repentance among the movers and shakers of the Christian ministry business could be the spark that revitalizes the work of the kingdom. In the words of Peter, "It is time for judgment to begin with the family of God" (1 Peter 4:17). I think I see it starting to happen, and I want to fan the flame—with prayer.

Sovereign Lord, start with me and my family. Examine me and my church. I choose to live in humility and submission to Your leadership. Don't ever let me back off of this commitment. Amen.

☩

If you're in ministry as a profession and what I've just said has set your teeth on edge, I understand. When someone waltzes into my sphere of influence and starts taking potshots, my first reaction is irritation, too. "I'm doing the best I can with what I've got," I say to myself. "If this hotshot can do it any better, he's welcome to it."

Yet, I suspect that for every person who snorts in disgust, hundreds will nod in agreement. A huge hunger has been growing beneath our "junk-food" habits. God is at work among His people awakening a new taste for His kingdom. In much the same way as the box-office-champion movies usually carry the relatively wholesome G or PG rating, so also the big blockbuster Christian publishing successes will continue to contain solid, kingdom-enhancing, life-transforming spiritual nutrition. God will always bless what builds His eternal kingdom in as many followers as possible.

Like the owner's servants in the parable of the weeds (Matthew 13:24-30), I am eager to pull all the weeds I see growing in the field of the kingdom. But my Lord can live with the mixed seed, and under His instruction so can I. The sorting of what is His kingdom "wheat" and what is our kingdom "weeds" will take place. But in His judgment it is too damaging to separate the true from the false—yet. Let's just make sure we aren't inadvertently cooperating with our Master's enemy. He loves to sow the seeds of selfishness in the field of God. The one piece of the field I have permission to weed is my own heart.

→ TWENTY-THREE ←
Passing the Fish Along

The great blue heron stood statuesquely in petrified alertness. Slowly his bladelike head rotated sideways, then suddenly speared downward beneath the water. The long, muscular neck recoiled, and the head reappeared with a herring firmly clamped in the long beak. He held it while it struggled futilely. Finally he worked it around to where the head was in his mouth. The throat expanded, the heron's head tilted back, he gulped, and the fish went down whole.

The heron must have found a hot spot because, from the beach house on Puget Sound where we were staying, I watched him catch and go through the swallowing process twice more. His fourth catch was the biggest yet, at least a foot long. It was time for a supergulp. He gave it a heroic effort, but the head of the fish was slightly larger than his gullet could handle.

The bald eagle had been waiting for this moment. He swooped out of the fir high above the beach and glided down upon the frustrated heron. The heron had obviously been watching, too, and made no attempt to argue over ownership of the fish. With majestic confidence, the huge bird of prey lowered his taloned feet and plucked the floating fish from the water. Wheeling on his magnificent wings, he glided back to the beach and settled on the sand to tear into a free lunch.

A golden eagle had also been watching the food-chain drama from a cedar spar farther down the beach. Now he launched into action. Considerably larger in size, he didn't hesitate to move in on his cousin. The bald eagle didn't give up as easily as the heron had, but attempted to outrun the golden bully. Fish firmly clutched in his claws, he beat his way out to sea with the larger predator calmly gaining on him.

You could see the exact moment when the bald eagle decided it wasn't worth a confrontation. He dropped the contested fish and immediately sheared off and glided back toward shore. The triumphant golden eagle nonchalantly picked up his prize and flew off to his perch to enjoy a stolen meal.

I have known spiritual leaders to operate in like manner—the stronger and more aggressive taking advantage of the smaller and weaker. With the birds and the beasts it is understandable. With humans who claim to be new creations in Christ Jesus, these strong-arm tactics take on a particular ugliness.

What happens when a spiritual leader mistakes his congregation's trust for a license to dominate them? What if he has no concept of the fact that kingdom authority is earned by demonstrating how to follow Jesus, not how to throw one's weight around? This chapter is written for people who are having trouble following their Leader while leading their followers.

THE KINGDOM IMPACT ON LEADERSHIP

The CEO of a sizable company ordered mandatory personality testing for everyone in his employ. He didn't submit to the testing himself, though. He had no intention of revealing anything of a personal nature. The new information gained by the psychological measuring device became a powerful tool for this leader. It offered a new set of criteria for evaluating and a potential means of manipulating and intimidating those who functioned under his authority.

This executive was following the law of the self-centered ego. Fundamental to successful domination of others is the axiom "While you conceal, force others to reveal." Egoism holds the truth cards close to the vest. The classic way to gain and maintain power and advantage over others is to hide who you really are and what your actual motives and objectives are. With this strategy, at times it may become necessary to appear transparent or create the illusion of openness in order to gain an advantage. Powerful people know how to skillfully create impressions that serve their purposes—while avoiding actual authenticity and transparency.

INFORMATION IS POWER

Non-kingdom leaders isolate and insulate themselves so that no one can put all the pieces together. Their wives, closest friends, relatives, and personal secretaries and work associates may have some of the pieces. But no one has enough pieces to get the real picture. This practice is instinctive. It's regarded as wise and "professional" by the leader. The significant downside of such an approach to leadership is that it is inevitably dangerous to the followers. Those dependent on such a leader will find themselves used, manipulated, coerced, deceived, betrayed, and discarded when of no further use.

The most significant challenge kingdom leaders face is how to protect their followers from the remaining strongholds and blind spots left over from their old kingdoms of self. What remains of their original arrogance and pride, their need to win and be right, their need to control and dominate, their obsession with protecting their options and agenda will always be painful to those under their authority.

PROTECTING THOSE YOU LEAD

Kingdom leaders can protect those under them in the organization by first and foremost submitting to the Leader of the universe. The safest human leaders are those who embrace God's higher power in voluntary humility and deep respect. Genuine followers of the Servant-King make safe leaders. Non-followers discourage and disillusion those entrusted to them. In fact, many believers have given up on following Christ because of human leaders who, while claiming to represent Him, violated their trust.

> *The safest human leaders are those who embrace God's higher power in voluntary humility and deep respect.*

The second step in protecting those you lead is to give a group of trusted others the truth about yourself. A leader under authority reveals himself. He deliberately collapses the appearance layer into the reality layer and exposes his true self.

When Jack was elected to the board of his church, he saw it as a huge responsibility. He was confident he could handle the assignment because he had been the president of his own company for several years.

He automatically began to lead in the church the way he had learned to do it in the world of business. The result was disastrous. He antagonized and offended almost everyone he was trying to supervise. His heavy-handed, "get-the-job-done" approach was resented. He was ready to quit when a wise fellow elder took him aside and suggested he humble himself and reveal his heart to his ministry team. "Let them see the real you. The passion you have for obeying Christ. The love you have for the church and for them. Stop driving the sheep, but rather lead them by example." Here's the pattern of leadership we are called to follow as Peter outlined it.

> Be shepherds of God's flock that is under your care, serving as overseers—not because you must, but because you are willing, as God wants you to be; not greedy for money, but eager to serve; *not lording it over those entrusted to you, but being examples to the flock.* . . . All of you, clothe yourselves with humility toward one another, because,
>
> > "God opposes the proud
> > but gives grace to the humble." (1 Peter 5:2-3,5,
> > emphasis added)

That timely advice made a huge change in Jack's life. He learned how to be a humbly transparent leader not only in the church, but also in his home and in his business, and is now one of the most loved and respected leaders in his church.

This transparency is what personal holiness and purity is all about. Genuine authenticity is precious and rare: precious because it effectively protects the followers of such a leader; rare because it is so seldom prized. Let me emphasize once again, this is not an affected style or illusionary trick used to lull subordinates into lowering their guard. Rather, this courageous openness and accountability is genuine in spite of how risky it feels for the leader.

In order to be effective, the leader's support team must include honest, gutsy, radical followers of Christ. He gives them the goods on himself and expects to receive the same transparency in return. The members of such a "truth-in-love team" are charged with the responsibility of protecting each other from getting trapped in blind spots. This watchdog role is strategically important—it protects the followers of these leaders from exploitation and abuse. Wise leaders see honesty, humility, transparency, and mutual submission as indispensable sources of safety for themselves and for their organizations. They have learned to regard ego-inflation, self-centeredness, arrogance, and obsession with control as deadly. Such a support team holds each of its members accountable *for maintaining an ego-proofed environment.*

The result in a Christian-run business, church, or ministry is a management team that is healthy. They are utterly ruthless with themselves when the eruptions of self-in-ascendancy strongholds show up and will, over time, largely free themselves of the diseases of management. The prima donna complexes, the competitive infighting, the political games, the macho cover-ups of personal insecurity, and the power trips gradually disappear. The disharmony, intrigue, and betrayal that paralyzes others is effectively neutralized. The turnover in the ranks is stopped. Leaders who submit to this kind of standard earn the admiration, respect, and gratitude of their followers. Followers who know they're serving a safe leader will contribute far more enthusiastically, even if it means personal sacrifice. They're free to give their best gladly rather than comply out of fear or manipulation.

COSTLY ATTRITION

I was part of a pastor's prayer group that disintegrated. There were eight of us in the beginning. Then Melvin had a moral lapse and broke his marriage vows with a woman he was supposedly counseling. We grieved over his failure. He had been a powerful preacher and a good friend.

Then it was Bert who broke down one Wednesday and confessed that he was addicted to pornography and had molested two young girls in his church. We were all in shock as we tried to help him and do damage control with his congregation.

Less than a year later, Robert stopped coming. When we inquired after his whereabouts, we found he had skipped town with his secretary and an undisclosed amount of his church's building fund. Three out of eight! Who would be next? It was one of the most traumatic and discouraging periods of my life. What you find in the last half of this chapter comes out of observations made and lessons learned in those painful days.

Christian leaders have fallen into immorality at an alarming rate in recent years. The chilling effect on the cause of Christ's kingdom is hard to calculate. All we know for sure is that our enemy, the Devil, has managed to take advantage of the situation and both promote and publicize clergy moral failure on a massive scale. Both the Christian and secular worlds have been exposed to extensive coverage of these embarrassing reports.

The reasons why more of this has been happening lately are not that hard to understand. A decadent, sexually permissive society certainly increases the temptation, but that alone doesn't explain the rate of moral decline among Christian leaders, for lust and indulgence have been with us from the beginning. My impression is that leaders of large churches and national and international parachurch ministries have been particularly vulnerable. Here's a scenario that offers an explanation for why such extraordinary leaders have fallen.

As the leader becomes successful he isolates himself and gradually begins to see himself as above the ordinary accountability of the average Christian. Cocooned by a growing staff and secretarial corps, he begins to think of himself as an exception. His important position is deemed worthy of "privileges." The perks of his growing power and influence in the organization, he considers to be his right and prerogative. He begins to get away with behavior that would be confronted were anyone else doing it. No one questions him. He's set it up so that he doesn't have to justify his actions to anyone.

About this time his wife becomes increasingly alarmed by the enlargement of his ego blind spots. She tries to tell him what she sees happening to him. He chooses to interpret her concerns as pettiness, jealousy, and disloyalty. The two of them drift apart emotionally and spend less and less time together. He buries himself in his work, where he is "appreciated and respected." She invests herself in the children or a career of her own.

Another woman, usually younger, begins to meet some of his needs. I say younger because a man at the successful stage of ministry leadership is usually at least in early middle age. Along with mid-life comes an impulse to see if he's still physically attractive. The new woman in his life admires him, affirms him, and treats him with thoughtfulness and respect. He begins to turn to her for affection and companionship.

She is attracted to his power, flattered by his attention, and feels swept along by a flood of emotions. They fall in love and secretly begin an affair. Eventually, their immoral relationship is discovered and exposed. The Christian leader and the woman are shamed, lose their reputations, and often their marriages. The leader loses his choice position and his credibility. The destruction is devastating to all concerned and . . . absolutely unnecessary!

There are other kinds of mistresses attracting the attention of Christian leaders. They have names like:

- Fanny Fame
- Polly Power
- Betty Bucks
- Rhonda Reputation
- Sophie Sought-After

They all tempt. They all have their own alluring, seductive influence. They all begin with seemingly harmless flirtations, then quickly become disastrous affairs.

The disillusionment and dashed trust of followers can be avoided. Christian leaders can intentionally *ego-proof* themselves. They can protect their wives, children, congregations, and ministry organizations from such painful betrayal. How? By taking the biblical doctrine of sin seriously. By setting up adequate precautions. No special privileges, no isolation, and no celebrity treatment.

I found U.S. Army captain Alek Milutinouk's observations as reported in the April 15, 1996 issue of *U.S. News and World Report* encouraging. He said that "the Bosnian Serb Army cannot comprehend the American concept of leadership, that our officers set the example and that we will not have anything better than our own soldiers. We took some Serbian commanders on a tour, and they were amazed that our brigade commander was living in a simple hex tent. When we go to dinner, our officers stand with their men."

Jesus could have written that policy—in fact, He did. "He who would be greatest among you must be the servant of all." (See Matthew 20:26.)

The accountability team mentioned earlier is an absolute must. Spiritual leaders cannot trust themselves to face the temptations of success all alone. Anticipating temptation and protecting those for whom you are responsible from your own potential failure is the responsibility of a godly leader, and is best accomplished in an accountability contract with other kingdom players.

Insisting on taking kingdom principles to their pragmatic conclusions produces a safe human leader. Wise kingdom leaders truly believe that they have strongholds and blind spots like every other believer. They also believe that theirs are even more dangerous than they would be in anyone else. They allow the Spirit of Truth to so control them that they cease to be a threat to those they love and lead. They blaze a trail for others to follow to the *repentance-saturated, humility-rich environment* of the kingdom in the power of their risen Lord.

Humility is safe. Egoism is dangerous. *No exceptions!*

TAKING ANOTHER STEP—
QUESTIONS FOR MEDITATION

1. Have you ever experienced personal revival? If so, think about the circumstances that surrounded it and identify the area of fresh repentance that instigated the emotional response.

2. Is there a particularly troublesome compartment of your life that has proven highly resistant to the Holy Spirit's control? Has it begun to influence other compartments you had once surrendered?

3. Which of these two strongholds is closest to your own profile of internal struggles?
   - "I'm worse than . . ."
   - "I'm better than . . ."

   Remember, "the lie" in both cases is in the idea that I am a special case—an exception to the general rule.

4. Who could you enlist to help you identify and dismantle your remaining strongholds and blind spots?

5. Does the mixed bag of kingdom of self under the guise of the kingdom of God bother you? What weeds do we have permission to pull?

6. If you're a Christian leader and recognize that you're in jeopardy, where can you go for help? Suggestion: Ask someone you know who is walking in consistent obedience to Christ to assist you. Pick someone strong enough to challenge you, yet loving enough to stick with you.

7. If you have a leader who has been seduced away from his or her kingdom loyalties, what should you do? Suggestion: Lovingly, with a broken heart, tell that leader what you see. Pray for him or her. Don't go away until that person forces you to.

8. How do you plan to protect those who look to you for leadership from what remains of your own ego issues?

PART FIVE

THE SAFE COMMUNITY

What Governs You?

There is one overriding factor that keeps a follower of Christ going for a lifetime in the process of repentance. It is referred to throughout the Bible as the "fear of the Lord." My intention in this chapter is to make sense of this fascinating fear factor in the context of the kingdom of God. We'll discover the liberating power of neutralizing our unhealthy fear-based behavior with a greater fear.

In the summer of 1994 great fires ravaged the western part of Washington. Months of little to no rainfall had turned the vast national and state forests into tinderboxes. Then came a series of electrical storms. Heat lightning struck at random and fire began to rage along the ridges and up the valleys.

Fire fighters responded to the call for help. Helicopters, special tanker planes, bulldozers—every possible means was utilized in an attempt to save the towns, ranches, and vacation homes in the path of the fire. In the end it came down to the oldest method in the book: fighting fire with fire. Backfires were started that burned from the fire lines toward the onrushing forest fires. When the great fires came to the territory that had been burned by the backfires, they ran out of fuel and died.

The Word of God uses a similar technique. The fear of the Lord is the answer to the problems we face when our other fears get out of control. As we learn to follow Jesus as a lifestyle, we become adept at fighting fear with a greater holy fear. In Psalm 34, King David issues an invitation, "Come, my children, listen to me; I will teach you the fear of the LORD." Let's accept his invitation and explore his instruction.

> Glorify the LORD with me;
>> let us exalt his name together.
>
> I sought the LORD, and he answered me;
>> *he delivered me from all my fears.*
> Those who look to him are radiant;
>> their faces are never covered with shame.
> This poor man called, and the LORD heard him;
>> he saved him out of all his troubles.
> The angel of the LORD encamps around those who *fear him,*
>> and he delivers them.
>
> Taste and see that the LORD is good;
>> blessed is the man who takes refuge in him.
> *Fear the LORD,* you his saints,
>> for those who *fear him* lack nothing.
> The lions may grow weak and hungry,
>> but those who seek the LORD lack no good thing.
>
> Come, my children, listen to me;
>> I will teach you *the fear of the LORD.*
>> (Psalm 34:3-11, emphasis added)

Most English Bibles include this translator's note immediately following the title: "Of David. When he pretended to be insane before Abimelech, who drove him away, and he left." This is a reference to a story in 1 Samuel 21:8–22:1. Some background is needed if we are to adequately appreciate the wisdom David offers to us.

David had not yet been established as king of Israel at this time, but he had been anointed by Samuel and was well aware of his future privilege. He had proven to be a courageous warrior. First, he became the champion of the army of Israel when he defeated Goliath the giant. Then the women sang in the homecoming victory parades, "Saul has killed his thousands, and David has killed his tens of thousands."

These accolades offended Saul and he began to develop resentment and animosity. Eventually, in jealous rage he sought to kill David. David fled into the wilderness without equipment or provisions. In 1 Samuel 21

David went to Ahimelech, the priest at Nob, looking for food. He was given the consecrated bread that had been in the presence of the Lord. Then in verse 8 we read:

> David asked Ahimelech, "Don't you have a spear or a sword here? I haven't brought my sword or any other weapon, because the king's business was urgent."
> The priest replied, "The sword of Goliath the Philistine, whom you killed in the Valley of Elah, is here; it is wrapped in a cloth behind the ephod. If you want it, take it; there is no sword here but that one."

This is David the giant killer. But, at this point in his life the giant of fear has him on the run. Since he escaped with only the shirt on his back, he takes this prized sword as his own from that time on. But Goliath's sword did not boost his courage.

His confidence is gone and he is afraid. In emotional disarray he flees to the land of the Philistines where Achish is king. (Achish and Abimelech are names for the same man.)

This is the court of an enemy, and suddenly he's recognized and captured. He has no doubts at all about what they're going to do to him, so he feigns madness, which at this point in his life wasn't hard to do. He's scared to death. He grovels and crawls, screams, cries, scratches the walls, and drools all over himself. What a pathetic state of humiliation! The great warrior of God, the hero of Israel, reduced to a slobbering, hysterical nut case.

Achish is disgusted and throws him out of his house. David flees to the cave of Adullam. There, alone with God, he writes Psalm 34 as he processes his disastrous battle with fear.

He begins with high praise and worship. Then, in verse 4, he states the motivation for his call to glorify the Lord.

> I sought the LORD, and he answered me;
>   he *delivered me from all my fears.* (emphasis added)

In verses 6-7 he continues the same thought,

> This poor man called, and the LORD heard him;
>   he saved him out of all his troubles.

The angel of the LORD encamps around those who fear him,
and he delivers them.

In the following diagram I've listed some of the more common
debilitating fears that plague us. This visual aid gives you a picture of a
person being pulled apart by fears. Like David, his fears are dominating
his thoughts and actions. This represents all of us. Every human being
is subject to the powerful influence of fear.

Diagram 24.1

Not long ago I was talking with an especially capable and highly
successful executive in his mid-thirties. He said, "I never thought I had
any worries when it came to my career until the president of our company called me in to tell me he was downsizing the company and was
unsure what he was going to do with my position." Suddenly this self-
confident, self-sufficient young man who seemed to have the world by
the tail was afraid. Without warning, his career, his income, his sense
of self-respect had spun out of his control. Until this point, arranging
his life his way had brought security.

Some of our fear magnets are more significant than others at different times in our lives. It's likely that, as in the case of the young busi-

nessman, one or more of them have already pulled us off balance. This pulled-apart experience is what happens sooner or later when we attempt to lead our own life.

When we follow David's hard-won advice and swap leadership roles with God, the picture looks quite different. David discovered there was only one escape from the paralyzing and controlling grip that fear had attained in his life. The one antidote was the development of a greater fear. As followers of the living God, we fight fear with fear! His stabilizing might is awesome. Those who run to Him and hide in Him "lack nothing"!

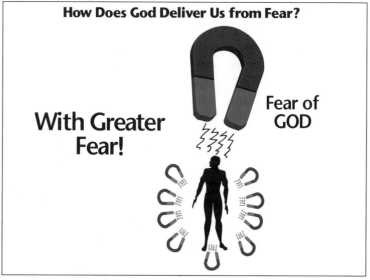

How Does God Deliver Us from Fear?

With Greater Fear!

Fear of GOD

Diagram 24.2

WHAT IS THE FEAR OF THE LORD?

This list is distilled from references to the fear of the Lord that appear throughout Psalms.

1. Reverence and respect for God as the all-powerful Leader of all else.
2. Certainty of inescapable accountability for behavior to God.
3. Practicing the presence of a Holy God.
4. Humbly following His leadership by obeying His Word.

How does the fear of the Lord help us bring other rampaging fears into healthy balance? By the way, I use the word *balance* because fear is not wrong or bad in itself. Fear of fire, for example, keeps us from playing with fire. Fear of failure motivates us to do our best and work hard. Fear becomes a serious problem only when it takes over. If fear is controlling us, God is not in His rightful place in our lives.

OVERCOMING FEAR WITH FEAR

David selects a key illustration to help us understand his lesson on the fear of the Lord. In verses 11-14 he explains how the fear of the Lord will affect the way we talk to each other. He indicates that God's control makes it possible to

keep your tongue from evil
and your lips from speaking lies. (verse 13)

The question is, what does this have to do with safely handling fear?

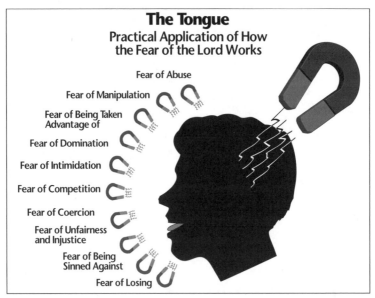

The Tongue
Practical Application of How
the Fear of the Lord Works

Fear of Abuse

Fear of Manipulation

Fear of Being Taken
Advantage of

Fear of Domination

Fear of Intimidation

Fear of Competition

Fear of Coercion

Fear of Unfairness
and Injustice

Fear of Being
Sinned Against

Fear of Losing

Diagram 24.3

What kinds of things come out of your mouth when you're afraid? Fear "flushes out" of us things we would never say at any other time.

Anger and fear are usually close companions. The combination, spilling out into our personal world through our tongue, can be a deadly pollutant.

Remember Carrie Fisher, who played Princess Leia in the *Star Wars* movies? She was the daughter of Eddie Fisher and Debbie Reynolds. Some time back the newspapers carried an interview she had given. She had been married five times and had just left her latest husband. Her explanation went like this: "Ever since my father left my mother for Elizabeth Taylor when I was two and a half years old, I have always been afraid that the men in my life will leave me. Only I cannot let that happen. I always leave them first."[1]

That's not an uncommon reaction. Wounded by the sins of others and acting out of fear, we tend to drive away the very people we want and need most. And we do it with our tongues. Our teacher, King David, insists that we can overcome fear-driven speech. I've pictured this solution as the bigger, more powerful magnet in Diagram 24.3.

IN HIS PRESENCE

What does the pull of the big magnet feel like? It feels like you're never alone. This illustration is dependent on the third point in David's definition of the fear of the Lord—practicing the presence of a Holy God. The saints of God down through the centuries have written of this secret to consistent obedience. Practicing the presence of the One with whom you want to be on your best behavior changes your choices. He *is* here— the One you care most about and honor above all others. He's in the car, in the kitchen, in the bedroom, in your thoughts, and in your heart. He's the same Lord who said,

> Never will I leave you;
>   never will I forsake you. (Hebrews 13:5)

Practicing the fear of the Lord is to live "under the influence" of omniscience in this world. My all-sufficient Leader is always with me. I can never do anything that He doesn't see. I can never say anything that He doesn't hear. There's no such thing as secret sin. Nothing is hidden.

> The eyes of the LORD are everywhere,
>   keeping watch on the wicked and the good.
>   (Proverbs 15:3)

This means that I can never get away with anything. So why try?

Through the years I've often been asked to mediate disputes. Sometimes these were between brothers and sisters, parents and children, husbands and wives, and occasionally between business partners. The reason they came to me was because both sides had respect for me. In other words, they had concluded that if I were present, they would probably control themselves and not act up so badly. Most of the time my presence has helped promote a civil discussion. This is the practical effect of the presence of someone whose opinion of us we value. It conditions our speech and our actions.

Do you remember the childhood experience of your mother or father's presence? As long as they were with you in the room, the temptation to get into forbidden things was nonexistent. It was when you thought you were alone that the cookie jar or the box of matches became so irresistible. The fear of authority and immediate accountability reinforced good behavior and deterred wrong behavior. Psalm 34 applies this principle to guarding our speech. Cultivating a strong awareness of the presence of God will always change what you allow to come out of your mouth. The present reality of "His eyes, His ears, His face, His closeness" are all mentioned next as David teaches us how the fear of the Lord motivates us.

It works because you and I *will* change if we're consciously living our lives in our majestic Leader's presence. If I'm aware that my Sovereign Master's eyes are ever upon me, His ears continually attentive to my every word, His face always before me, then I am living in the fear of God. I have adjusted to constant accountability. I am welcoming constant exposure. I am "[walking] in the light, as he is in the light" (1 John 1:7).

Let me caution you. This isn't about merely looking like good Christians so we won't embarrass or irritate God. The fear of the Lord brings *real* change. Jesus called the same followership mentality *abiding* (John 15). Maintaining awareness of your connectedness to your Leader not only conditions your behavior, it gives you confidence, security, and rest. Even when things aren't going well or feeling pleasant, His presence is our refuge and our hope. Andrew Murray, who taught us so much about depending on God, put it this way in his book *Mighty Is Your Hand:*

> What we are talking about, then, is the absolute assurance that a child has in a good father—and for the Christian, this means we may live freely as children, having a confidence that is deeply

rooted in respect for the character and the word of the Father. It is not at all like slavish, cringing fear. It is the simple *belief* that God governs every aspect of our lives in goodness and love, and so we fear to trust in anything else.[2]

We can either be driven by fears or governed by fear. Fear-driven lives are out of control. Fear-governed lives are surrendered to the ever-present supervision and companionship of the Lord of all. The exciting results pour from Psalm 34.

Those who look to him are radiant. (verse 5)

Taste and see that the LORD is good;
      blessed is the man who takes refuge in him. (verse 8)

Those who seek the LORD lack no good thing. (verse 10)

Whoever of you loves life
      and desires to see many good days,
keep your tongue from evil. (verses 12-13)

The LORD is close to the brokenhearted
      and saves those who are crushed in spirit. (verse 18)

The LORD redeems his servants;
      no one will be condemned who takes refuge in him.
            (verse 22)

These are all benefits of entering into the fear of the Lord. For David this is what lifestyle followership was all about. It means treating God as though He really is God! It's living with the awareness of a supernatural, sovereign, omnipotent, omniscient, omnipresent God above you, beside you, and within you at all times.

David "lifts our eyes" off of our circumstances (where they naturally tend to be fixed) and sets them on the Lord. He is more real than even our pain! When we "see Him" beside us as well as above us, terrors like loss, limitation, death, and rejection lose their power over us. We see Him, powerful and merciful, working all things together for His good purposes and our ultimate good.

The fear of the Lord lifts not only our eyes but our lives above our circumstances. The final book in the Bible has much to say about a powerful level of followership called *overcoming*. This kind of consistent faithfulness is a result of abiding in Christ. Revelation 2–3 and 21 all make extravagant promises to those who follow through.

The fact is, every Christian has a unique obstacle course to run. We each have things "on our plate" to deal with that are different from what others have on theirs. Overcoming means not letting what is producing your degree of difficulty stop you from following Jesus. Sickness, an unhappy marriage, rebellious children, financial reversal, a job you hate, cantankerous neighbors, a disappointing church — whatever it is, it can and must be overcome.

Even when our loving Leader challenges us by rocking our little world, He is *with us*. He shakes us to wake us — and delivers us from trusting in ourselves and worldly securities. He intends for the roots of our souls to sink deep into the soil of His constant supervision and companionship. He is the only adequate ground of our being. We have not arrived at the destination of His good intentions for us until we find our rest in Him.

This understanding and appreciation of the fear of the Lord has significantly affected and changed my life. It's so obvious, so simple, and yet so profound. I have embraced a friendly fear that has delivered me from tyrannical phobias. His presence, which admittedly seemed fearsome at first, has become the most precious companionship I've ever known. The other side of the fear of the Lord is the affirmation and affection of the Lord. That's what we'll take a look at next.

NOTES
1. Carrie Fisher, quoted in *The Seattle Press*, no date.
2. Andrew Murray, *Mighty Is Your Hand* (Minneapolis, Minn.: Bethany House, 1994), p. 25.

→ TWENTY-FIVE ←
The Beauty of Kingdom Community

As His kingdom comes within us, we are forced to change our thinking about the nature of love. We've been deeply conditioned by the world's definition of love. Modern Western culture sees love as primarily a feeling. Popular perception has concluded that it is a relational affection that rides on emotion. The Bible informs us that love is first a command to be obeyed and then an emotional response.

It was Jesus who introduced the leadership/followership concept of love. First He gave the Beatitudes and the kingdom-above-coming-near orientation. Then after three years of explaining the priority and the value of His kingdom, He laid out His definition of love. In the Upper Room, shortly before His crucifixion, He said:

> If you love me, you will obey what I command. (John 14:15)

> Whoever has my commands and obeys them, he is the one who loves me. He who loves me will be loved by my Father, and I too will love him and show myself to him. (John 14:21)

> If anyone loves me, he will obey my teaching. My Father will love him, and we will come to him and make our home with him. (John 14:23)

> If you obey my commands, you will remain in my love, just as I have obeyed my Father's commands and remain in his love. (John 15:10)

You are my friends if you do what I command. (John 15:14)

When we resolve the trust question in favor of the King of kings, a true, from-the-heart obedience follows, and a relationship begins that God calls genuine love. But it is never possible to separate the relationship of affection from followership. God loves to relate to those He leads. That's why we can trust Him completely, no matter what. God's love language is obedience. God feels loved when He is obeyed. To profess love and refuse to obey is to communicate opposites to Him.

This is not all that hard to understand. Parents also measure love by obedience. When children happily trust that their parents want only the best for them, they relax in their parents' authority, and love flows freely. The attitude of submission toward a trustworthy leader causes the love relationship between the leader and follower to flourish. If the child says "I love you" but consistently violates parental instruction, the dad and mom will come to doubt the verbal profession. Their child has a "self-centered" idea of love that's not genuine love at all.

> *We choose to love Him when we voluntarily choose to trust and obey Him.*

The breathtaking surprise is not so much that God is good, but that He is majestically submissive in an infinite humility of love. He *is* love (1 John 4:16)! His internal structure functions in such a way that causes Him to be relationally centered. He thrives on love relationships. In fact, that's why He took the risk of creating beings with the capacity of freedom of choice. We exist because God desires to love and be loved voluntarily. We choose to love Him when we voluntarily choose to trust and obey Him. When the love of God is poured out upon a church full of obedient followers, it becomes highly visible and attractive.

THE BULL'S-EYE

When I first met with Rick and Stephanie, they seemed unusually nervous and anxious to be out the door. After several months Stephanie called me one morning, and her story cleared up the question in my mind. "When I came to this church I was suspicious and cynical about churches. I had two bad experiences in the last two congregations where I had been a member. Both times I lowered my guard and trusted people. I thought they really believed the Bible and were committed to practicing it. It seemed like things were going along fine, in both groups, until conflict exploded. In each of those churches powerful personalities collided and refused to be reconciled. The results were unbelievable pain and ugliness. So, as I was saying, when I came to your church I expected to find the same sickness. But, praise God, this has proven to be a real sanctuary. No pun intended."

Stephanie and her husband are part of the walking wounded. Each year dozens of disillusioned casualties of local church wars arrive at the church I serve. Some are literally spiritual stretcher cases. Their friends carry them to the services on substitute faith. They're too afraid to come on their own.

After a few months or years they begin to recover and heal. They speak of "coming home" and of finally "feeling safe." Why would a kingdom-oriented church be a haven of unity and harmony?

The answer is obvious. When the majority of people in a local church are living humble lives of ongoing repentance, and Jesus Christ is embraced as their Supreme Leader, the bickering and competitive power struggles are minimal. Where Jesus is consistently obeyed, peace reigns. The Holy Spirit is free to pour out a spirit of cooperation and camaraderie that ignites the joy of the abundant life.

RELATIONAL MATURITY IS THE GOAL

This relational atmosphere of genuine Christian love is no accident. As Robert T. Henderson says in his powerful kingdom book, *Joy to the World*, "True repentance will be culture creating. It is in the prayers of the community of repentance that we come to understand, not only the tangled motives in us individually, but, by the Spirit, to perceive the liberating grace of God."[1] The most intentional objective of the leadership team and the working nucleus of a church should be love. Where there is an adequate foundation of obedience and love, it is safe to trust.

The target on the wall in safe churches will look something like this:

The outer ring of the target is truth. Everything we aim at must be defined by the Word of God. The second ring is transformation. The truth must change our behavior. It sets us free to be all that God intends us to be. The center of the target is love. When we obey God's Word we not only behave correctly, we thrive on relational maturity.

The truth changes us in the context of loving our marriage partner, our parents, our children, our friends, our neighbors, and our brothers and sisters in Christ. When the humility of Christ rules our hearts, we discover the beauty of how to love as safe selves. He makes us easy to live with. Those closest to us are able to attest to the fact that we really are growing up to become mature in the image of our Lord. Our progress isn't just measured by an increase in knowledge or in personal disciplines. The deepest kind of maturity is seen in how we love.

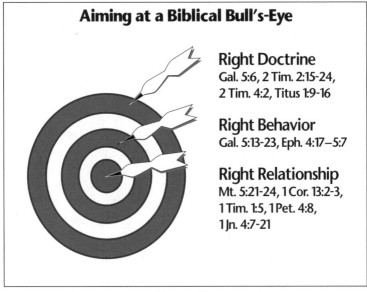

Aiming at a Biblical Bull's-Eye

Right Doctrine
Gal. 5:6, 2 Tim. 2:15-24,
2 Tim. 4:2, Titus 1:9-16

Right Behavior
Gal. 5:13-23, Eph. 4:17–5:7

Right Relationship
Mt. 5:21-24, 1 Cor. 13:2-3,
1 Tim. 1:5, 1 Pet. 4:8,
1 Jn. 4:7-21

Diagram 25.1

This is so important that, in our church, we have the bull's-eye diagram in the church constitution. We see it as essential to be clear about our objective. We're not perfect. We still see some relational failure. But overall, we're excited and thrilled with the healthy relational flavor of our spiritual family. It's working the way the Word of God promises it will when we simply follow directions and make "the greatest of these" the greatest of these (1 Corinthians 13:13)!

THE VALUE OF REPETITION
You've probably figured out by now that the "castle graphic" is my favorite visual for teaching about the kingdom. I consistently use king-

dom imagery as the theme message into which I plug the remainder of biblical truth. The result is a frame of reference that our church family understands and finds helpful. We share a common "kingdom vocabulary" like the one Jesus used with His disciples.

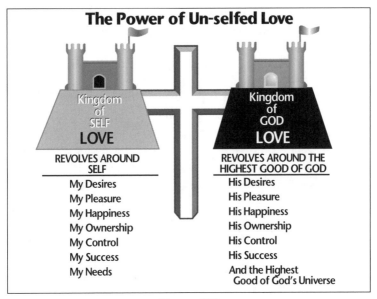

Diagram 25.2

This next series of illustrations explains the mind-set that can develop among followers of Christ when the kingdom of God is consistently taught.

Life in the kingdom is God-centered. We don't think first of getting our needs met and our problems solved. We concentrate on what makes God happy, what gives our Lord pleasure, and what makes Him look good. That always turns out to be the best choice for us as well. On the surface it may look like this choice of kingdoms is an either/or situation (my happiness versus God's happiness). That's exactly why it's so hard for us to let go of a love that revolves around ourselves. It feels like the safest course of action to maintain our own kingdoms. But the surrender choice that explodes into the eternal realm of love is where true safety and satisfaction lie.

It's important to understand that our old sin nature (the kingdom of self) never fails to be hard on relationships. When others are expected to orbit around my "planet of self," they tolerate it only as long as it fits into their trajectory. On the other hand, Christocentric living sets us free from the gravitational pull of self-interest. It allows us to genuinely care about others and take their best interests to heart. When this permeates the thinking of a church, people will begin to experience the remarkable quality of a love life that is normal under the control of God's Spirit.

It is my experience that you cannot review these truths too often. The shrouding of the kingdom message that we discussed in chapter 18 is a constant and very real threat. The Adversary is relentless in his attempts to snatch away the seed concepts of the kingdom. We have to keep reminding each other that repentance and submission are good for us. Repentance feels just as threatening the thousandth time you give up and take sides with God as it did the first time. It shouldn't surprise us when the old nature of self-centeredness takes every new loss of control like it was the end of the world.

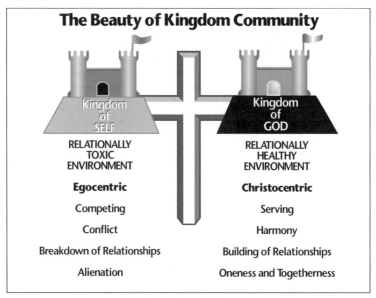

Diagram 25.3

The truth is that the kingdom seeds of fresh surrender, trust, and repentance are planted with pain. It hurts to allow our Lord to dismantle our selfish dreams, schemes, and agendas. But the harvest of righteousness is magnificent! As God's Spirit receives territory He has claimed for Christ and His kingdom in our hearts, the benefits are tremendous. The lid comes off and the news gets out! The kingdom community of eternity future is already here in those churches where the reign of King Jesus is alive and well.

The Kingdom Orchard

Kingdom of GOD

A RELATIONAL ENVIRONMENT

1. Seeds of Repentance and Submission Are Planted

2. Grace Germination Takes Place

3. Spontaneous Growth Develops

4. The Relational "Fruit of the Spirit" Results
   —in the Individual
   —in the Church Community

Diagram 25.4

BLESSED ARE THE PEACEMAKERS

My intent in this chapter has been to give you a feel for the relational health that is normal among kingdom-oriented Christians. I want to show you one more graphic in order to reflect more accurately on kingdom life in the real world. Numerical growth can put great pressure on church workers, finances, facilities, and programs. Growth forces many changes and, as we all know, change is threatening. Some have an easier time with it than others. If not understood and carefully supervised, the healthy conflict that change brings can become toxic. The process of maintaining relational maturity looks something like diagram 25.5 (page 232).

As we've been discussing, healthy communities of followers of Christ are extremely attractive. As unbelievers and dissatisfied believers find them, mostly by word of mouth, these churches continue to grow. The growth forces change and suddenly there is conflict. There are honest differences of opinion about what should be done next. This is where a group's spirit of humility and repentance is tested. Will they honor Christ and insist on pleasing Him, or will they fight for what they want without regard for what happens to the kingdom community?

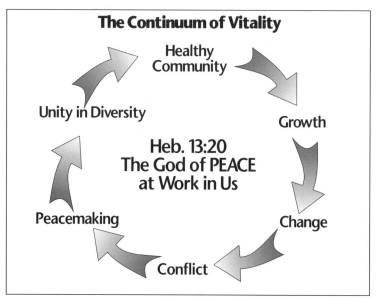

The Continuum of Vitality

Healthy Community

Growth

Unity in Diversity

Heb. 13:20
The God of PEACE
at Work in Us

Change

Peacemaking

Conflict

Diagram 25.5

It is here, at the conflict stage of the cycle, that the relational effects of kingdom principles shine with the glory of our future home. Humble followers of Jesus submit to each other. But their unity should not be confused with uniformity. Honest differences can exist side by side if our egos have been made safe by our Master's control. Mutual submission fueled by the eternal Spirit's gracious power turns into peacemaking. Then unity in diversity brings us back into healthy community. Churches that are safe kingdom communities can go through this continuum of vitality many times without stalling out from conflict.

Healthy conflict resolution is a wonder to most people these days. I've watched new arrivals attend congregational meetings where there are tough issues and strong opinions on both sides. They expect the worst and are incredulous when the issues are resolved with dignity and gracious unity. Several months ago my church family was trying to decide whether or not to continue with our master site plan and build for the fifth time in fourteen years. After the business meeting a new member came up to me with tears streaming down his cheeks. "That was so beautiful. I'm so proud to be a part of a church that behaves with such maturity!" He was overwhelmed with the corporate manifestation of the leadership of Jesus. He was seeing the transforming power of God creating kingdom community—and he found it breathtaking.

We are diverse in our backgrounds, our personalities, and our gifting. But we are triumphantly one in Christ! The miracle of unity among strong, capable people is a wonderful sight. It thrills you to your toes. People want to see it and get in on it. And so the "mustard seed" of the kingdom keeps on growing and becoming a mighty sheltering tree—just as Jesus promised it would.

NOTE
1. Robert T. Henderson, *Joy to the World* (Grand Rapids, Mich.: Zondervan, 1991), pp. 94-95.

⇥ TWENTY-SIX ⇤
The Sensational Kingdom Fragrance

Church shopping is a name given to one form of Christian discontent. Every summer a wave of restless believers rolls out on the annual church search. Their regular commitments to the Sunday school, the choir, and other programs in their "old" church have relaxed for the vacation season, and they feel free to look around and check out their options.

As my staff and I interact with these folks in transition, we've learned a great deal about what is behind their frustration. They usually have a list of their sources of dissatisfaction: mediocre, uninspiring preaching; inability to break into the closed ranks of the church power structure; poor children's or youth ministry; a new pastor who has instituted changes; or the catchall "we aren't getting our needs met."

Sometimes these people are refugees. Painful frustration and disillusionment spill out from between tight lips; church conflict has dislodged them from their former loyalties. Sometimes their lives contain an embarrassing secret that they're convinced their old church community would not handle very well. Sometimes it's just plain boredom and the notion that there must be more to being part of a church than what they've thus far seen.

"What is it that you're hoping to find?" we ask. The "needs" of the marriage or family are the easiest to identify and use as justification for their quest. Listening between the lines, we began to recognize a recurring theme: peace, joy, and love seem to be the underlying longing of these seekers. Many are searching for a kingdom community —

a healthy place to follow what C. S. Lewis calls "the safe but not tame" leadership of Jesus.

THE FRAGRANCE

When they do catch a whiff of the kingdom, they inevitably find it fascinating. This fragrance of Christ and His kingdom is referred to in 2 Corinthians 2:14-16.

> But thanks be to God, who always leads us in triumphal procession in Christ and through us spreads everywhere the fragrance of the knowledge of him. For we are to God the aroma of Christ among those who are being saved and those who are perishing. To the one we are the smell of death; to the other, the fragrance of life. And who is equal to such a task?

It's in the air. The fragrance of life permeates the atmosphere of a healthy church. Not only are the inadequately churched attracted, but the spiritual noses of the unchurched start twitching as well. The aroma of the knowledge of Christ is never merely intellectual. It is primarily relational—sweet perfume of the heart. Once experienced, it becomes necessary. It is the smell of home, the fragrance of relational health and wholeness, the safe scent of the kingdom of God among His people.

The fragrance of life permeates the atmosphere of a healthy church.

No church is perfect. No church is completely mature in its ability to lovingly provide safe community. This is particularly true if the church is growing. New arrivals take time to get up to speed with the operating principles and relational dynamics of the church. At any given time there are people at all different stages of growth and maturity.

A kingdom community is how I refer to a healthy church with a significantly higher than average ratio of de-fanged and de-clawed egos. They have committed to living in the humility of Christ with each other—working in harmony toward His goals, which are higher than any individual's *ego* fulfillment. If most of the people in a body of believers are humbly living out lifestyle submission to Christ, they smell like it!

THE TASTE

When John first came in contact with the church, he was hurt, angry, and disillusioned. He had experienced a consistent pattern of rejection in his life. His parents divorced when he was eleven. His wife of six years left him for another man. The final straw was the betrayal of his best friend, who was also his business partner. He was cynical and alienated when he first attended, and looking for the "smoke and mirrors," as he put it.

The longer he stayed and the closer he looked, the better the church proved to be. This was not reassuring to him. He grew feverish in his determination to uncover the seamy underbelly of hypocrisy that he was sure had to be there. He tested the people who welcomed him into their homes. He pushed them with his doubter's questions designed to discredit their faith. He poked them in the eye with his angry aura of superiority. He threw his well-rehearsed accusations and critical judgments in their faces—and they still treated him with kindness and would not back away. He deliberately baited them with opportunities to speak disparagingly of others and express disloyalty and discontent with their leaders. For a full year, they refused to rise to the bait.

Finally he came to the conclusion that what he thought he saw was reality after all. His reluctance turned to ecstasy. He had found a kingdom community. The credibility and integrity of the relationships made Jesus look so attractive that John decided he wanted to get in on it. He later said, "If the Lord Jesus could produce the quality of true community that I have experienced, then Christianity must be real. I knew I was risking the biggest letdown in my disappointment-prone life, but I was too hungry for genuine love not to place my life in Christ's hands." The taste of the kingdom drew this man to pledge allegiance to his eternal King. He is now a changed and changing man.

THE FRUIT

What is it that catches the attention of the hungry-hearted when they encounter the church of the living God? It is nothing more or less than the fruit of the Spirit! The ministry of the Holy Spirit within those yielded to His control is most clearly exhibited in the way He transforms relationships.

In our preoccupation with the individual in modern culture, the evangelical Christian world has adopted a tendency to privatize the

Christian life. We encourage personal disciplines, a personal "quiet time," a personal prayer life, personal introspection and evaluation through journaling, personal witness, and personal growth into Christ-like maturity. As a result of this focus on the individual, we view key spiritual-formation passages as designed for separate units. The nine qualities of the fruit of the Spirit given in Galatians 5:22-25 *are* for individuals, but *even more* for the kingdom community:

> But the fruit of the Spirit is love, joy, peace, patience, kindness, goodness, faithfulness, gentleness and self-control. Against such things there is no law. Those who belong to Christ Jesus have crucified the sinful nature with its passions and desires. Since we live by the Spirit, let us keep in step with the Spirit.

The fruit of the Spirit is what happens in a group when God is in control. He never leaves us the same as we were before the initial repentance transaction. He always changes us, conforming us to the image of His dear Son. The changes are lifestyle changes, but they must be understood as primarily relational in their real-world impact. Christ changes the way we love. As we follow Him, He enlarges our capacity to treat each other with value, respect, and resilient affection.

As you and I respond to the grace of God by faith, we step out on the finished work of Christ and make a leadership swap. We change sides. We decide it is inappropriate for us as limited creatures to continue to play God. We realize that it is ludicrous for us to run the show ourselves, trusting in our own perceptions of what's "right" for us. We welcome heaven's management contract. Our leadership dysfunction is resolved. We are now followers with childlike trust. God is now God to us. His kingdom has come in our "earthly" bodies as it is in heaven.

THE KINGDOM ARRIVES

What does God's leadership look like? Its most visible and powerful form is always relational. God's leadership produces love! In a safe kingdom community, working at healthy relationships is a given—and it's not optional. Fickleness disappears. Long-term fidelity and faithfulness emerge and come to the forefront.

I'm sure you've noticed how selfishness and self-centeredness always break down relationships. It's an unbearable, salt-in-the-wound experience to live with someone who thinks of himself or herself first. A marriage of two self-centered people quickly produces a tug of war. He wants his way, she wants hers. His ego competes with hers; her needs, desires, and agenda collide with his. The resulting battle of the wills rubs them both raw to the emotional quick. It is into conflicted situations like this that the kingdom comes with peaceful resolution. Following Jesus disarms our power struggle with Him and then with others.

In a safe kingdom community, working at healthy relationships is a given—and it's not optional.

When you've begun to follow Jesus and His Spirit is filling and controlling you, you will change in your relationships with those who are closest to you. You're now trusting Him first, open to His coaching and grooming. You're following the safe leadership of your Lord in ways that produce harmony and unity. This *must* affect your personal life circle. But it will also contribute significantly to the relational environment of your church. You don't have to respond with irritation to the irritators! You can accept and be patient with the immature and the weak. The church, in turn, can encourage and help you in your relational growth process. Together we grow. Together we bear delicious relational maturity. Together we become a display window for heaven.

So there is the center of the target: Following Jesus inevitably produces love. This is true for the individual. It should be even more powerfully true in groups of growing believers. A fruit basket on your kitchen table with a few apples, a peach or two, several bananas, and a bunch of grapes looks good. But if you walk through the produce section in a grocery superstore, the impact on your senses is overwhelming. Aisle after aisle, bin after bin, display after impressive display—the variety and abundance of the fruit are staggering.

That's exactly what happens to people who find a true kingdom community. They're enthralled with the sheer abundance of the Spirit's fruit. The cumulative sensory effect of a feast and a smorgasbord is a tremendous attraction. Fruit-producing churches cannot be hidden. The word gets out. Happy, satisfied people talk to their friends. Word of mouth spreads the news that the kingdom is arriving on earth. The church receives the kind of attention an ice cream stand gets on a hot beach.

WORM RESISTANCE

This is not a short-shelf-life kind of produce, nor is it plastic fruit that merely looks good. The fruit of the Spirit is designed by God to flourish in a hostile environment. Kingdom community manifestations are hardy and tough. They can stand the test of real-world difficulties and problems.

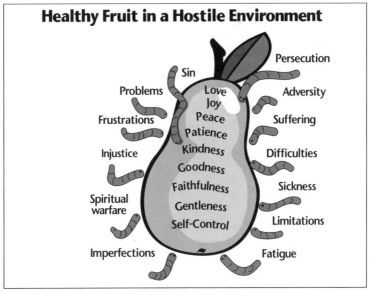

Diagram 26.1

In diagram 26.1 I have used one fruit made up of nine qualities because the word for fruit in Galatians 5 is singular in the original language. This is really the fruit of love broken down into its flavors.

The "worms" are the influences and challenges that come against us all. Every Christian experiences the kinds of difficulty and hardship that are represented here. The good news is that the fruit of the Spirit is able to thrive in the midst of adverse circumstances. For example, let's say your brother forces you out of the business in which you've been partners. Not only that, but he manages to convince the rest of the family that it was all your fault. Insult is added to injury when you find out that your parents have taken you out of their inheritance. The unfairness of the situation is so overpowering that you feel like it's driving you crazy. Should such a difficult situation cancel out your ability to produce the fruit of the Spirit? Is it okay to set aside your relational cooperation with your divine Leader in order to retaliate in a hard-nosed way? Won't you lose out if you don't fight for your rights?

The fact is, the fruit of the Spirit can stand such a plague of "worms." If you continue to obey *you cannot lose.* God will see that justice is done—He's gone on record with that promise. It may not be in this life, but so what? It's the next life that matters most anyway.

On the other hand, if you cave in and let the worms eat your fruit, *you cannot win.* You can sue your brother and campaign for vindication in your family. When the smoke clears you may have even gained some money, but you will have lost the relationships. The redemptive course that leaves the option of reconciliation open is always found in sticking with the Spirit's supervision. The evidence of divine power at work in us at the relational level is unmistakable. On our own we cannot begin to produce it. The "worms" are just too ravenous in devouring love relationships. Only the sustaining faithfulness of God at work in us can produce the beauty of love, joy, peace, patience, kindness, goodness, faithfulness, gentleness, and self-control in spite of a relentlessly hostile world.

NO LOVE = NO VALUE

I close this subject with a familiar passage from one of the most loved chapters of the Bible. After the Twenty-Third Psalm and the Sermon on the Mount, 1 Corinthians 13 consistently shows up in national surveys as a top-ten all-time favorite. It's called the Love Chapter and has inspired tough and tender Christian relationships since it was first penned.

> If I speak in the tongues of men and of angels, but have not love, I am only a resounding gong or a clanging cymbal. If I have the gift of prophecy and can fathom all mysteries and all knowledge, and if I have a faith that can move mountains, but have not love, I am nothing. If I give all I possess to the poor and surrender my body to the flames, but have not love, I gain nothing. (1 Corinthians 13:1-3)

Think with me about the implications of God's cut-to-the-chase analysis. This passage means that you can be a superstar kind of big-league Christian. You can have the appearance of spiritual commitment.

You can be supergifted, seem like a big-time success, and have all the credentials of Christian celebrity status. But if it is a *superficial shell*, motivated by your ego needs, it is useless. God cannot credit your accomplishments to the kingdom work of His Spirit. You've made the tragic mistake of attempting to build your own self-centered kingdom under the umbrella of God's kingdom. God won't sanction the best of human effort if it is out from under His control. It won't produce kingdom fruit because that comes from the heart and focuses attention and affection on Christ, not us.

What a warning! We're all capable of doing Christian ministry stuff in the energy of the flesh. We can be convincing and impressive. We can master the art of appearances. Our ability to wow our hearers can be brilliant. "But," Jesus explained, "God looks on the heart, not the outward appearance." The test is love. Not love measured by *emotional profession* or *impressive activity*, but love measured by *consistent humble obedience*.

EGO-PROOFED RELATIONSHIPS

"What do you mean, God?" I defensively react. Even the suggestion that my motivation might be suspect is enough to set my teeth on edge. My first instinct is usually to justify myself, and that only reveals the extent of my self-oriented mind-set.

"Okay," God replies, "this is what I'm after. Just so there's no confusion, this is how true kingdom followers operate relationally. In the process of serving Me, they demonstrate safe egos. They protect the people in their life circle from the anti-relational behavior of the old life." In 1 Corinthians 13:4-8, God makes clear what He does not want and then carefully spells out what He does want.

Love is patient, love is kind. It does not envy, it does not boast, it is not proud. It is not rude, it is not self-seeking, it is not easily angered, it keeps no record of wrongs. Love does not delight in evil but rejoices with the truth. It always protects, always trusts, always hopes, always perseveres.

Love never fails.

Again I react. "Woe is me. I am uncovered. My eyes have seen the King, the Lord Almighty!" If your heart responds like mine, you are on your face in shame and embarrassment, yet at the same time, in awe and wonder. This is a description of how God loves you and me. Safe, humble, likable, approachable, tough, tender, holy love! Terrifying! Why? Because it is *the standard*. Utterly impossible. Light years beyond us.

Dave and Sandy sat in numbed silence. Their marriage counselor had just had them read the Love Chapter aloud to each other. They found it discouraging.

"We could never be like this," Sandy blurted out. "We've already proven that knowing what we should be like doesn't help. We both know how we would like to be treated ourselves. We just can't seem to change the painful control games we constantly play with each other."

Dave nodded in agreement and stared at the floor.

The counselor laughed gently and said, "That's what I was hoping you'd say. You are now at the best possible place to begin your recovery process. You're absolutely right. You can't love like this . . . yet. But with God's leadership your track record will steadily improve."

He then showed how they were revealing the fact that they had never relinquished control of their lives to God. Although claiming to be Christians, they had consistently refused to give up their obsession with having their own way. Their marital problems were a wake-up call designed by God to get their attention. It was time for them to invite the Author of the 1 Corinthians 13 kind of love to take over.

The counselor handed them each a sheet with a prayer printed on it. "Read this prayer to yourselves and if it strikes you as an appropriate pattern for your response to God, go ahead and pray it. Feel free to add any thoughts of your own. I'll give you a few minutes of privacy." The prayer went as follows:

> O Lord, I see what You are after. It feels so good to know that I
> am loved this way by You. It feels so hopeless to expect that my
> ego will ever be so safe. But You are right to expect this kind of
> relational purity from me. My ego-enlargement and self-assertion
> don't belong in Your kingdom. I contaminate my relationships. I
> would pollute heaven. Have mercy upon me, my Savior. Fill me,
> Holy Spirit. Precious Father, lead me into love. Amen.

They chose to begin letting God lead them that day, and it wasn't long before the Holy Spirit was infusing them with His relational excellence. If you recognize that you need to head in the same direction, why not take a moment right now and make use of this prayer yourself. The Spirit can bear this love fruit in the hostile environment of a nonrelational world—if He has your permission and cooperation.

Nose Prints on the Window

I currently have four grandchildren. If I had known how much fun they would be, I would have had them before we had our own kids. I love having them around. But little kids are sure messy. They spit up on my ties, get my stereo covered with sticky candy residue, and smudge up my office windows. The Venetian blinds make it difficult for them to see inside, so they press their little faces against the glass in order to determine if I'm there. On a sunny day the nose prints on my windows tell me how often they've been to see me lately. I treasure those nose prints. I'm reluctant to wipe them off.

In the book of Acts there is a description of the tremendous experience of true community in the young Christian church. The relational warmth and camaraderie were palpable. It hung in the air like the smell of jasmine on a warm summer night. It radiated from hearts on fire with love for Jesus and for each other. It's no surprise that the watching world was eager to get in on it. Their nose prints on the windows of the early church revealed how attracted they were to the breathtaking marvel of the kingdom of God among men.

> They devoted themselves to the apostles' teaching and to the
> fellowship, to the breaking of bread and to prayer. Everyone
> was filled with awe, and many wonders and miraculous signs
> were done by the apostles. All the believers were together and
> had everything in common. Selling their possessions and

goods, they gave to anyone as he had need. Every day they continued to meet together in the temple courts. They broke bread in their homes and ate together with glad and sincere hearts, praising God and *enjoying the favor of all the people.* And the Lord added to their number daily those who were being saved. (Acts 2:42-47, emphasis added)

That phrase "enjoying the favor of all the people" reveals the nose-print longing that I'm talking about. It expresses the universal desire in the hearts of humanity for the safety and harmony of the kingdom. Harmony like that can only come as we submit to *one* Leader. There is a memory in our very cell structure of "paradise lost." Like all the rest of creation, we "groan" inwardly over the missing peace of the human puzzle (Romans 8:22).

Even counterfeit community is amazingly magnetic. David Koresh and his Branch Davidian community in Waco, Texas, are an example of this phenomenon. After a prolonged standoff with government law enforcement authorities, nearly one hundred people, many of them children, lost their lives as the compound went up in flames. The government agencies' role in this tragedy will probably continue to be debated for years to come. My interest is in how David Koresh managed to attract such a committed following. My hunch is that it was not just his fiery apocalyptic preaching and his charismatic personality that drew people to him. It was the fascinating promise of close community. The family atmosphere was a beacon in the night to those from broken homes and broken marriages. Even a cult commune has intense appeal in a culture of alienation. When division and bitter conflict are the norm for most people, any promise of a haven from the storms of life has potent drawing power.

> *The "pillar and foundation of the truth" upon which the gospel is displayed to the world is healthy churches!*

How much more inviting is the charm and beauty of the true community that our Creator designed us to enjoy! When the kingdom comes on earth as it is in heaven, we can expect the stimulation of intense interest. Healthy love relationships are always a source of wonder and admiration. When they're collected into a sizable community of unity and companionship, they develop an almost irresistible appeal.

This is the tremendously important part of evangelism that has been disregarded today. Our witness to the world was intended to be served up on the silver platter of heavenly community, literally the household of God on earth. The "pillar and foundation of the truth" upon which the gospel is displayed to the world is healthy churches (1 Timothy 3:15)!

WHEN COMMUNITY IS UNSAFE

It breaks my heart whenever I hear two complaints. The first one comes from nonChristians who at one time in their lives had contact with an evangelical church.

The following monologue is a compilation of bits and pieces of some of the stories that I've listened to. The main ingredient is the disillusioning effect of disappointment with those who say Jesus is their Savior and Lord.

> I grew up in one of those born-again Christian homes. We went to church every time they opened the doors. It seemed to be important to my parents, but it sure didn't stop them from fighting. As far back as I can remember, my father threw temper tantrums and my mother complained and criticized. Then when I was ten years old the church we were part of got into a nasty conflict over whether or not to build a larger building. When the smoke cleared, the church had split right down the middle and my family had been chewed up and spit out in the process. My dad was on one side of the battle, and my mom was on the other, which was par for the course. They were separated for two years. Then they divorced, and I ended up living with my mom. She dropped out of church but tried to send me and my sister to the youth group. I wouldn't have anything to do with that whole scene then or since. If there was anything to Christianity, I would have seen it or sensed it. I remember church with a great deal of anger and frustration. They are just a group of people who like to fight.

Many, if not most, conservative Bible-teaching churches have had their internal wars. Their survival, in spite of an astonishing propensity for toxic conflict, can only be attributed to the sustaining grace of the Holy Spirit. What we as an evangelical movement have failed to face up to is the multitudes who have been turned off and who have left our ranks in disgust. Every crummy little church squabble has long-term consequences. God gets a black eye, people get destroyed, faith gets pulverized, and worst of all, children and young people get inoculated against the gospel. The sad fact is that they have never really seen it.

> *Every crummy little church squabble has long-term consequences.*

The second complaint that tears me up is the one I hear from nonChristians who refuse to give Christianity a hearing because of the obnoxious behavior of professing Christians they have met. Once again the expressions that follow are a blend of several conversations.

> My impression of the Christians I have met is pretty much negative. They have all seemed rather smug and sure of themselves, like they're the only ones who are right and everyone else is wrong. It's irritating to talk with someone who seems to think he has all the answers when you haven't even asked a question. I think I would find it easier to hear what Christians had to say if they felt some empathy and sympathy for my background and worldview. I've not yet met a Christian who was a good listener. I don't want to be talked down to, and I want to be taken seriously. I have some great friends who like me and accept me the way I am. Why would I want to risk losing them in order to join a group of people whose only interest in me is recruitment to their way of thinking about God?

That kind of report hurts, as well it should. We work hard with the best of intentions, only to earn that kind of reputation. Certainly, not all Christians relate to and communicate with those outside the faith in counterproductive ways. There are believers who are careful to treat their nonChristian friends with respect and sensitivity. Yet a great deal of damage has been done by those who zealously witness without taking time to establish an adequate base of relationship. Jim Petersen, the author of *Living Proof*, is right on target when he says, "The process begins with the development of a friendship. . . . We draw nonChristians into our lives and step into theirs. As the relationships expand, so does the gospel."[1] Authentic love relationships that reflect the compassion of Jesus for every person are indispensable. The place where we're supposed to learn and grow in our ability to love is the local church.

BACK TO THE FUTURE

That brings me back to the embryo church in Acts 2. Here is a description of the main attraction in God's kingdom showcase. A healthy young church is doing what it does best—loving. This was relational integrity that stood the test of intense inspection. The ingredients of true kingdom community are clearly outlined.

The apostles' teaching. It would be safe to assume that the apostles' teaching was identical to that of their risen Lord. The book of Acts starts with a summary of the forty days of last-minute training that Jesus gave His leadership team after His resurrection.

> After his suffering, he showed himself to these men and gave many convincing proofs that he was alive. He appeared to them over a period of forty days *and spoke about the kingdom of God.* (Acts 1:3, emphasis added)

The theme of His teaching and theirs was the kingdom. The newly opened entrance to the realm of heaven was their passion. The Holy Spirit's arrival with the sound of a mighty rushing wind and tongues of fire was the signal for which they had been told to wait. His power, His life, and His fruit immediately began to reproduce the kingdom of God on earth.

Decades after Pentecost we see that the apostolic message is still unchanged. The apostle Paul was a preacher of the King and His kingdom until the day he died. I like the way Eugene Peterson translates the last verse in the book of Acts in *The Message.* He adds the energy that Paul had in his teaching. "[Paul] urgently presented all matters of the kingdom of God. He explained everything about Jesus Christ. His door was always open."

Fellowship and hospitality. The second ingredient in the mix of the church of the first century was relational openness. The apostles taught the kingdom; those who received it and entered in practiced a lifestyle of open arms to each other and open hearts to the rest of the world.

When God's people are devoted to the teaching of the kingdom, the rest of the things listed in Acts 2:42-47 are produced:

- Fellowship
- Eating meals together, especially the communion meal
- Prayer
- Wonders and miraculous signs
- The sharing of material possessions
- Generosity toward anyone in need
- Gladness and praise

As the watching world observed that kind of humble, selfless, generous love, they approved of it. Many of them decided to get in on real community themselves. "And the Lord added to their number daily those who were being saved."

I've been watching the same process take place in genuine kingdom communities today. We now have a name for it: "body evangelism"— meaning the witness of the whole Body as it works and fellowships together. The beauty of the queen-elect, the bride of Christ, is still enormously attractive. God the Spirit still delights in using healthy communities of the King to show those who have not yet repented what they are missing. In fact, it is my conviction that it's His favorite way of drawing people to Himself. They feel the warmth and security of heaven through the love they experience when the church is living out its kingdom lifestyle.

SUPERNATURAL EVENTS

Should we still expect to see the wonders and miraculous signs that were present among the first Christians? I don't think any Spirit-filled believer would be so bold as to deny God the right to exercise His power when and where He chooses. In the kingdom, the King is in control. He can be expected to do what only God can do. This is especially true in light of His promises to answer prayer.

We pray—we humbly accept His invitation to come to Him with our concerns and petitions—and He answers. How is it possible for God to answer requests for His assistance and intervention without demonstrating His supernatural power? Can you believe in prayer and not believe in answered prayer? In my estimation it is unthinkable that our great King would refuse to exercise His authority over sin, Satan, and the realm of created things on behalf of the followers He loves. He is God! We should never be surprised when He does Godlike things in a Godlike way.

Does this mean that we join what has been called "the signs and wonders movement"? No. We join the kingdom of God, nothing more, nothing less. In the kingdom we live by faith. What seems normal to us seems extraordinary to others. We expect deep conviction and the melting of cold hearts, and the miracle happens. We expect the elders to pray over the sick who come to them. And without question God still heals as James 5 promises He will.

AN UNRECOGNIZED MIRACLE

One of the more significant signs of God's activity can be seen when He turns selfishness into generosity. Turning water into wine is child's play when compared to changing the hearts of human beings with regard to money and possessions. Religious people give to create an impression with others and leverage with God. Jesus deliberately exposed the inferior motivation behind the giving of the Pharisees and religious authorities of His day (Matthew 6:1-4).

Kingdom people give because they're no longer building their private kingdoms. Part of their worship involves continually transferring ownership of all that they have to their Master. The more you see that it really is God's kingdom you're helping build in hearts, and not man's kingdom, the more your values change. Jesus applauds the practice of "selling all that you have" in order to possess the pearl of great price (see Matthew 13:45-46). It makes no sense to hoard and accumulate for *time* what you can give away and keep for *eternity*. When the kingdom is the focus of a believer's value system, the hold of wealth and possessions radically diminishes. Jesus said it this way:

> "Do not be afraid, little flock, for your Father has been pleased to give you the kingdom. Sell your possessions and give to the poor. Provide purses for yourselves that will not wear out, a treasure in heaven that will not be exhausted, where no thief comes near and no moth destroys. For where your treasure is, there your heart will be also." (Luke 12:32-34)

The early church "had everything in common. Selling their possessions and goods, they gave to anyone as he had need" (Acts 2:44-45). "No one claimed that any of his possessions was his own, but they shared everything they had. . . . There were no needy persons among them" (Acts 4:32,34).

This is supernatural behavior. It takes "much grace" for God to pry our fingers from their death grip on the material substance upon which we base our independent self-sufficiency. We can know beyond the shadow of a doubt that the kingdom is arriving in our hearts when our generosity flourishes as it did for the saints of old.

THE CLASSIC GIVER

Remember Zacchaeus, the skinflint? I deliberately left him out of the chapter entitled "No Formula" (chapter 18) because his story fits so well here. First let's review the story.

> Jesus entered Jericho and was passing through. A man was there by the name of Zacchaeus; he was a chief tax collector and was wealthy. He wanted to see who Jesus was, but being a short man he could not, because of the crowd. So he ran ahead and climbed a sycamore-fig tree to see him, since Jesus was coming that way.
>
> When Jesus reached the spot, he looked up and said to him, "Zacchaeus, come down immediately. I must stay at your house today." So he came down at once and welcomed him gladly.
>
> All the people saw this and began to mutter, "He has gone to be the guest of a 'sinner.'" . . .
>
> Jesus said to him, "Today salvation has come to this house, because this man, too, is a son of Abraham. For the Son of Man came to seek and to save what was lost."
> (Luke 19:1-7,9-10)

What was the evidence that Zacchaeus had repented and placed his life under new management? In his case it was a new generosity, a new trust in God to meet his needs. He gave half of his possessions to the poor immediately. He committed himself to pay back *four times* the amount he had cheated taxpayers. This restitution would be taken out of the half that remained of his estate. It's likely that bankruptcy loomed as a possibility. But what a powerful example of what it means to be "poor in spirit" and yet rich in the kingdom of heaven!

This is what embracing the kingdom of God has always done. Jesus' announcement that salvation had arrived in that home may surprise some. There had been no mention of what we have come to view as "the gospel." Did Zacchaeus buy his way in? No. He acknowledged Jesus as his Lord and Master. The question of who was in control of providing for him and his family was settled. The spontaneous expression of this man's surrender was his willingness to stop squeezing others for money and trust fully in the Father. Generosity flowed from his surrendered heart. Kingdom followers of Jesus do not calculate the cost. Their lives and possessions are laid at the feet of their King. Someday even their rewards and crowns will be gladly placed there as well.

This is not tithing, where God is given 10 percent and we keep 90 percent of what we make. This is gratitude expressing itself in miraculous generosity. One hundred percent giving is normal behavior in the kingdom. All that we have is placed at God's disposal. We are entrusted to manage His resources for Him.

How far we have strayed from kingdom generosity in our churches! It is beyond human comprehension what God could do on this planet if those who claim to be His would exchange keys with Him. By that I mean, He gets the keys to my kingdom treasures and I get His keys to His kingdom treasures. If the total resources of evangelical Christians were released under the direction of the Holy Spirit, every worthy ministry objective could be adequately funded with a surplus left over. The world could be radically influenced as Christians exchanged treasure with God. Why not? Why not now?

If you were a nonChristian, what would it take to impress you with the desirability of the kingdom? What would so intrigue you that your nose print would be there on the window beside the others who were "just looking"? Would people who give their lives away yet never run out of resources amaze you? The burning bush out of which God spoke to His servant Moses was on fire yet not consumed. It was a fascinating spectacle then and it still is today. When the people of God are aflame with His kingdom, their lives burn with generosity and magnanimous sharing but are never depleted. Like the miraculous jar of oil that filled every jar in the neighborhood (2 Kings 4:1-7), Christian love keeps flowing out with a generosity motivated and resourced by the Spirit of God.

The followers of Jesus look the same in their obedience today as they always have in the past. The kingdom message our Lord taught still has a "Zacchaeus effect" wherever it is understood and fully received. The question that most challenges me personally is: What does my giving tell me about my followership of Jesus? And is my generosity the kind of kingdom miracle that my Lord can use to attract new followers to Himself?

NOTE
1. Jim Petersen, *Living Proof* (Colorado Springs, Colo.: NavPress, 1989), p. 120.

Finishing Strong

Most Christians believe that our great King is returning to this earth — in power and great glory. The question is: What should we be doing while we wait? If perhaps we're the generation that will witness the second coming of our majestic King of kings and Lord of lords, how should we prepare ourselves? The New Testament has given every generation of Christ's followers the task of answering that question, for "no one knows the day or the hour" (see Mark 13:32).

One of the most fascinating studies I've ever done has been to examine all the passages in the New Testament that specifically speak to the end times. I like to think of these unique sections as "my mail," as I prepare personally for ushering in the kingdom.

In this chapter I'd like to read some of the mail addressed specifically to the Christians who "love His appearing." You'll notice that all of the bad behavior listed in these verses has existed throughout the past two thousand years. The warnings about the end of the age seem to predict a worsening of what has gone on before. Apparently, the mystery of iniquity will deepen.

> But, dear friends, remember what the apostles of our Lord Jesus Christ foretold. They said to you, "In the last times there will be scoffers who will follow their own ungodly desires." These are the men who divide you, who follow mere natural instincts and do not have the Spirit.

But you, dear friends, build yourselves up in your most holy faith and pray in the Holy Spirit. Keep yourselves in God's love as you wait for the mercy of our Lord Jesus Christ to bring you to eternal life. (Jude 17-21)

In the volatile and climactic time in history that ushers in the arrival of the kingdom on earth, the instructions to the waiting followers are clear.

1. Build yourself up in faith.
2. Pray in the Holy Spirit.
3. Keep yourself in God's love.

The first two instructions are the means of accomplishing the last one.

The unmistakable expectation of God in the end times is, "Christian, relate to Me." The cry of God's heart is, "My faithful servants, My beloved children, love Me! Communicate with Me. Commune with Me. Give Me your attention. Stay close to Me." For Spirit-led followers, love relationships are our most prized possessions. Should it surprise us that God feels the same way?

THE NEW ICE AGE

Why would God ask us to pay special attention to our love relationship with Him in the last days? The Word of God doesn't leave us puzzling over this. First of all, love is what He's been after all along. His purposes for creating us were clearly relational from the inception. As history is readied for His closing act, His desire for our love is frustrated by a strengthening of competing affections. Other loves leave little room in our hearts for divine love.

But mark this: There will be terrible times in the last days. People will be *lovers of themselves, lovers of money*, boastful, proud, abusive, disobedient to their parents, ungrateful, unholy, *without love*, unforgiving, slanderous, without self-control, brutal, *not lovers of the good*, treacherous, rash, conceited, *lovers of pleasure rather than lovers of God*—having a form of godliness but denying its power. Have nothing to do with them. (2 Timothy 3:1-5, emphasis added)

Did you notice all the references to love? What does God predict people will love in the days just prior to the return of Christ? Themselves! The self-enthronement that has been fermenting in us since the departure of our first parents from Eden will become the order of the day. What has always been tragically true will break out with renewed vigor. Global selfishness will flourish.

Is this sounding like a match to the trends of recent days? Maybe this *is* our mail. The Holy Spirit is warning us that a spiritual ice age will be present at the end of the "last days" era. The hearts of the majority of people will be cold and hard toward God. On the other hand, the climate of the culture will be steamy hot, especially when it comes to the pursuit of self, money, and pleasure. The Holy Spirit predicts that this will adversely affect the love of Christians for their Lord. Wouldn't it make sense that God would raise up Spirit-led fires of fresh repentance in order to thaw out the cooling hearts of His people?

Second Timothy 3 was written to believers. The warning implies that believers will get caught up in this preoccupation with self-love. Notice, the people being described here are still religious people. They have "a form of godliness but [deny] its power." Whenever the Bible talks about the power inherent in the gospel, it's talking about the power to change, about the Holy Spirit's dynamic work in producing transformation of life.

God doesn't give us power over other people through the development of godliness. He gives us power over ourselves; power over our old self-in-control nature; power to stop practicing sinful behavior and to start practicing godly behavior. In the last days people will still hold to the form of biblical Christianity but refuse to let it change them. Church history establishes this as a debilitating pattern that has plagued us all along. Can we accurately say that the pattern is getting worse? I think we can, and here's why.

We've never had so many knowledgeable Christians as we have today. There's more excellent Bible teaching available than ever before, and more personal study and small-group Bible studies. Christian schools have multiplied. Christian bookstores have proliferated. Christian radio and television stations have sprung up around the world with offerings that run the spectrum from legalism to slushy grace. Yet, in spite of all the available support material, Christians are having a terrible time letting the truth influence them in ways beyond superficial cosmetic changes.

The vibrant excitement and radical commitment of kingdom follower-ship seems to be spotty, if it's there at all. The point is, a strong case could be made that if ever it could be said that people were "always learning but never able to acknowledge the truth" (2 Timothy 3:7), it would be today. Learning the truth and putting it into practice are two different things. Keeping ourselves in the love of God is a tough assignment in a world where the self-love message is steadily getting stronger.

AN ANCIENT VOICE

The Pacific Northwest has become one of the world centers for the new age movement. One of the most successful channeling groups operates here with wide acceptance. One evening I happened to catch ABC's "20/20" reporting on the channeling phenomenon. Barbara Walters was interviewing a woman by the name of J. Z. Knight who has made quite a name for herself in the channeling business. The spirit that Ms. Knight claims to be channeling is supposedly a male warrior from Atlantis. She calls him Ramtha and believes that he is thirty-five thousand years old.

Barbara Walters wanted to know, "What is the fascination all about? What is the message of wisdom that Ramtha communicates?"

I watched as J. Z. Knight went into her trance. All of a sudden, she took on the characteristics of a male. She sounded like a man and had the body language and movements of a man. People were on the edge of their seats soaking in the whole drama. Women were sitting in the front rows with tears rolling down their faces. They were absolutely enthralled by what they were seeing and hearing. This is what I hurriedly wrote down as the raspy voice gave its message: "God is within you. Love yourself. If you pray to anyone, pray to yourself. You are God. Focus your attention and loyalty on yourself. You need to do what you really want to do. Go ahead and enter into the greatest love of all . . . love yourself."

While I was watching, it dawned on me that I was witnessing the doctrines of demons that Paul warned Timothy about (1 Timothy 4:1). What was depressing was how unlike an "exorcist" movie it was. It was weird stuff—but set to ego-music, the narcissistic melody of self-deification was hypnotic.

You may be saying to yourself, "This doesn't relate to me. I would never be taken in by such blatantly twisted philosophies." Is that so? Do you honestly think you can remain unmoved by the *identical ideas* permeating the television programs and movies you watch, the music you listen to, and the books, magazines, and newspapers you read? Let's face it, we're getting our egos massaged no matter which way we turn—even in church. And that's exactly why the Word of God is asking us to surrender to the holding power of an overriding affection. Without it we'll all get sucked into the quicksand of self-absorption.

THE POWER OF ROMANCE

In this present age the wheat and the weeds will be permitted to grow side by side. Jesus was emphatic about that (Matthew 13:24-30). The love of self, money, and pleasure will flourish side by side with the love of God. Two kingdoms with two violently opposite value systems will compete for our loyalty and our affection. The siren song of selfism, enticing us to the mirage of human potential and self-sufficiency, will blast from the twin speakers of the culture and the media. The still, small voice of the Holy Spirit of God will quietly hum the oldies but goodies of heaven—the love songs of eternity—deep within our hearts. Whitney Houston's "Greatest Love of All" will compete with "My Jesus I Love Thee."

From beginning to end, following Jesus comes down to love. Who do you love the most? The greatest romance is developing alongside and in contrast to the tacky affairs of the kingdom of self. But it must be remembered that love is a choice and a process of choices. It is hard work to stay focused and single-minded in the face of multiple options. God's call to those who are committed to following Him throughout the age is: "Keep yourselves in [my] love as you wait" (Jude 21).

> *This is more than staying in love with your Leader. This is staying in your Leader's love for you!*

This is more than staying in love with your Leader. This is staying in your Leader's love for you! This is refusing to doubt in days of darkness what He has shown you in the light. Holding firm in old age what He taught you in your youth. Closing the door on the suspicions whispered by pain and loss that He is less than good. Shutting out the roar of the traffic of injustice and unfairness. Squelching the rumor that He doesn't care. Hanging up on the obscene phone calls of lust and greed that promise you what He alone can satisfy. This is hanging in there—refusing to stop following, no matter what! And why not?

> If God didn't hesitate to put everything on the line for us, embracing our condition and exposing himself to the worst by sending his own Son, is there anything else he wouldn't gladly and freely do for us? And who would dare tangle with God by messing with one of God's chosen? Who would dare even to point a finger? The One who died for us—who was raised to life for us!—is in the presence of God at this very moment sticking up for us. Do you think anyone is going to be able to drive a wedge between us and Christ's love for us? There is no way! Not trouble, not hard times, not hatred, not hunger, not homelessness, not bullying threats, not backstabbing, not even the worst sins listed in Scripture:
> "They kill us in cold blood because they hate you.
> We're sitting ducks; they pick us off one by one."
> None of this fazes us because Jesus loves us. I'm absolutely convinced that nothing—nothing living or dead, angelic or demonic, today or tomorrow, high or low, thinkable or unthinkable—*absolutely nothing can get between us and God's love* because of the way that Jesus our Master has embraced us. (Romans 8:31-39, MSG, emphasis added)

This I can get into: a love that will not let me go—no matter what! The last chapter contains some final thoughts on how to maintain the greatest love of your eternal life.

→ T W E N T Y - N I N E ←
Rediscovering the Kingdom

When my wife and I took a sabbatical and spent six weeks visiting missionaries in Europe, we asked one question of every Christian we met: "What is God doing in your country?" We deliberately did not ask, "What are you as an individual doing?" or "What is your church or mission organization doing?" We weren't interested in hearing about human activity unless those doing it were convinced that God was in it.

The answers we received to that question were not encouraging. We didn't meet any Christian leaders who thought God was doing much through them or in their local area. The answers were always about what they had heard God was doing somewhere else, in another city or even another country. The more we asked, the more we found the same handful of names cropping up.

God was at work, but it seemed there were very few followers He could trust. There were thriving, productive ministries in every country. Yet, right alongside each demonstration of God at work were dozens of ineffective, going-through-the-motions, weak, and even sick ministries.

The main difference between the two was *worship* and *prayer*. Without exception, the work where the blessing of God was clearly evident was riding a wave of believing prayer and refreshing, Spirit-empowered, Christ-exalting worship.

The language of prayer and worship was the same in every place where there was life and life transformation. I noticed that it was without exception *kingdom language*. The authority of Jesus Christ was understood, and the leaders were walking in submission and humility with their Lord. There's much to learn here.

LISTEN TO THE INTERCESSORS

Intercessors are followers of Jesus who have the gift of faith. They are self-aware about God calling them to a ministry of stand-in-the-gap prayer. I'm beginning to recognize a true intercessor when I hear one. They are impressed with God! The way they talk to Him makes it clear that they have an overwhelming sense of His power and authority. They pray as if He really is in control. They have a deep childlike humility and faith. I cannot take it upon myself to judge the prayers of my Christian brothers and sisters, but I do sense which ones are actually in touch with God.

> *The work where the blessing of God was clearly evident was riding a wave of believing prayer and refreshing, Spirit-empowered, Christ-exalting worship.*

Many prayers are full of the speakers' own egos. There's the sound of the self telling God what to do. Many are self-conscious prayers for the benefit of others in the room. But some are kingdom prayers. They're full of wonder, awe, and admiration—exactly as one would expect in a conversation between a creature and his Creator, between a great and mighty King and His obedient servants.

There's nothing put-on about such praying. Its style cannot be imitated. It's the fresh, clean breeze of the humility of Jesus in us, blowing upward to the Father from an eager-to-please, ready-to-obey heart. Not only is there respect and profound gratitude toward God, there's also the passion of almost unutterable love. True prayer warriors *like* God. They would rather be with Him than with any other person.

Sarah is a friend of God. You can hear the warm affection in the tone of her voice when she's talking to her heavenly Father. As I sit with her in the one-room nursing home "apartment" she calls home, I'm drawn closer to the heart of God. I marvel at her tender choice of words. I love the comfortable companionship. She laughs and cries when she prays. She gets choked up and overwhelmed with joy. My strongest impression is that this elderly woman of faith is grateful to God at a level I never even knew was possible. Without question Jesus is her absolute authority and closest friend. As I enter into His presence with Sarah as my prayer partner, I experience the most soul-satisfying kind of spiritual intimacy.

I could tell you of kingdom glimpses received while praying with Ben and his Tuesday morning prayer group. Or take you along to the four-day prayer and worship "summits" of the Northwest Renewal movement and have you enter the richness of kingdom-loving prayer.

I love to pray with true kingdom intercessors. The fever of "glory to Jesus," "hallelujah," and "praise God" lingo is either thoughtfully appropriate or pleasantly absent. It doesn't sound religious or pretentious. It's simple, creative, loving, yet reverent communication with our Leader. It delights in Him, waits before Him, listens to Him, and such prayer is wonderfully visited with His presence.

The prayer warriors among us are, without exception, kingdom followers. They're calling us to get ready for the arrival of our conquering King. As the curtain begins to close on the church era of history, the Holy Spirit is clarifying the vision of the eternal kingdom. This is strongest among those who are called to intercessory prayer.

WORSHIP WITH THE WORSHIPERS

Another place where the resurgence of the kingdom theme of Jesus is being rediscovered is in the worship reformation that is sweeping through the churches. A huge change that is far more than style or musical taste has been taking place. The understanding of what worship actually is has been undergoing immense renovation.

A good song leader can get rousing singing from a group the way a cheerleader gets applause from a stadium of sports fans. A good music director is expert at orchestrating instruments and voices in gorgeous combinations and exquisite varieties of sound.

But worship leaders are something else entirely. They are primarily true worshipers themselves. They bring to a worshiping community an unerring sense of the presence of God. They guide you to the throne room of the universe, *because they let the vision of majestic holiness take over.* The music is only the medium of experience and expression. In essence, the worship leader opens the eyes of our inner selves to God by causing us to focus on His high, holy attributes.

The language of worship is, without exception, kingdom language. This is not new. It's always been this way. The ancient psalms of Israel are crammed full of the King and His kingdom. The great hymns of the past two thousand years of church history are preoccupied with the reign of God. The new worship music continues in the same theme. Worship is all about calling one another to come back under the rule of God. It is bowing down before the glory of our matchless King. It is voluntary humility, repenting again and again. It is the sweetest ecstasy, the deepest soul-shaking catharsis, the most powerful reality check that sane humans can experience. Think with me about the anointed songs of the worship renewal that has been sweeping through the churches. I've selected four representative worship choruses that have become familiar to a sizable portion of Christians.

"When I Look into Your Holiness" (Psalm 34:5)[1]
When I look into Your Holiness,
When I gaze into Your loveliness
When all things that surround become shadows in the light
    of You
I worship You, I worship You.
The reason I live is to worship You.
I worship You, I worship You.
The reason I live is to worship You.

"Great Are You Lord" (Jeremiah 10:6)[2]
Holy Lord, most Holy Lord, You alone
Are worthy of my praise. Holy Lord, most Holy Lord,
With all of my heart I sing
Great are You Lord, Great are You Lord
Great are You Lord, most Holy Lord!

"Blessed Be the Lord God Almighty" (Revelation 4:8)[3]
Father in heaven how we love You.
We lift Your name in all the earth.
May Your kingdom be established in our praises
As Your people declare Your mighty works.
Blessed be the Lord God Almighty
Who was, and is, and is to come.

Blessed be the Lord God Almighty
Who reigns forever more.

"You Are Crowned with Many Crowns"[4]
You are crowned with many crowns
And rule all things in righteousness.
You are crowned with many crowns
Upholding all things by Your Word.
You rule in power and reign in glory!
You are Lord of heaven and earth!
You are Lord of all.
You are Lord of all.

I could go on and on. I included just a taste of some familiar worship songs to demonstrate the spirit and flavor of the kingdom that permeates them. I'm convinced that the worship renewal movement, along with the prayer movement, is the leading edge of a return to the kingdom dream of Jesus. Kingdom-style evangelism and discipleship in true Kingdom community churches and parachurch ministries must come next.

GET READY . . .

On a practical level it has been prayer and worship that has kept my grasp of the Word of God on target. The apostle Paul was so right: "Knowledge [especially theological knowledge] puffs up" (1 Corinthians 8:1). There's something about the capable intellect that can't seem to resist the inclination toward superiority and pride. Knowledge *about* God is the basis of Pharisaism. Knowledge *of* God is the path of humility, repentance, and love.

I love the way the Holy Spirit led Eugene Peterson to translate Jesus' words in John 4:23-24 in *The Message* (emphasis added):

It's who you are and the way you live that count before God. Your worship must engage your spirit in the pursuit of truth. That's the kind of people the Father is out looking for: those who are simply and *honestly themselves* before him in their worship. God is sheer being itself—Spirit. Those who worship him must do it out of their very being, their spirits, *their true selves*, in adoration.

What is God doing today? He's calling His people to rediscover His kingdom. As His kingdom develops within us we'll be getting ready for the kingdom around us. We'll be like a bride making joyful preparations for her bridegroom's arrival to escort her to the wedding. We'll be keeping ourselves in the love of God by thriving on obedience to His leadership. We'll be ready, eagerly anticipating His return to set up His kingdom and our eternal home. What a glorious vision and yet, at the same time, what an incredible present reality. In following Jesus we are rehearsing for our grand entrance.

Is that our Beloved's voice at the door?

NOTES

1. "When I Look into Your Holiness," words by Wayne and Cathy Perrin. Copyright © 1981 Integrity's Hosanna! Music/ASCAP. All rights reserved. International copyright secured. Used by permission. c/o Integrity Music, Inc., P.O. Box 851622, Mobile, AL 36685.

2. "Great Are You Lord," words by Steve and Vikki Cook. Copyright ©1984 Maranatha! Music (Administered by The Copyright Company, Nashville, TN). All rights reserved. International copyright secured. Used by permission.

3. "Blessed Be the Lord God Almighty," words by Bob Fitts. Copyright ©1984 Integrity's Hosanna! Music/ASCAP. All rights reserved. International copyright secured. Used by permission. c/o Integrity Music, Inc., P.O. Box 851622, Mobile, AL 36685.

4. "You Are Crowned with Many Crowns," words by John Sellers. Copyright ©1984 Scripture In Song (a division of Integrity Music, Inc.)/ASCAP. All rights reserved. International copyright secured. Used by permission. c/o Integrity Music, Inc., P.O. Box 851622, Mobile, AL 36685.

TAKING ANOTHER STEP—
QUESTIONS FOR MEDITATION

1. What do you believe about God's goodness and His sovereign control?

2. If you were released from the effects of an unhealthy fear, could you become an overcoming follower?

3. The "friendly fear" of the Lord that sets us free from the tyranny of our other fears is a powerful resource. Have you discovered the practical "deliverance" side of surrender to your Lord's leadership?

4. If you've been adversely affected by unsafe Christian communities, you are not alone. In your disappointment and hurtful memories it is easy to "throw the baby out with the bath water." This might be a good time to forgive and release any residue of bitterness that remains. It would be a tragedy if the distrust created by dysfunctional community kept you from finding the joy of true kingdom community. Will you try again? Hope again?

5. If your church resolved conflict in a healthy, loving way, would you be more likely to invite others to join in the safe community you are enjoying? What can you do to initiate healthy conflict resolution?

6. If you've contributed to the breakdown of unity and the peace-making process in your church, repent immediately and clean up your part of the mess. You won't want to face your Lord with bloody knuckles and fingernails. I know you think you're in the right. Both sides always do. Could it be that what remains of your own control and ego issues has drawn you into conflict that is destroying your King's reputation?

7. Is the fruit of the Spirit too good to be true? Can followers of Jesus actually treat each other like this consistently? What would unbelievers do if they saw such relational health?

8. Have you ever had the miracle of generosity happen to you? (How about God's grace?) Have you ever had it happen in you and through you? If you became a "giver," would it be noticeable?

9. There has never been a sharper contrast between the love of self and the love of God than there is today. Do you feel the self-saturated spirit of the media and the culture? How are you keeping yourself in love with your Lord?

10. How has thinking about the kingdom message of Jesus refocused your mission and vision?

11. One of these days you'll wake up as usual in your familiar surroundings but by evening be home in heaven! Are you ready to meet your Leader face-to-face? What changes immediately come to mind when you visualize His eyes looking intently into yours? What is the first thing you want to say to Him when you see Him in person?